MUSLIM CIVILIZATION

The Causes of Decline and the Need for Reform

M. UMER CHAPRA

THE ISLAMIC FOUNDATION

Published by
THE ISLAMIC FOUNDATION,
Markfield Conference Centre, Ratby Lane, Markfield,
Leicestershire LE67 9SY, United Kingdom
E-mail: publications@islamic-foundation.com
Website: www.islamic-foundation.com

Quran House, PO Box 30611, Nairobi, Kenya

PMB 3193, Kano, Nigeria

Distributed by: Kube Publishing Ltd.
Tel: (01530) 249230, Fax: (01530) 249656
E-mail: info@kubepublishing.com

2nd impression, corrected 2008/1429 H

British Library Cataloguing-in-Publication Data
Chapra, M. Umar (Muhammad Umer), 1933-
Muslim civilization: the causes of decline and need for reform
1. Civilization, Islamic – 2. Islamic renewal
I. Title
909'.097671

ISBN 978 1 84774 466 4 *casebound*
ISBN 978 1 84774 461 9 *paperback*

Typeset by: N.A.Qaddoura
Cover design by: Nasir Cader

To my late
brother Ibrahim and sister Aisha,
may Allah shower His blessings on them,
for the sacrifices they made for me and
the whole family

بسم الله الرحمن الرحيم

CONTENTS

Foreword vii

Preface ix

Introduction: Some Crucial Questions 1

1. Ibn Khaldūn's Theory of Development and Decline 17
2. Factors that Contributed to the Rise of the Muslims 34
3. Factors Responsible for Muslim Decline 45
4. Economic Decline 68
5. Decline in Education, Science and Technology 96
6. Social Decline 133
7. Some Lessons (*'Ibar*) from Muslim History 149
8. Failure to Learn the Lessons 158
9. The Need for Reform 164

References 195

Index 217

TRANSLITERATION TABLE

Arabic Consonants

Initial, unexpressed medial and final:

ء	ʾ	د	d	ض	ḍ	ك	k
ب	b	ذ	dh	ط	ṭ	ل	l
ت	t	ر	r	ظ	ẓ	م	m
ث	th	ز	z	ع	ʿ	ن	n
ج	j	س	s	غ	gh	هـ	h
ح	ḥ	ش	sh	ف	f	و	w
خ	kh	ص	ṣ	ق	q	ي	y

Vowels, diphthongs, etc.

Short:	ـَ a	ـِ i	ـُ u
Long:	ـَا ā	ـِي ī	ـُو ū
Diphthongs:		ـَوْ aw	
		ـَيْ ay	

FOREWORD

History is not merely a chronicle of events; more importantly it is a gallery of pictures unveiling successive scenarios of mankind's achievements and failures, excellences and depravities, sublime heights and abysmal falls. It is a record of humanity's long march towards tomorrow, the past merging into the present and opening avenues for the future. It is a mirror in which one can see vibrant episodes of the rise and fall of nations and civilizations through an interplay of ideas, personalities, institutions, communities and societies.

History also presents much more than an unending galaxy of pictures and mirrors reflecting the ebb and flow of events and rise and fall of nations and civilizations. While unfolding for the human eye, these fascinating scenes, it also confronts the mind with challenges. One is prompted to reflect, analyze and delve deeper beneath the surface to discover the causative forces behind all historical phenomena. This is a process through which one moves from the dynamics of history to the realm of the philosophy of history. This opens up for mankind a world of opportunities to learn from the past, so as to reshape the present and pave the way for a better future. History's heights and downfalls both have their lessons, which can be ignored only at mankind's peril.

The Qur'ān invites mankind to reflect upon history so that it draws lessons, mend its behaviour and seek its tryst with destiny. The renowned historian Ishtiaq Qureshi puts it succinctly when he says, that the Qur'ān "does not look upon the present as merely transient, nor upon the past as the sum total of merely so many transients and insignificant presents. ... [It] draws attention repeatedly to the misdeeds of previous people and their destruction as the result of these misdoings"[1]

Reflection on the factors responsible for the rise and fall of peoples, communities and nations are germane to the Qur'ānic way of thinking:

> *(O Muḥammad) We narrate these (historical) anecdotes of Messengers to you that We may strengthen your heart through them. In these anecdotes come to you the Truth, and Exhortation, and a Reminder for the believers.*
>
> (Qur'ān 11:120)

> *We raised a Messenger in every community (to tell them): "Serve Allah and shun the Evil One". Thereafter Allah guided some of them while others were overtaken by errors. Go about the earth, then, and observe what was the end of those who rejected the Messengers.*
>
> (Qur'ān 16:36)

> *Have they not seen how many a people We have destroyed before them? People whom We had made more powerful in the earth than you are and upon whom We had showered abundant rains from the heavens and at whose feet We caused the rivers to flow? And then (when they behaved ungratefully) We destroyed them for their sins, and raised other peoples in their place.*
>
> (Qur'ān 6:6)

1. Qureshi, Ishtiaq Husain, "*Historiography*" in M.M. Sharif (ed), *A History of Muslim Philosophy*, Vol. II, Karachi; Royal Book Co., 1983, pg 1198.

> *And indeed before your time, (O Muḥammad) many a Messengers has been scoffed at: but those who mocked at them were encompassed by the Truth they had scoffed at. Say: "Go about journeying the earth and behold the end of those who gave the lie (to the Truth).*
>
> (Qur'ān 6:10-11)

The Qur'ān has emphasized moral as well as material factors responsible for the rise and decline of nations. It has invited mankind to understand the Divine design embedded in historical processes. It has also assigned to man and woman the role not only to learn from history but also to fashion it. The dynamic principle of *istikhlāf* (vice-regency and stewardship) defines the role of human beings on this earth. Their historic mission, as individuals and as a community of believers, is to strive continuously to live by and establish the Divine Will in history's space and time. The position of the Prophet Muḥammad (Peace be upon him) as the last prophet spells out for him and the Muslim *Ummah* a unique role in history. The Qur'ān puts it clearly:

> *Indeed We have sent forth Our Messengers with clear Messages, and We sent down with them the Book and the Balance, so that men may establish Justice.*
>
> (Qur'ān 57:25)

The responsibility of the *Ummah* has also been very clearly stated:

> *We have made you a mid-most (just) community*
>
> (Qur'ān 2:143)

> *O believers! Be establishers of Justice, Witnesses for God*
>
> (Qur'ān 4:135)

The Muslim *Ummah* is a nation with a mission which upholds a vision for mankind. It is required to undertake, individually and collectively, active struggle to establish justice within and without, so as to enable humanity to seek the Good in this world and in the Hereafter. If the *Ummah* fulfils its responsibility, in accord with the Divine guidance and following the *uswah* (life example) of the Prophet Muḥammad (Peace be upon him), then it is destined to achieve peace and prosperity in this world and success and salvation in the life to come.

> *Allah has promised those of you who believe and do righteous deeds that He will surely bestow upon them power in the land as He bestowed power on those who preceded them, and that He will establish their religion which He has been pleased to choose for them, and He will replace with security the state of fear that they are in. let them serve Me and associate none with Me in My Divinity.*
> (Qur'ān 24:55)

The most distinct and defining aspect of Muslim civilization is that it is based on faith and is inspired by a vision of Man, Society and Destiny based on Divine guidance. It is characterised by the integration of the spiritual with the material, and the moral with the mundane. Life is one organic whole. Human problems have to be solved through a holistic approach, and not through any partial or piecemeal approach to human life and its problems. The *élan vital* of Muslim civilization consists in this vision and the mission to change the world in accord with this vision through a process of sharing and establishing model personalities, societies and cultures.

The real strength of Muslim civilization had always been in the simultaneous pursuit of moral excellence and material strength, prosperity and security. All the phases of the rise and expansion of Muslim civilization were characterised by the dynamic operation of this *élan*: whenever this balance was disturbed, the forces of decline and disintegration weakened the fabric of Muslim society and led to its downfall. Throughout its historic march, spread over fourteen centuries, Muslim history has witnessed many periods of strength and weakness, of rise and fall, as also of ebb and flow and rout and rally. Yet what has been unique throughout is the inner resilience of the Islamic *élan* and its articulation in different space and time situations. After every decline, there has been a fresh wave of revival characterised by efforts of renovation and regeneration that responded creatively to the challenges of the time.

Every episode of rise and revival drew its strength afresh from the original sources, the Qur'ān and the Prophetic practice (*Sunnah*). Every such effort represents elements of continuity all along while catering for the demands of change. There was always continuity of vision and mission, but their articulation in forms tuned in to new needs and situations represents the hallmark of the Islamic venture in history. The strategy for Islamic revival has always included remobilization of the spiritual, moral, material and technological forces. In turn, this led invariably to raising a generation of individuals imbued with this vision and committed to the restructuring of society and to harnessing all sources of power in the service of Islamic ideals. A careful reading of the history of the last fourteen centuries reveals this dynamic nature of the Muslim ethos which has expressed itself in different space/time scenarios.

This ethos of Islamic history and civilisation has been described by contemporary Muslim thinkers as *Tajdīd wa Iḥyā'* (renovation and revival).[2] Earlier thinkers have also addressed this issue in the context of their own historic situations. Some of the more prominent and outstanding thinkers who have examined this aspect of Muslim

2. See Mawdudi, Abul Ala, *A Short History of the Revivalist Movement in Islam*, Lahore, Islamic Publications, 3rd Edition, 1976; ibid: *Khilafat-o-Mulukiyyat*, Lahore, Islamic Publication, 1996; ibid, *The Islamic Movement:Dynamics of Values, Power and Change*, (ed and translated by Khurrum Murad), Leicester, The Islamic Foundation, 1984. Also see Nadvi, Abul Hasan Ali: *Tarikh Dawat-o-Azeemat*, 6 Volumes, Lucknow, India, Majlis Tahqiqat-o-Nashariyyat-e-Islam, 1969-1984.

civilization were Abū Yūsuf (113-182 AH/731-798 AD), Abū'l-Ḥasan ibn Muḥammad al-Māwardī (364-450 AH/974-1058 AD), Abū Ḥāmid Muḥammad al-Ghazālī (451-505 AH/1055-1111 AD), Aḥmad ibn 'Abd al-Ḥalīm ibn Taymiyyah (661-728 AH/1263-1328 AD), Ibn Khaldūn (732-808 AH/1332-1406 AD), Shāh Walīullāh Dihlawī (1114-1176 AH/1703-1762 AD), and Jamāl al-Dīn Afghānī (1254-1315 AH/1838-1897 AD).

It is interesting that despite differences in historical contexts, there is agreement among these scholars about the factors responsible for the decline of Muslim civilization as well as in respect of their insights about the strategies and modalities for revival, renovation and resurgence. All of them agree that Muslim decline was never because of Islam but due to departures from it. They re-emphasized the original vision and priorities and strived to correct the distortions produced by neglect of the balance between the moral/spiritual and material/technological aspects of the Islamic equation. Strategies for revival focussed on re-understanding of the original vision, reaffirmation of the *Ummah*'s mission, promotion of education and character building, and simultaneous mobilization of material, economic and technological resources for the reorganization of society on the principles of *shūrā* (consultation and accountability), *'adl* (justice and socio-economic equity) and unity and self-reliance. These constituted the sum and substance of the essentials for revival and reconstruction, regardless of the form they had to assume because of distinct historic contexts. The real strength lied in loyalty to Allah and His Prophet, moral integrity of the individual and the prosperity and security of society. This is achieved through the harnessing of competitive political, economic, technological and military power. While the manifestations of these revivalist strategies may have differed in different epochs, the above essentials constituted their common parameters.

My dear friend and colleague, Dr. Umer Chapra, has blazed a new trail by examining the contemporary state of Muslim history and civilization, drawing upon the historical experience of the *Ummah* in general and applying the tools of historical analysis developed by Ibn Khaldūn in particular.

Ibn Khaldūn's work provides one of the most comprehensive models for understanding the rise and fall of civilizations in general and of Muslim civilization in particular. His work not only identifies the factors responsible for the emergence and growth of civilizations and for their decline and disintegration but has also applied this analytical model to the understanding of the problems faced by the Muslim society and the pathways for its revival and development. Ibn Khaldūn has analyzed historical data with an incisive mind and philosophic vision. He has also tried to look upon the strengths and weaknesses of human society in the light of values, principles and insights contained in the Qur'ān and *Sunnah* and the ways in which they were operationalised in Muslim history.

One key lesson derived from Islamic history has been beautifully summed up by Iqbal when he said that it is Islam that has saved the Muslims in their hours of crisis, and not *vice versa*. Throughout history Islam has remained the ultimate source of inspiration and the most decisive rallying point for revival and regeneration.

This line of thought is diametrically different from the approach advanced by most of the Orientalists and Western scholars of Islamic history. They have generally tried to put the blame for Muslim decline, in some form or other, on Islam and its value framework, ignoring all together that the source of revival in all major episodes of Muslim history had come from none other than Islam itself. In fact some of them have gone to the extent of pronouncing the virtual demise of Islamic civilization, painting Muslim civilization as a legacy, a thing of the past, and not as a living, vibrant and evolving reality and a pace-setter for the future.

This approach has been challenged by contemporary Muslim scholars and it is also belied by the powerful waves of Islamic resurgence in almost all parts of the world. This flawed approach to Islamic history and civilization has been given a new twist in the literature produced by the "terror industry" which has overshadowed the intellectual and media horizon after the tragic events of 9/11. It is a pressing need of the hour that a more honest, objective and realistic effort is made to understand the nature of Muslim civilization, the real state of present-day Muslim society and to undertake a sympathetic and fact-based analysis of contemporary Islamic resurgence. It deserves to be acknowledged that some efforts are being made in the western world to look upon the Muslim situation in a more realistic manner and also to explore avenues of dialogue and co-operation between Islam and the West despite the dominant discourse which is obsessed with theories and prophecies of conflict and confrontation. I would like to refer in this respect to the works of thinkers like Marshall Hodgson,[3] John Esposito,[4] John Voll,[5] and Hans Kung,[6] among others. Their works provide some silver lining to an otherwise dismal horizon. Dr Umer Chapra's present work, however, is unique and outstanding as it breaks new grounds by presenting the Muslim viewpoint with a high degree of astute scholarship, academic integrity and penetrating insights.

3. Hodgson, Marshall G.S, *The Venture of Islam; Conscience and History in a World Civilization*, 3 Volumes, Chicago: University of Chicago, 1974.
4. Esposito, John, L (ed) *The Oxford History of Islam*, Oxford University Press, 1999. Also, Esposito, John, L and John. D. Voll *Makers of Contemporary Islam*, New York, Oxford University Press, 2001.
5. Voll, John, D *Islam: Continuity and Change in the Modern World*, 2nd Ed, Syracuse University Press, 1994.
6. Kung, Hans, *Islam: Past, Present and Future*, Oxford: One World, 2007. Hans Kung has tried to capture the dynamics of rise and fall and ebb and flow of Muslim civilisation in the form of six paradigms: original Islamic community; Arab empire; classical paradigm of Islam as a world religion; paradigm of Ulema and Sufis; Modernization paradigm; and contemporary (post modern) paradigm. He acknowledges:

   'We must recognize that, for all the historical currents and counter-currents, in the various constantly shifting historical images and lived-out realizations of Islam there is an abiding element to which we shall have to devote all our attention: its basic components and basic perspectives stem from an origin that is by no means random but is given with a quite specific historical personality, a holy scripture. This remains an enduring norm. Hans Kung (2007) page 20

Umer Chapra's major contributions lie in the field of economics, particularly Islamic economics. His excursions into history and philosophy of history also seem to have branched out for his strides into the landscapes of economics. His first major work, *Towards a Just Monetary System* (1985) which has won for him the prestigious King Faisal International Prize (1990) deals with the fundamentals of Islamic finance. It is a pioneering study on the issue of *Ribā* in a modern financial and economic context. It is a scientific exposition of the Islamic rationale for the prohibition of *Ribā* and an original contribution towards developing major contours of a *Ribā*-free monetary system. Chapra has ably demonstrated that, on counts of stability and equity, a *Ribā*-free financial system is not only feasible but also superior to interest-based systems. It seems his mind remained puzzled on the issue as to how can a *Ribā*-free monetary system operate in isolation. It could be fully operationalised and could produce its optimal results only in an economic system whose entire landscape is Islamic. This seems to have prompted his quest to study the Islamic economic system in its entirety and also examine it in the context of the contemporary economic systems of capitalism, socialism and the welfare state. The efforts of this research and reflection were presented in his second major work, *Islam and the Economic Challenge* (1992). This thoroughly researched and well-written book contains highly incisive discussions on capitalism, socialism, welfare state and the Islamic economy.

While making this comparative study, Chapra has also dealt with issues involved in the implementation of an Islamic economic system in the contemporary Muslim context. He tried to focus on the need to develop a comprehensive strategy for the application of the Islamic approach to the economy of Muslim countries. Chapra has emphasized that this new approach cannot produce desirable results unless there are fundamental changes in the objectives and modalities of policies and socio-economic programmes pursued in the Muslim world, which should also be coupled with a thorough restructuring of their economic institutions and mechanisms. An Islamic financial and economic scheme can bear fruits only as part of an overall reform and restructuring programme for the economy.

This seems to have brought him to the next stage of reflection: the problems of social change and the search for historical models for the reconstruction of society and economy. The focus in his third major work: *The Future of Economics: An Islamic Perspective* (2000) was widened to explore these areas. In this book he has tried to grapple with the complex problems of the interface between economy, society and history. He also drew heavily on Ibn Khaldūn's model for socio-economic change which provides a major key to the understanding of the past as a prelude to planning for the future. It was his quest for a new economy based on Islamic values and principles that prompted him to dwell at length on issues of political economy: the role of the state, the processes of social change, and dynamics of history. In this discussion he also discovered the need to emphasize the centrality of *Maqāṣid al-Sharīʿah* (objectives of the Sharīʿah: the protection of *dīn*, intellect, life, posterity and wealth) in dealing with the specifics of *fiqh*. In the matrix of his analysis some other factors also become prominent, particularly the issues of freedom, human rights, justice, good governance, accountability and fighting corruption and the eradication of poverty and ignorance. That is how Chapra seems to have moved along with economics onto the realms of history, sociology and politics. The results of this intellectual pilgrimage can be seen in his present study, *Muslim Civilization: Causes of Decline and Need for Reform*.

Muslim Civilization: Causes of Decline and Need for Reform is a multi-disciplinary study and has to be read and understood in the context of the author's earlier works. This volume, while focussing on the causes of Muslim decline, the nature of Muslim contemporary crisis, and the need for reform, also spells out major elements of a comprehensive strategy for reform and reconstruction. The roles of ideas, individuals, institutions, social movements and state have come into sharp focus. This strategy is rooted in the moral, spiritual and ideational vision of Islam and the ideological and political ambitions of the Muslim *Ummah*. The main building blocks of the proposed strategy consists of the mobilization of economic, sociological, political, technological and structural factors for the reconstruction of Muslim society and state.

Another important feature of this study is that it addresses issues which deal with Muslim civilisation in the context of the current global matrix. The author emphasises the multi-dimensional nature of the challenges and makes a reasoned plea for a comprehensive strategy as against the existing partial strategies for reform. Chapra's advocacy of a holistic approach is in keeping with the historic ethos of the Muslim *Ummah*. This is also in consonance with the longings of humanity that is afflicted by the fruitless efforts to find solutions to economic, social and political problems without bringing about a fundamental shift from the dominant secular and liberal paradigm. A shift which provides a new paradigm that integrates moral and material dimensions and assigns centrality to justice and equity for all human beings.

Clarity of vision is the first major requirement for any worthwhile strategy for reform. Umer Chapra has successfully spelled out a vision for an Islamic society and economy to be carved out under the umbrella of the Islamic paradigm. Efforts to rebuild society in the light of this paradigm are the destiny of the Muslim *Ummah* in the twenty-first century. Vision and action are major planks of this strategy; for vision without action remains a dream, and action without vision is a nightmare and a recipe for disaster.

Chapra's approach has the merit of being morally motivated and man-centred. Justice and well-being for all human beings is the ultimate destiny that beckons mankind. Strategies that emanate from secular and materialistic paradigms ignore these vital dimensions. Chapra pleads for a thorough integration of the moral and spiritual dimensions with the material and technological ones. Human resource development becomes the premium mobile for the establishment of a just socio-economic order. Development and the harnessing of material and technological resources are means to that end, and not ends in themselves. Chapra has rightly emphasized the importance of freedom, equality of opportunities, transparency and accountability at all levels and justice and tolerance as essential elements of any worthwhile strategy for reform. Education and research must reign prominently in this strategy as would be comprehensive programmes for scientific and technological development. Democracy and participatory mechanisms would be the soul of such a system. The ultimate objective is justice for all and the unity and self-reliance of the *Ummah* in a pluralistic, competitive and non-hegemonic world. The challenges of corruption, consumerism and ecological neglect would also have to be addressed. While the individuals remain the real pivot of the system, the role of moral filters, price mechanism, other socio-economic institutions and a positive role of the state are major pillars of this new system. Umer Chapra has identified all the major ingredients of a viable strategy for change so as to enable Muslim civilization to reach a new height while maintaining its distinct identity and becoming a blessing for the *Ummah* and humanity. I have no reservation in suggesting that Umer Chapra's scholarly quartet, particularly the final volume on Muslim civilization is a major contribution towards the development of Islamic socio-economic thought in our times and is bound to open up new vistas for intellectual discourse and discussion within the community of Muslim scholars and dialogue with the rest of the world. These ideas also provide a viable basis for fresh policy formulation and political and socio-economic restructuring of Muslim society.

Leicester
November 16th, 2007

Khurshid Ahmad

PREFACE

We have not sent you except as a blessing for mankind.

(Qur'ān 21:107)

Every nation has a direction [or vision] towards which it turns; you, therefore, try to excel in all that is good.

(Qur'ān 2:148)[1]

If Islam can be shown to be capable of providing fruitful vision to illuminate the modern conscience, then all mankind, and not only Muslims, have a stake in the outcome.

(Marshall Hodgson)[2]

The vision that the Qur'ān gives to Muslims is that of being a blessing for mankind (Qur'ān, 21:107). The Muslim world, however, reflects a picture which is not in harmony with this vision. It has gone through

1. This translation is based on an explanation of the verse in the commentary (*Tafsīr al-Kabīr*) by Fakhr al-Dīn al-Rāzī (d. 606/1209), Volume 4, pp. 131-3. See also footnote 123 in Asad's translation of the Qur'ān.
2. Hodgson, 1977, Volume 3, p. 441.

a persistent process of decline over the last several centuries which has taken it away from the realization of this vision.

This raises the question of what the causes of this failure are. I tried to answer this, briefly, in two chapters (3 and 6) of my book, *The Future of Economics: An Islamic Perspective*. However, since these chapters were part of a work on Economics, they may primarily have attracted the attention of economists, even though the subject is of concern to many others, particularly social and political scientists and reformers. The Islamic Foundation, therefore, urged me to discuss the causes of decline more comprehensively in a separate title, one that would draw the attention of a wider circle of readers than just economists and one that would also suggest a practical reform programme. In response to this request, I have substantially revised and expanded those earlier chapters and added some others along with a more comprehensive concluding chapter on the needed reform. I hope this might set into motion a discussion on the causes of Muslim decline and the reforms that are needed to help fulfill the Qur'ānic dream of making the Muslims a blessing for mankind.

I am extremely grateful to Prof. Robert Whaples, Dr. Murad Hofmann, Prof. Anas Zarqa, Prof. M. Nejatullah Siddiqi, Dr. Sami Al-Suwailem and Prof. Khurshid Ahmad who carefully read the manuscript's preliminary draft and made valuable comments which have proven very useful in my revisions. Consequently, the final product reflects a number of their precious insights. None of them has, however, seen the final draft and I am, therefore, myself responsible for any errors that may still remain. The views expressed in this book are my own and do not necessarily reflect those of either the institute where I am now working or the one where I worked in the past.

I have benefited significantly from a number of books and papers which I have read over the last several years. It was, however, not possible to give credit to all of them in the list of references, which primarily includes those works I have cited. Inclusion of all the books and papers from which I have benefited would have required a much longer bibliography, one that may not have been economically feasible. This does not in any way, however, mitigate the value of their contribution to the current title. I have also benefited from the translations of the Qur'ān by Abdullah Yusuf Ali and Muhammad Asad, and of Ibn Khaldūn's *Muqaddimah* by Rosenthal (1967) and Issawi (1950), even though I have not reproduced their translations. Translations of *aḥādīth, fiqh* and other Arabic literature quoted in this book are my own. However, I have benefited from the insights of my daughter, Dr. Sumayyah, in making some of these translations. I wish to thank Dr. Abdul Latif Bello who has been very kind in providing me with statistical data on Muslim countries and, thereby, saving a great deal of my time. My thanks are also due to Dr. Manazir Ahsan, Director General, Islamic Foundation, Leicester, UK, who tirelessly urged me to complete this volume, which was taking rather longer than anticipated because of other engagements. The completion of this work, therefore, owes a great deal to his persistent reminders. Last, but not the least, I wish to record my gratitude to Mrs. Susanne Thackray for her excellent editorial input.

Wherever two years are shown separated by an oblique sign after a classical Muslim personality, dynasty or event, the first year refers to the lunar Hijri calendar, while the second refers to the Gregorian. Although this makes the reading a little cumbersome, it was considered necessary to help the reader realize when that individual or dynasty existed or when the event took place after the Prophet (pbuh).

As with my previous writings, my debt to my wife, Khairunnisa, is immense and immeasurable. A substantial part of the credit goes to her for her constant help and encouragement and for taking over a number of my household responsibilities to enable me to complete this book. I am also indebted to Shaikh Mohammad Rashid and Mohammed Rasul Hoque for the valuable secretarial assistance they have provided in the book's preparation.

Jeddah **M. Umer Chapra**
10 Jumādā I 1428 H
27 May 2007

INTRODUCTION: SOME CRUCIAL QUESTIONS

The Muslim world is currently passing through a difficult phase in its history. Even though it has more than one-fifth of the world's population and is rich in natural resources, it produces only around 8 percent of the purchasing power adjusted GNP of the world. It is plagued by illiteracy, poverty, unemployment and extremely difficult macro-economic imbalances. It is far behind major industrial, and even some developing countries in almost all fields of life, including the economic, political, educational, technological and military. Even in terms of realization of the *maqāṣid al-Sharīʿah* (objectives of the Sharīʿah), it presents a sorry picture.[1] In place of moral strength, the need-fulfilment of all, socio-economic justice, and brotherhood that one would expect to prevail in a Muslim society, one finds that there is moral decadence, deep-rooted inequalities of income and wealth, conflict and disunity. While even the basic needs of a considerable proportion of the population remain unsatisfied, the rich and upper middle classes live in luxury. The existence of poverty alongside affluence tends to corrode the fabric of brotherhood and social solidarity and serves as one of the prime causes of crime and violence, social unrest and political instability. Some of the powerful industrial countries are trying to exploit this weakness to dominate Muslim countries, particularly those that are rich in natural resources or that occupy a strategic geographic position.

This gives rise to a number of questions. One of these concerns the factors that have led the Muslim world to this weak position after having enjoyed a glorious past stretching over several centuries. Efforts to answer this question bring into focus another important question about the factors that enabled Muslims to perform extremely well in the earlier centuries of Islam. Did Islam play a positive role in the earlier rise of Muslims? If this earlier rise was due to Islam, then why has it now become ineffective in enabling the Muslims to improve their condition? Could it be that while Islam was able to contribute to their rise in the past, it is no longer capable of enabling them to respond successfully to the newer challenges they face in modern times? If, however, Islam is not the cause of Muslim malaise, then what is to blame? Once the cause or causes of Muslim decline are determined, then there arises the question of what can be done to reform the Muslim world and enable it to rise again.

A number of scholars[2] have emphasized different internal as well as external factors that led to the decline of Muslims, particularly after the twelfth century. Some of the most important of these are moral degeneration, loss of dynamism in Islam after the rise of dogmatism and rigidity; decline in intellectual and scientific activity; internal revolts and disunity along with continued external invasions and warfare that ravaged and weakened the economies, created fiscal imbalances and insecurity of life and property, and reduced investment and growth; decline in agriculture, crafts and trade; exhaustion or loss of mines and precious metals, and natural disasters, such as plague and famine, which led to a decline in the overall population and demand followed by the weakening of the economy.

While the adverse impact of all these factors cannot be denied, it should be expected that a living and dynamic society can discuss and freely analyze all these factors, and not only develop but also implement a proper strategy to effectively offset their adverse effects at least in the long-run, if not in the short-run. Why, then, were the Muslims unable to do this? Was there something that prevented them from responding successfully to the internal as well as external challenges that they faced? It is necessary to weave all these factors together, as an interrelated chain of events, into a philosophy of development to show how most of them were triggered by some major cause in a manner that made it difficult for society to stop the decline without coming to grips with the cause that triggered the decline.

There is no doubt that numerous efforts were made over the last several centuries to stop this decline. Accordingly, Muslim decline has not been a straight-line phenomenon. There have been a number of ups and downs. However, because the primary cause persisted, the reversals continued and the process of decline gained momentum until it reached its trough in the nineteenth and the first half of the twentieth century. The objective of this exercise is not to show that, if the trigger mechanism in the historical process of decline had not come into operation, the decline may not have taken place. No society has been able to sustain continued progress for 1,400 years and it is wishful thinking to expect the Muslim world to be an exception. The primary focus of this exercise is, therefore, the future and not the past. The future is, however, so closely linked with the past that unless we correctly identify all the forces of decay and show how they were triggered and how they built momentum through mutual interaction over the years, it will not be possible to suggest an effective strategy for accelerating future development in Muslim countries.

Some crucial factors responsible for a society's rise or fall

Seeking guidance from the Qur'ān and the Sunnah

This makes us cast around for some of the crucial factors that are responsible for a society's rise or fall. For this purpose, the inherent tendency of a Muslim is to turn towards the Qur'ān and the Sunnah for guidance. According to the Qur'ān, the most important factor in society's rise or fall is the human being himself. The Qur'ān clearly states that "God does not change the condition of a people until they change their own inner selves" (13:11; see also 8:33), and that "corruption has appeared everywhere because of what *people* have done" (30:41, italics added). This implies that human beings are themselves the architects of their fate. They are not only the end but also the means of their development and, as the Qur'ān rightly points out, they can have nothing more than what they strive for (53:39). Their rise and fall can, therefore, be rationally explained by analyzing their own motivations, efforts, characters and capabilities. Toynbee also reflected this same idea by stating: "Civilizations die from suicide, not by murder."[3]

Human beings do not, however, operate in a vacuum. There are a number of factors that influence them and affect their performance. The most important of these is their own motivation. They need to have the right motivation – motivation to do their utmost not only to improve their own condition, but also to push forward the frontiers of their society's development. Their motivation is, however, affected by a number of factors, the most important of which is the extent to which their effort helps improve their own well-being. Therefore, one of the primary conditions for sustained development is that the fruits of development must be shared *equitably* by all the people in society, irrespective of their colour, sex, age, position, wealth or religion.

This raises the question of what it is that helps fulfil this condition for development. This is where the society's worldview and institutions come into the picture. If the worldview and institutions are such that they ensure justice and fairness at all levels of society, economy and polity, to enable all individuals to fulfil their material as well as non-material needs,[4] then there will be social solidarity as well as sustainable development. If the resources provided by this development are not wasted in conflict, war and extravagance, but rather used to improve the moral, physical and intellectual qualities of the people, enhance their knowledge base and technology, raise savings for investment after fulfilling basic needs, and develop their socio-economic, judicial and political institutions, then there will be further development and improvement in people's well-being. This will enhance their motivation to work hard and efficiently and promote further development. Justice, therefore, needs to be a key factor in the analysis of development and decline.

Therefore, while Islam has stressed the role of human beings themselves in their own development, it has simultaneously placed maximum emphasis on justice (Qur'ān, 57:25; 5:8; 4:58; 42:15; 6:15; 16:90; 6:115). If there is no justice, there can be no development (Qur'ān, 20:111). Injustice serves as the most venomous poison for development by adversely affecting human motivation as well as the socio-economic and political environment through a complex process which it is difficult to predict precisely. Even if a country manages to develop in spite of injustice, this development may not be sustainable in the long-run. There will be a rise in discontent, conflict and disunity, leading ultimately to decline.

Justice, however, demands certain socially agreed values, institutions or rules of behaviour which everyone accepts as given and abides by them conscientiously. Some of these are: sanctity of life, property and honour, truthfulness, honesty and integrity, fairness, willingness to learn, work hard and help the needy, and devotion to duty. The presence of these qualities among people promotes the honest fulfilment of all contracts and socio-economic and political obligations and, thereby, social solidarity.[5] No society can manage to develop or sustain its development if the moral quality of its people is low and social solidarity among them is weak.[6]

However, unless moral development is complemented by economic development, it may not be possible to expand the knowledge and technological base of society, increase savings and investment, and accelerate development. Lack of development will, in turn, frustrate society's effort to ensure justice and the well-being of all. This will adversely affect the motivation to work hard and efficiently and, thereby, hurt development.

One factor which is crucially important for the moral, physical and intellectual development of individuals is the proper upbringing of children. For this purpose, Islam, like other major religions, emphasizes the crucial importance of the family. If the family fails, it may be difficult to offset the setback. Families will, however, not succeed in fulfilling their responsibility if, firstly, the parents do not themselves have the qualities of character that need to be inculcated in children and, secondly, there does not prevail in the family an atmosphere of love and affection, and mutual care and respect. The husband and wife need to not only respect each other but also faithfully fulfil their mutual obligations. If, instead, any one of them tries to boss over the other and neglects his/her responsibilities, there is likely to be an atmosphere of tension and conflict which, if not corrected, may ultimately lead to divorce and disintegration. This, in turn, tends to have a damaging effect on children's moral, psychological and intellectual development.

In addition to proper upbringing, children (both boys and girls) also need education to learn the skills in demand and to be able to push forward their society's knowledge and technological base. Well-equipped and well-staffed schools, colleges and universities with adequate research facilities are indispensable for this purpose. If these do not exist, there will be a setback. If future generations are of a lower standard than the preceding ones, and do not have command over a continually improving knowledge base and technology, society will have set itself on a declining path. This places proper upbringing along with education, research and advancement in technology among the most crucial factors for development.

It is also necessary to have freedom of thought, expression and enterprise. Without these, people will not have the initiative and drive that are needed to be innovative and to push forward the frontiers of their society's knowledge and technology. One of the important missions of the Prophet (pbuh) was to free mankind from the chains that bind them (Qur'ān, 7:157). Shackles of any kind, whether physical or mental, can be a hindrance to development. People should be free to think and act freely, provided that they do not cross the bounds of moral values. It is also important to avoid confrontation, conflict and war as much as possible because these not only generate insecurity and tension but also divert resources away from nation-building activities and, thereby, frustrate the realization of the *maqāṣid al-Sharī'ah.*

No society can hope to develop its entire knowledge base and technology itself. It has to take advantage of developments elsewhere. It may not, however, be able to do this if it has a superiority complex, is not tolerant of differences of opinion, does not encourage enterprise and innovation, and is not willing to remove its weaknesses by analyzing their causes, adopting remedial measures, and readily accepting beneficial ideas from other cultures and civilizations. The acquisition of useful knowledge and technology from anywhere and the ability to develop it further to suit its own circumstances and goals has to be one of society's ideals. The Prophet (pbuh), therefore, exhorted Muslims to "seek knowledge even if it is from China", because "wisdom is the lost asset of a Muslim; he is the most deserving of it whenever he finds it".[7] Without such an attitude towards knowledge acquisition, a society may not be able to gain the momentum that it needs.

The values and institutions that a society has, may be of little value if they are not effectively and impartially enforced on everyone, irrespective of their status or wealth. Two factors help greatly in such enforcement. One is people's deep faith in the rightness of their values and worldview and their willingness to abide by them of their own volition. This is more likely to happen if the values and worldview have a Divine origin. This helps create in them an inner urge to live up to these values even if this means a sacrifice of self-interest. Any man-made worldview and value system is unlikely to command such unswerving loyalty. The second factor is an effective role taken by the government to enforce these values impartially on all so that no one is able to get away scot-free. The Prophet (pbuh), clearly recognized this role of government by saying that "God restrains through the sovereign more than what he restrains through the Qur'ān."[8] The Qur'ān can only give values, it cannot, by itself, enforce them. It is the moral and legal responsibility of the state to enforce society's values and ensure justice. In addition, the government also needs to provide the infrastructure and facilities that the people need to perform their tasks more efficiently. This essentially calls for what is nowadays commonly referred to as good governance. This was emphasized by the Prophet (pbuh) by his saying that: "Anyone who has been given the charge of a people but does not live up to it with sincerity, will not taste even the fragrance of paradise."[9] Good governance is indispensable for sustainable development. A corrupt and incompetent government can dilute the favourable effect of all the other factors and serve as a serious obstacle to development.

There is a greater chance of good governance if honest and competent people hold key positions, and there are also checks and balances on them. Although this may at times be possible even under authoritarian rule, it is normally more likely to be the case in a democracy with a representative parliament, the proper accountability of all officials, an honest judiciary, and a free press. The existence of all these should enable society to utilize its resources more effectively for overall development. Development will, in turn, provide the resources needed by the government to defend the country against external threats, enforce law and order, ensure justice, and provide the social and economic infrastructure that is necessary for ensuring sustainable development.

The need for an explanatory model for development and decline

The above discussion shows that even though the rise or decline of a society depends on the human beings themselves, they are in turn, influenced by a number of factors that are mutually interdependent and influence each other over a long period that is difficult to predict precisely. One could add a number of other factors to those indicated above. However, even if a comprehensive list were prepared, it would not necessarily yield a theory that can explain a society's rise or decline. It is though important to show which of these factors triggers the rise and how the effect of this is transmitted to other factors, enabling them all to contribute to the development of an otherwise dormant society. Conversely, what is it that triggers the decline and how is the effect of this transmitted to other factors, leading to the overall decline of a society that has already attained a high level of development. This is what a theory is expected to do. Only a theory which accomplishes this will help us in our task of explaining the rise and decline of Muslim society.

Given that many scholars, including Ibn Khaldūn (d. 808/1406)[10] and Gibbon (d. 1208/1794) in the past, and Spengler (1947), Schweitzer (1949), Sorokin (1951), Toynbee (1957), North and Thomas (1973), Kennedy (1987) and a number of others in modern times, have discussed the rise and fall of civilizations the construction of a new model may be justifiable only if the existing models are not satisfactory. It would be preposterous to say that none of these models provides valuable insights: they all do in different ways. This raises the question, then, of which model to choose.

Ibn Khaldūn's model of socio-economic and political dynamics spelt out in his *Muqaddimah* or Introduction [to History], and briefly discussed in the next chapter, not only takes into account most of the factors discussed above in the light of the Qur'ān and the *Sunnah* but also shows the factor that triggered the Muslim society's rapid rise from its humble beginnings in the Arabian bedouin environment and the factor that triggered its decline thereafter.[11] The *Muqaddimah* is the first volume of Ibn Khaldūn's seven-volume history, briefly called *Kitāb al-'Ibar* or the Book of Lessons [of History].[12] The last of these seven volumes is his autobiography (*Al-Ta'rīf bi Ibn Khaldūn*), which provides considerable insight into the deteriorating socio-economic and political conditions prevailing in his time, conditions that led to the development of his philosophy of history.

It is rightly said that necessity is the mother of invention. This is also true of the philosophies of history or intelligent interpretations of historical events, which have generally appeared when the need arose before, during, or after periods of crisis in the life of nations.[13] Ibn Khaldūn must also have felt the same need to write what Sorokin considers to be, in step with Toynbee, "one of the greatest philosophies of history ever written".[14] He lived in very difficult times resulting from the decay that had overtaken Muslim society. The 'Abbāsid caliphate had come to an end in 656/1258, around three-quarters of a century before his birth, after the pillage, burning and near destruction of Baghdād and its surrounding areas by the Mongols. A number of other calamities, including the Crusades (488-690/1095-1291), Mongol invasions (656-758/1258-1355), and Black Death (740s/1340s) had also weakened most of the central Muslim lands. In addition, the Circassian Mamlūks (784-922/1382-1517), during whose period Ibn Khaldūn spent nearly a third of his life, were corrupt, inefficient and followed policies that could not but accelerate the decline.

As a result of all these adverse developments, the condition of the Muslims was, in general, very sad. Ibn Khaldūn's family was no exception. It was also suffering, like other Muslims, from deteriorating living conditions and was compelled by force of circumstance to migrate from Spain to Tunis a few years before the consummation of the *Reconquista* (Christian reconquest). Ibn Khaldūn was, thus, born in Tunis in 732/1332 and not in Seville (Ishbīliyah), where his family had been domiciled for almost seven hundred years prior to its migration. While he was still in his early teens, the scourge of Black Death claimed the life of his parents as well as that of many relatives, close family friends and teachers.[15] Consequently, he had to undergo a great deal of suffering. However, the Maghrib (North Africa west of Egypt), of which Tunis is a part, was also in a state of political turmoil as a result of wars between different dynasties. The resultant upheavals forced Ibn Khaldūn to move from place to place, including Fez (the capital of Morocco), Tlemcen (Algeria), Andalusia (Spain), and Bijāyah or Bougie (Algeria).

Under these circumstances, it would be strange if a person of his moral and mental calibre were not in search of an effective strategy to bring about a reversal of the declining tide.[16] As a social scientist of extraordinary intellectual capacities,[17] he was well aware that the reversal could not be dreamed of without first drawing lessons from history and determining the factors that had led the Muslim civilization to bloom out of its humble beginnings in the cradle of Arabian bedouin society and to decline thereafter. He was of the view that the future resembles the past just as water resembles water[18] and, therefore, it should be possible to predict the future by analyzing the past. Hence, the primary task of historiography (*'Ilm al-Ta'rīkh*) was not to confine itself merely to just a recording of historical events. It was rather to analyze the causes and origins, or the hows and whys, of the various phenomena in human history so as to be able to predict what might happen in the future.[19]

During this process of moving from place to place, Ibn Khaldūn was looking for an opportunity to express his ideas about historiography in writing. He found this opportunity when he was able to stay, for four years (776-780/1374-78), in Qal'at Ibn Salamah, a secluded fort in what is now Algeria. Here, he completed the preliminary draft of the *Muqaddimah* and some parts of the *Kitāb al-'Ibar*. He then moved to Tunis where he stayed from 780-784/1378-1382 to consult references in libraries with the purpose of finalizing this monumental work of history. He finally moved, in 1382, to Cairo where he received a warm welcome as a result of his reputation which had already spread there. He spent the rest of his professional life there until his death in 808/1406 at the age of 74.

A number of objections may be raised against the use of Ibn Khaldūn's model. One of these is that it is very old. Why should one use an old model when more recent ones are available? This objection would hold ground only if the model is unable to help us in our objective of analyzing the rise and fall of Muslim societies. The fact, however, is that this model uses scientific cause and effect analysis to derive the principles that lie behind the rise and fall of a ruling dynasty or state (*dawlah*), or civilization (*'umrān*).[20] It is powerful enough to enable us to answer questions about why the Muslim world rose rapidly and continued to rise for several centuries and why it declined thereafter to the extent that it lost its *élan vital*, and not only became largely colonized but also unable to successfully respond to the challenges that it faced. Furthermore, his model is based on the Islamic worldview and not only takes into account all the above-mentioned factors that are responsible for the rise and decline of a society but also shows, through the use of circular causation, how one factor triggers the rise or fall and how the effect of this is transmitted to all other factors. Consequently, instead of being couched in a secularist framework, the *Muqaddimah* gives a central place to the reform of human beings as well as their society and the institutions that affect them. It emphasizes the importance of justice, social solidarity and economic well-being in the sustained overall development of a society, and the role that moral values and their effective enforcement by the political authority play in this whole process. It is difficult to find any other model that is in such great harmony with the ethos of Islam.

A second objection to the use of Ibn Khaldūn's model may be that it gives the impression of being concerned with the rise and fall of dynasties. This objection may be valid but only if we forget to remember the real objective behind Ibn Khaldūn's writing of the *Muqaddimah*. As a committed and well-meaning Muslim, his ultimate focus was not the perpetuation of rule by any specific dynasty. It was rather the survival of the Muslim civilization through a reversal of the decline that had set in. He couldn't have cared much if a specific dynasty fell as a result of its corruption and inner weaknesses. This was inevitable. He was, however, worried that, if dynasties continued to fall, one after the other, it would have an adverse impact on the whole Muslim civilization. Consequently, there is a clear advantage in benefiting from his insights and by making his model a base for the analysis.

A third objection to the use of Ibn Khaldūn's model may be that the *Muqaddimah* seems to use an organic theory of development according to which "old age is a chronic disease" and there is no cure for the decay once it has set in.[21] It continues, as it does in the case of the human body. This impression may result from the fact that Ibn Khaldūn was discussing the rise and fall of dynasties. However, dynasties come and go whilst civilization needs to be saved from perishing. Even in modern times, while one or two corrupt and incompetent governments may not do excessive harm to a given country, a successive series of such governments may jeopardize that country's future. Therefore, Ibn Khaldūn's verdict about dynasties need not necessarily be true of civilizations, and it is the latter with which we are concerned. Dynasties may collapse and never bloom again in step with what Danilevsky and Spengler perceived.[22]

For civilizations, it should be possible to have more than one period of blossoming and decline. Ibn Khaldūn would perhaps not have written the *Muqaddimah* if he had not been optimistic about the reversal of the declining tide of Muslim society. There is no natural law that every civilization having once blossomed must necessarily wither away without any chance of revival. This is also the verdict of the religious worldview which underlies Ibn Khaldūn's model. The missions of the messengers of God would not have been meaningful if a reversal was not possible. All of them tried to reform their societies by reforming the human beings and the institutions that affected them. This implies that a reversal is possible if people reform both themselves and their institutions.

However, while I have used Ibn Khaldūn's model, it would be impudent not to take into account the insights of a number of other scholars who have also written on this subject. This is especially necessary because six hundred years have passed since Ibn Khaldūn wrote the *Muqaddimah*. A number of changes have taken place since then in all walks of life. It is, therefore, necessary to make adjustments to his model[23] in response to the changed realities around the world, including Muslim countries, by benefiting from the insights of other scholars. This should also help improve the analysis.

Notes

1. There has been a substantial discussion of the *maqāṣid* in *fiqh* literature, some of the most prominent exponents being al-Māturīdī (d. 333/945), al-Shāhī, (d. 365/975), al-Bāqillānī (403/1012), al-Juwaynī (d. 478/1085), al-Ghazālī (d. 505/1111), Fakhr al-Dīn al-Rāzī (d. 606/1209), al-Āmidī (d. 631/1234), ʿIzz al-Dīn ibn ʿAbd al-Salām (d. 660/1262), Ibn Taymiyyah (d. 728/1327) and al-Shāṭibī (d. 790/1388). For a modern discussion of these, see: Masud, 1977; al-Raysūnī, 1992, pp. 25-55; Nyazee, 1994, pp. 189-268. For a brief discussion see, Chapra, 2007 (forthcoming).
2. Some of these include: Hitti, 1958; Arsalan, 1962; Issawi, 1966 and 1970; Lambton, 1970; Saunders (ed.), 1966; Inalcik, 1970, and Inalcik and Quataert, 1994; Musallam, 1981; Zakariyyah Bashir, 1977; Najjār, 1989; al-Samarra'i, 1993; Kuran, 1997 and 2004 and Abū Sulaymān, 1991 and 2005. Lewis, (1962) gives the views of Luṭfī Pāshā, Kochu Bey, Ḥājjī Khalīfah, Ḥuseyn Ḥazarfenn and Sārī Mehmed Pāshā on the causes of Ottoman decline
3. Toynbee, 1935, Volume 4, p. 120.

4. Material needs include: proper nourishment, clothing, education, housing, medical care, transport, and honest means of livelihood. Non-material needs include: justice, freedom, security of life, property and honour, social equality, family and social harmony, and freedom from crime, tension, insecurity and anomie.
5. All these qualities are now generally accepted as necessary for development. See for example, Myrdal, 1968, Volume 1, pp. 57-69.
6. The Qur'ān emphatically pronounces that "he succeeds, who adopts righteousness" (87:14; see also 91:9-10). Individual righteousness promotes social capital, which is now considered to be crucial for development. See, for example, Dasgupta and Serageldin, 2000; Zaheer, Evily and Perrone, 1998 and Gintis, 2002.
7. The first *ḥadīth* is reported from Anas ibn Mālik by al-Bayhaqī in *Shu'ab al-Īmān* (Volume 2, p. 254:1663). The second *ḥadīth* is reported from Abū Hurayrah by al-Tirmidhī in the *Kitāb al-'Ilm* of his *Jāmi'*. This is a weak *ḥadīth* but is, nevertheless, widely quoted because of its harmony with Islam's ethos. What it implies is that no one has a monopoly over wisdom. It is the common property of all mankind and Muslims should feel free to acquire it, irrespective of where they find it.
8. Cited by al-Māwardī, 1955, p. 121.
9. Al-Bukhārī, from Ma'qil ibn Yasār, Volume 9, p. 80, *Kitāb al-Aḥkām*.
10. Wherever two years are indicated in the text, the first one refers to the Hijrah year and the second to the Gregorian year. If only one year is given, it refers to the Gregorian year unless indicated otherwise. If a year is not preceded by the letter d (died), then it refers to the year in which the book or paper being referred to was published and not the year in which the author died.
11. Several different editions of the *Muqaddimah* are now available in Arabic. The one I have used is that published in Cairo by al-Maktabah al-Tijāriyyah al-Kubrā without any indication of the year of publication. It has the advantage of showing all the vowel marks, which makes the reading relatively easier. The *Muqaddimah* was translated into English in three volumes by Franz Rosenthal. Its first edition was published in 1958 and the second edition in 1967. Selections from the *Muqaddimah* by Charles Issawi were published in 1950 under the title, *An Arab Philosophy of History: Selections from the Prolegomena of Ibn Khaldūn of Tunis (1332-1406)*. Even though I have given the reference to Rosenthal's translation (R) wherever I have referred to Ibn Khaldūn's *Muqaddimah* (M), the translations used in this paper are my own.
12. The full name of the book in Arabic (given in the References) may be freely translated as 'The Book of Lessons and the Record of Cause and Effect in the History of Arabs, Persians and Berbers and their Powerful Contemporaries.'
13. Sorokin, 1951, p. 4.
14. Ibid., p. 5.
15. Ibn Khaldūn, *Al-Ta'rīf*, p. 37.

16. Talbi, 1986, p. 808.
17. Toynbee, 1935, Volume 3, pp. 321-322.
18. *Muqaddimah*, p. 10; R: I, 17.
19. *Muqaddimah*, pp. 3-7 and 9-34; R: I, pp. 6-14 and 15-68. See also Muhsin Mahdi, 1964, p. 31.
20. For a more detailed discussion of this model, see the next chapter and also Chapra, 2000, Chapter 5, pp. 145-172.
21. *Muqaddimah*, pp. 293 and 294; R: II, 117.
22. Spengler, 1947, and Sorokin, 1951, p. 164.
23. Some of these adjustments are indicated in Chapter 1 after the discussion of Ibn Khaldūn's model.

I

IBN KHALDŪN'S THEORY OF DEVELOPMENT AND DECLINE[1]

Ibn Khaldūn's entire model is condensed to a substantial extent, though not fully, in the following advice extended by him to the sovereign:

1. The strength of the sovereign (*al-mulk*) does not materialize except through the implementation of the Sharīʿah[2]...;
2. The Sharīʿah cannot be implemented except by the sovereign (*al-mulk*);
3. The sovereign cannot gain strength except through the people (*al-rijāl*);
4. The people cannot be sustained except by wealth (*al-māl*);
5. Wealth cannot be acquired except through development (*al-ʿimārah*);
6. Development can not be attained except through justice (*al-ʿadl*);
7. Justice is the criterion (*al-mīzān*) by which God will evaluate mankind, and
8. The sovereign is charged with the responsibility of actualizing justice (*Muqaddimah* (M): p. 39; Rosenthal's translation (R): Volume 1, p. 80).[3]

The entire *Muqaddimah* is an elaboration upon this advice, which consists of, in Ibn Khaldūn's own words: "eight wise principles (*kalimāt ḥikamiyyah*) of political wisdom, each one dovetailed with the other for mutual strength, in such a circular manner that the beginning or the end is indistinguishable" (M: p. 403; R: I, p. 82).

The strength of this model lies in its multidisciplinary and dynamic character. It is multidisciplinary because it links all important socio-economic and political variables, including the sovereign or political authority (G), beliefs and rules of behaviour or the Sharīʿah (S), people (N), wealth or stock of resources (W), development (g), and justice (j), in a circular and interdependent manner, each influencing the others and, in turn, being influenced by them.[4]

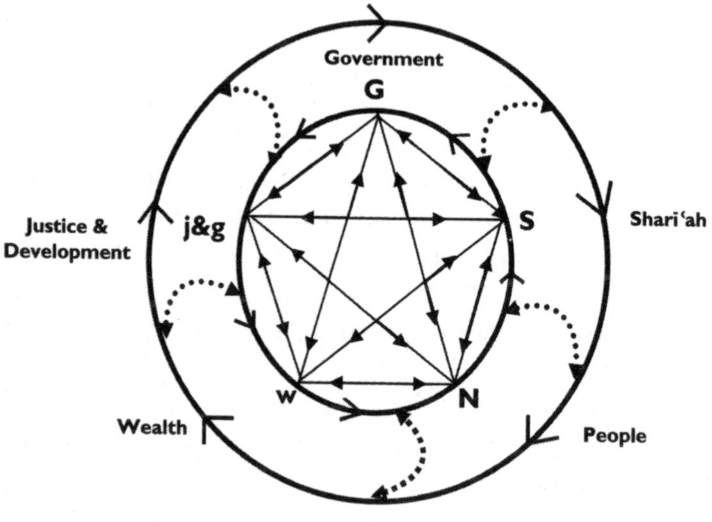

Since the operation of this cycle takes place through a chain reaction over a long period of three generations, or almost 120 years, circular causation as well as dynamism is introduced into the whole analysis. This helps explain how political moral, institutional, social, economic, demographic, and historical factors interact with each other over a long period of time to lead to the development and decline, or the rise and fall, of a state or civilization.

In a long term analysis of this kind, there is no *ceteris paribus* clause because none of the variables is assumed to remain constant. One of the variables acts as the trigger mechanism.[5] If the other sectors of society react in the same direction as the trigger mechanism, the decay will gain momentum through an interrelated chain reaction such that it becomes difficult, over time, to identify the cause from the effect. If the other sectors do not react in the same direction, then the decay in one sector may not spread to the others and either the decaying sector may be reformed over time or the decline of the civilization may be much slower.

The role of the human being (N)

The centre of Ibn Khaldūn's analysis is the human being[6] because the rise and fall of civilizations is closely dependent on the well-being or misery of the people. This is, in turn, dependent not just on economic variables but also on the closely interrelated role of moral, institutional, psychological, political, social, and demographic factors through a process of circular causation extending over a long period of history (M: pp. 39 and 287; R: I, p. 80 and II, p. 105). This emphasis on the human being is in keeping with the Qur'ānic verses quoted in the Introduction, which state that, "God does not change the condition of a people until they change their own inner selves" (13:11), and that "Corruption has appeared everywhere because of what *people* have done" (30:41, italics added). These two verses along with many others emphasize the role of human beings themselves in their rise and fall. This is why all God's Messengers (including Abraham, Moses, Jesus and Muḥammad) came to this world to reform human beings and the institutions that affect their behaviour.[7]

The role of development (g) and justice (j)

If human beings are the centre of analysis, then development and justice become the most crucial links in the chain of causation. Development is essential because unless there is a perceptible improvement in the well-being of the people, they will not be motivated to do their best (M: p. 287; R: II, p. 109). Moreover, in the absence of development, the inflow of scholars, artisans, labour and capital that need to take place from other societies to boost development further may not take place (M: pp. 362-3; R: II, pp. 271-6). This too may make it difficult to sustain development and may ultimately lead to a decline (M: p. 359; R: II, p. 270).

Development in Ibn Khaldūn's model does not refer merely to economic growth (M: p. 39 and pp. 347-49; R: I, p. 39 and II, pp. 243-49). It encompasses all-round human development such that each variable enriches the others (G, S, N, W, j, and g) and is in turn enriched by them, contributing thereby to the true well-being or happiness of people and ensuring not only the survival but also the civilization's rise. Economic development cannot be brought about by economic forces alone in isolation of the non-economic and spiritual forces of society. It needs moral, social, political and demographic support. If this support is not available, economic development may not be triggered, and if it is available, it may not, however, be sustainable.

Development is, however, not possible without justice. Justice, like development, though is also not conceived by him in a narrow economic sense but rather in the more comprehensive sense of justice in all spheres of human life. Ibn Khaldūn clearly states: "Do not think that injustice consists in only taking money or property from its owner without compensation or cause, even though this is what is commonly understood. Injustice is more comprehensive than this. Anyone who confiscates the property of someone else or who forces him to work for him, or presses an unjustifiable claim against him, or imposes on him a duty not required by the Sharīʿah, has committed an injustice. Collection of unjustified taxes is also injustice; transgression on another's property or taking it away by force or theft constitutes injustice; denying other people their rights is also injustice" (M: p. 288; R: II, pp. 106-7). "One of the greatest injustices and the most destructive of development is the unjustifiable imposition of tasks on people and subjecting them to forced labour" (M: p. 289; R: II, pp. 108-9). Justice is considered so crucial by Ibn Khaldūn for development that he entitled a whole section as 'Injustice Triggers the Destruction of Civilization' (M: pp. 286-90; R: II, pp. 103-111). This is why justice and development are juxtaposed in the above diagram. "The extent to which property rights are infringed determines the extent to which the incentive to earn and acquire it goes…If the incentive is gone, they refrain from earning" (M: p. 286, R: II, p. 103). This adversely affects people's efficiency, innovativeness, entrepreneurship, drive and other qualities, ultimately leading to society's disintegration and decline.

Justice in this comprehensive sense leads to the development and strengthening of *ʿaṣabiyyah*, which has variously been translated as 'social solidarity', 'group feeling' or 'social cohesion'. Justice promotes social solidarity by ensuring the fulfillment of mutual obligations and an equitable sharing of the fruits of development, and thereby, the well-being of all. This helps create mutual trust and cooperation, without which it is not possible to promote division of labour and specialization, which are necessary for the accelerated development of any economy (M: 41-43; R: I, 89-92). The absence of justice tends to generate discontent among people, dishearten them, and adversely affect their solidarity. This, in turn, not only adversely affects their motive to work but also saps their efficiency, entrepreneurial drive and other good qualities needed for development, ultimately leading to society's disintegration and decline.

The crucial role that trust plays in development is now being rightly emphasized by economists[8] and has become a part of 'conventional wisdom' or 'embeddedness'. Ibn Khaldūn used the word *'aṣabiyyah* for what is, to a great extent, currently referred to as 'social capital' or 'social infrastructure'.[9] However, some scholars have raised objections against the use of the word 'capital' for something that is abstract and cannot be possessed, like the physical capital of individuals.[10] Therefore, Ibn Khaldūn's use of the expression *'aṣabiyyah* or 'social solidarity' seems to be a better alternative.

The role of institutions (S) and the government (G)

Justice, however, necessitates certain rules of behaviour called institutions in Institutional Economics and moral values in religious worldviews. They are the standards by which people interact with, and fulfill their obligations towards, each other (M: pp. 157-58; R: I, pp. 319-21). All societies have such rules based on their own worldview. The primary basis of these rules in a Muslim society is the Sharī'ah. "Divine Laws command the doing of good and prohibit the doing of what is evil and destructive" (M: p. 304; R: II, p. 142). They are, therefore, according to Ibn Khaldūn, "for the good of human beings and serve their interests" (M: p. 143; R: I, p. 292). Their Divine origin carries the potential to help promote their willing acceptance and compliance and to serve as a powerful cement for holding a large group together (M: pp. 151-52; R: I, pp. 305-8 and 319-22). This can help curb socially harmful behaviour, ensure justice, and enhance solidarity and mutual trust among people, thereby promoting development.

The Sharī'ah cannot, however, play a meaningful role unless it is implemented fairly and impartially (M: pp. 39 and 43; R: I, p. 80 and pp. 91-92). The Sharī'ah can only give rules of behaviour, it cannot itself enforce them. It is the responsibility of the political authority to ensure compliance through incentives and deterrents (M: pp. 127-28; R: I, pp. 262-63). The Prophet (pbuh) clearly recognized this by saying: "God restrains through the sultan (sovereign) more than what he restrains through the Qur'ān."[11] For Ibn Khaldūn, political authority has the same relationship to a civilization as form has to matter (M: pp. 371 and 376; R: II, pp. 291 and 300). "It is not possible to conceive of political authority without civilization and of civilization without political authority" (M: p. 376; R: II, p. 300). However, Ibn Khaldūn clearly emphasizes "good rulership is equivalent to gentleness" (M: p. 188; R: I, p. 383). "If the ruler is tyrannical and harsh in punishments... the people become fearful and depressed and seek to protect themselves by means of lies, ruses and deception. This becomes their character trait. Their perceptions and character become corrupted... They may conspire to kill him" (M: pp. 188-2; R: I, p. 383).

While Ibn Khaldūn emphasizes the role of the state in development, he does not, in step with other classical Muslim scholars, support a totalitarian role for the state. He stands for what has now become characterized as 'good governance'. Recognition of private property and respect for individual freedom within the constraints of moral values is a part of Islamic teachings and has always been prevalent in Muslim thinking. The job of the state in the writings of almost all classical Muslim scholars, including Ibn Khaldūn, is, in addition to defence and the maintenance of law and order, to ensure justice, the fulfillment of contracts, the removal of grievances, the fulfillment of needs, and compliance with the rules of behaviour.[12] In other words, the state must do things that help people carry on their lawful business more effectively and prevent them from committing excesses and injustices against each other.

Ibn Khaldūn considers it undesirable for the state to get directly involved in economic activity (M: p. 281; R: II, p. 93). Doing so will not only hurt the people by reducing their opportunities and profits (now termed as crowding out the private sector) but also reduce the state's tax revenue (M: pp. 281-83; R: II, pp. 93-96). Thus, the state is visualized by Ibn Khaldūn as neither a *laissez faire* nor a totalitarian state. It is rather a state which ensures the prevalence of the Sharīʿah and serves as an instrument for accelerating human development and well-being.[13] The slant towards nationalization came into the thinking of some Muslim writers under the influence of socialism, and was exploited by ambitious generals and politicians in several Muslim countries to serve their own vested interests. Socialism, however, brought nothing but misery to nearly all those Muslim countries where it was imposed through military *coups*.[14]

The role of wealth (W)

Wealth provides the resources that are necessary for ensuring justice and development, the effective performance of its role by the government, and the well-being of *all* people. Wealth does not depend on the stars (M: p. 366; R: II, p. 282), or the existence of gold and silver mines (ibid.). It depends rather on economic activities (M: pp. 360 and 366; R: II, pp. 271 and 282), the largeness of the market (M: p. 403; R: II, p. 351), incentives and facilities provided by the state (M: p. 305; R: II, pp. 143-4), and tools (M: pp. 359 and 360; R: II, pp. 270-72), which in turn depend on savings or the "surplus left after satisfying the needs of the people" (M: p. 360; R: II, p. 272). The greater the activity, the greater will be the income. Higher income will contribute to larger savings and greater investment in tools (M: p. 360; R. II, pp. 271-2), which will, in turn, contribute to greater development and wealth (ibid.). Ibn Khaldūn emphasized the role of investment further by saying: "And know that wealth does not grow when hoarded and amassed in safes. It rather grows and expands when it is spent for the well-being of the people, for giving them their rights, and for removing their hardships" (M: p. 306; R: II, p. 146). This makes "the people better off, strengthens the state, makes the times prosperous, and enhances the prestige [of the state]" (M: p. 306; R: II, p. 146). Factors that act as catalysts are low rates of taxation,

(M: pp. 279-81; R: II, pp. 89-91), security of life and property (M: p. 286; R: II, p. 103), and a healthy physical environment amply provided with trees and water and other essential amenities of life (M: pp. 347-9; R: II, pp. 243-8).

Wealth also depends on division of labour and specialization, whereby the greater the specialization the higher the growth of wealth. "Individual human beings cannot by themselves satisfy all their needs. They must cooperate for this purpose in their civilization. The needs that can be satisfied by the cooperation of a group exceed many times what they can produce individually. ... [The surplus] is spent to provide luxury goods and to satisfy the needs of inhabitants of other cities. They import other goods in exchange for these. They will then have more wealth... Greater prosperity enables them to have luxury and the things that go with it, such as elegant houses, clothes and utensils, and the use of servants and carriages... Consequently, industry and crafts thrive" (M: pp. 360-61; R. II, pp. 271-72). However, since human beings do not allow their labour to be used free of charge (M: p. 402; R: II, p. 351), division of labour will take place only when exchange is possible (M: p. 380; R: II, p. 311). This requires well-regulated markets which enable people to exchange and fulfill their needs (M: pp. 360-2, R: II, pp. 271-76).

A rise in incomes and wealth contributes to a rise in tax revenues and enables the government to spend more on people's well-being. This leads to an expansion in economic opportunities (M: p. 362; R: II, p. 275) and greater development, which, in turn, induces a natural rise in population and also the immigration of skilled and unskilled labour and scholars from other places (M: pp. 362-3; R: II, pp. 271-6), thus further strengthening the human and intellectual capital of that society. Such a rise in population boosts the demand for goods and services, and thereby promotes industries (*al-ṣanā'iʿ*), raises incomes, promotes sciences and education (M: p. 359 and 399-403; R: II, pp. 270 and 346-52), and further accelerates development (M: pp. 363 and 403; R: II: pp. 277 and 351-52). In the beginning, prices tend to decline with the rise in development and production. However, if demand keeps on rising and the supply is unable to keep pace with it, scarcities develop, leading to a rise in the prices of goods and services. The prices of necessities tend to rise faster than those of luxuries, and prices in urban areas rise faster than those in rural areas. The cost of labour also rises and so do taxes. These lead to a further rise in prices, which creates hardship for people and leads to a reversal in the flow of population. Development declines and along with it prosperity and civilization (M: pp. 168 and 363-5; R: I, pp. 339-42 and II: pp. 276-85).

A decline in incomes leads to a decline in tax revenues, which are no longer sufficient to cover state spending. The state tends to impose more and more taxes and also tries to gain excessive control over all sources of power and wealth. The incentive to work and earn is adversely affected among farmers and merchants, who provide most of the tax receipts. Hence, when incomes decline, so do tax revenues. The state, in turn, is unable to spend on development and well-being. Development declines, the recession deepens further, the forces of decay are accelerated and lead to the end of the ruling dynasty (M: pp. 168 and 279-82; R: I, pp. 339-42 and II, pp. 89-92).

If one were to express Ibn Khaldūn's analysis in the form of a functional relationship, one could state that:

$$G = f(S, N, W, j \text{ and } g)$$

This equation does not capture the dynamics of Ibn Khaldūn's model, but does reflect its interdisciplinary character by taking into account *all* of the major variables discussed by him. In this equation, G or the political authority has been shown as a dependent variable because one of Ibn Khaldūn's main concerns was to explain the rise and fall of dynasties, states or civilizations. According to him, the strength or weakness of a dynasty depends on the strength or weakness of the political authority which it embodies. The survival of the political authority depends ultimately on the well-being of the people, which it must try to ensure by providing a proper environment for actualizing development as well as justice through the implementation of the Sharīʿah. If the political authority is corrupt and incompetent and not accountable before the people, it will not perform its functions conscientiously. Consequently, the resources at its disposal will not be utilized effectively and the services that need to be provided to facilitate development will not become available. Development as well as well-being will then suffer. Unless there is development, the resources needed to enable society as well as the government to meet the challenges they face and to actualize their socio-economic goals will not expand.

The role of the trigger mechanism

However, while a normal cause and effect relationship is not necessarily reversible, the circular and interdependent causation in human societies emphasized by Ibn Khaldūn generally tends to be so. (This is indicated in the diagram by means of arrows and dots.) Any one of the independent variables and, in particular, development, which is the main theme of this paper, may be treated as a dependent variable with the others being considered independent. This implies that the trigger mechanism for the decline of a society may not necessarily be the same in all societies. In Muslim societies, with which Ibn Khaldūn was concerned, the trigger mechanism was the failure of the political authority which, unfortunately, continues in most Muslim countries until the present time (as will be seen in Chapters 3-6), and has led to the misuse of public resources and their non-availability for the realization of justice, development and general well-being.

Therefore, while all factors play an important role in the development and decline of a society, the trigger mechanism has a crucial role. The trigger mechanism in other societies may be any of the other variables in Ibn Khaldūn's model. It could, for example, be the disintegration of the family, which was not a problem in Ibn Khaldūn's time and which he did not, therefore, mention in his analysis. It is, however, an integral part of N (the people) and is now having a greater manifestation in the Western world even though all societies are affected by it in varying degrees. Such disintegration, if it continues unchecked, may first lead to a lack of proper upbringing of children and then to a decline in the quality of human beings, who constitute the bedrock of any civilization. It may not, then, be possible for that society to sustain its economic, scientific, technological and military supremacy. The trigger mechanism could also be the weakness of the economy resulting from a faulty economic system based on unhelpful values and institutions, as happened in the Soviet Union. It could also be the absence of justice, educational and health facilities, and access to venture capital, which may lead to the inefficient performance of human resources and, thereby, to sluggish development, as is the case in many developing countries, of which the Muslim world is an integral part.

Ibn Khaldūn did not, thus, commit the mistake of confining himself to economic variables alone to explain development and decline. He rather adopted a multidisciplinary and dynamic approach to show how the interrelated relationship of social, moral, economic, political, historical and demographic factors leads to the rise and fall of societies. This is what can also explain why some countries develop faster than others, what makes development sustainable, and when people realize true well-being. Fortunately, Development Economics has gradually started taking into account the roles of almost all these variables as well as their mutual interaction through circular causation.

Nevertheless, Ibn Khaldūn's concept of a trigger mechanism has not been fully utilized. Without this concept, even the emphasis on property rights by North and Thomas (1973), to explain the rise of the Western world does not take us very far. Property rights have been there in most societies, and particularly so in the Muslim world because of the Islamic emphasis on them. However, all societies do not necessarily develop. The reason is that property rights, like other institutions, carry no weight unless they are enforced. What is it, then, that led to their enforcement in Western societies? It was perhaps the emergence of democracy which led to political accountability. This led to the enforcement of institutions, of which property rights are a crucial part. It is, therefore, political accountability resulting from democracy that acted as the trigger mechanism for the enforcement of property rights and justice. This led to development. North and Thomas perhaps realize this themselves to a certain extent when they state that innovation, economies of scale, education, capital accumulation, etc., are not causes of growth; they are growth.[15] Using the same logic, one could argue that enforcement of property rights, is also an effect rather than a cause. Property rights were enshrined in Christian values but were not enforced. If it were not for democracy, property rights may not have been enforced.

Ibn Khaldūn did not commit the neoclassical economists' mistake of being concerned primarily with short-term static analysis by assuming other factors to be constant when changes are constantly taking place in these factors in all human societies through a chain reaction even though these changes may be so small as to be imperceptible. Nevertheless, their influence on economic variables continues to be significant and cannot be ignored. Therefore, even though economists may adopt the *ceteris paribus* assumption for convenience and ease of analysis, multidisciplinary dynamics of the kind used by Ibn Khaldūn also need to be simultaneously utilized because of the help they give in formulating socio-economic policies that help improve the overall long-run performance of an economy and raise the well-being of its people. Neoclassical Economics is unable to do this because, as North has rightly asked: "How can one prescribe policies when one doesn't understand how economies develop?" He, therefore, considers Neoclassical Economics to be "an inappropriate tool to analyze and prescribe policies that will induce development".[16] Since Ibn Khaldūn formulated a brilliant model for explaining the rise and fall of a society, Toynbee was right in declaring that in terms of "both breadth and profundity of vision as well as sheer intellectual power", Ibn Khaldūn, in his *Muqaddimah* to his *Universal History*, "conceived and formulated a philosophy of history which is undoubtedly the greatest work of its kind that has ever been created by any mind in any time or place".[17]

Even though I have used Ibn Khaldūn's model, I have found it necessary to introduce some changes to it. This is because, as mentioned in the Introduction, a number of changes have taken place in all walks of human life. Societies, polities and economies have all experienced radical changes. First, while taking into account the role of the people, it is necessary to bear in mind that they do not constitute a solid whole. They represent an aggregate of different components, including men and women, scholars, a political elite and lay people; families, tribes, and social and economic groups, and society as a whole. Ibn Khaldūn took some of these into account but not all.

Secondly, even though the economies of the central Islamic lands had started declining, they were still pretty strong compared with their competitors and their relative position was certainly not as weak as it is in modern times. One of the primary reasons for this weakness is the gap in education and the knowledge and technology base. This gap will take a long time to fill even if these societies try in earnest to implement the socio-economic and political reforms necessary.

Thirdly, the tremendous expansion in the human knowledge and technology base has greatly lightened the burden of household chores for women and freed them to play a much greater role in the educational, intellectual, and socio-economic uplift of their societies. If they are not enabled to play this role, they will feel frustrated and their society's development will also be adversely affected. However, if they are enabled to play their role effectively, then they may not be able to attend as much to the upbringing of their children as they did in the past. This raises the question of what alternative measures need to be taken to fill this vacuum. Furthermore, international endeavours in science and technology have made it necessary for both male and female members of society to acquire much greater knowledge and to spend much more time for this purpose than was necessary in the past. This demands far more resources now than was necessary before. It is not possible to mobilize such resources unless families, societies and the government all join hands. *Zakāh* and *awqāf* will also have to play an important role, particularly for the purpose of imparting knowledge and skills to the poor.

Fourthly, it has become indispensable for the *'ulamā'* to keep abreast of changing modern realities, so that the *fiqh,* which is a part of the Sharī'ah, evolves in a way that enables Muslims to successfully face the newer challenges. Although *fiqh* had already become somewhat stagnant by Ibn Khaldūn's time, it has become more so now because of the long period of Muslim decline coupled with foreign occupation. *Fiqh*, thus needs to be extricated from its stagnant position so that it can play the same dynamic role that it played in earlier centuries.

Fifthly, even without nationalization and central planning, the role of governments is much greater now and they are required to contribute more effectively to justice, the socio-economic infrastructure and development than was necessary in the past. Even the scope of both justice and development has expanded substantially. In the close-knit societies of the past, the existence of tribes, guilds, fraternities and Sufi orders strengthened social solidarity, which helped enforce formal as well as informal rules of behaviour. This promoted honesty and fairness in dealings and, thereby, played an important role in ensuring justice and general well-being. Since all these have now become weaker as a result of increases in population, extensive urbanization, and the greater mobility of people, the vacuum needs to be filled by families, *'ulamā'*, *madrasahs*, schools, institutions of higher learning and the government.

Finally, it is not wealth alone but also the economy as a whole that needs to be incorporated into the model. This will bring in all its components such as the market, the monetary and financial system, and the public and private sectors, the focus being on the realization of both efficiency and equity in the use of resources All this shows that there is a greater need for reform now of not only the people but also of all the institutions that affect them.

Notes

1. This Chapter draws heavily on Chapra, 2000.
2. The term Sharī'ah refers literally to the beliefs and institutions or rules of behaviour of any society, but has now become associated with those prescribed by Islam.
3. The same advice is repeated on p. 287 (R: II, 105). Ibn Khaldūn himself says that his book is a *tafsīr* (elaboration) of this advice (M: p. 403; R: I, p. 82), which was given by Mobedhān, a Zoroastrian priest, to Bahrām ibn Bahrām and reported by al-Mas'ūdī in his *Murūj al-Dhahab*, (Meadows of Gold), 1988 (Volume 1, p. 253). Ibn Khaldūn acknowledges this fact, but also simultaneously clarifies that, "We became aware of these principles with God's help and without the instruction of Aristotle or the teaching of Mobedhān" (M: p. 40; R: I, p. 82).
4. For a more detailed picture of Ibn Khaldūn's model, see Chapra, 2000, pp. 145-172. See also Spengler, 1964; Boulakia, 1971 and Mirakhor, 1987.
5. The words used by Ibn Khaldūn throughout the *Muqaddimah* are *mu'dhin* and *mufḍī*, which mean 'inviting' or 'leading' towards something. However, I have used the expression 'trigger mechanism', which is now more commonly used in English to convey the same meaning.
6. Rosenthal, 1967, p. 19.
7. According to the Qur'ān, God has sent a chain of messengers to all people at different times (see, for example, 13:7, 16:36 and 40:78). Thus, according to Islam, there is a continuity and similarity in the value systems of all Revealed religions to the extent to which the Message has not been lost or distorted over the ages.
8. Arrow, 1973; Etzioni, 1988; Fukuyama, 1995 and Hollingsworth and Boyer, 1998.
9. See Dasgupta and Serageldin, 2000.

10. See, for example, Arrow, 2000; Solow, 2000 and Bowles and Gintis, 2002.
11. Al-Bayhaqī, 1990, from Anas ibn Mālik, Volume 5, p. 267, No. 6612.
12. The functions of the state are discussed by Ibn Khaldūn in a number of places in the *Muqaddimah.* He states in one place, for example, that: the ruler "must defend and protect the subjects, whom God has entrusted to him, from their enemies. He must enforce restraining laws and prevent them from committing aggression against each other's person and property. He must ensure the safety of roads. He must enable them to serve their interests. He must supervise whatever affects their livelihood and mutual dealings, including foodstuffs and weights and measures, to prevent cheating. He must look after the mint to protect the currency used by people from forgery.... A noble wise man has said that 'moving mountains from their places is easier for me than winning the hearts of people'," (M: p. 235; R: II, p. 3).
13. Ibn Khaldūn classifies political authority into three kinds. The first is the 'natural or normal' (*ṭabīʿī*) authority which enables everyone to satisfy self-interest (*al-gharaḍ*) and sensual pleasures (*al-shahwah*); the second is the rational political authority (*siyāsah ʿaqliyyah*), which enables everyone to serve this-worldly self-interest and to prevent harm in accordance with certain rationally derived principles, and the third is the morally-based political authority (*siyāsah dīniyyah* or *khilāfah*) which enables everyone to realize well-being in this world as well as the Hereafter in accordance with the teachings of the Sharīʿah (M: pp. 190-1; R: I, pp. 387-88). If one were to use modern terminology for these three different forms of governments, one could perhaps call them the secular *laissez faire* or passive state, the secular welfare state, and the Islamic welfare state or *khilāfah.* (For the Islamic welfare state, see Chapra 1979 and 1992, Chapters 1, 3 and 5.)
14. Desfosses and Levesque, 1975.
15. North and Thomas, 1973, p. 3.
16. North, 1994, p. 359.
17. Toynbee, 1935, Volume 3, pp. 321-322.

2

FACTORS THAT CONTRIBUTED TO THE RISE OF THE MUSLIMS

It is now time to apply the above analysis to determine the factors that acted as a trigger mechanism in the rise of Arabian bedouin society. When the Prophet Muḥammad (pbuh) started preaching the message of Islam, this society faced a socio-economic, political and international environment that was too unfavourable to allow, if we use Toynbee's thesis, the flowering of a vibrant civilization. The primary characteristics of this society were bitter internecine feuds, paucity of resources, a harsh climate, difficult terrain, and excruciating poverty, combined with flagrant inequalities of income and wealth. There was very little education and hardly any sign of accelerated development in the near future. Furthermore, this society did not possess the intellectual sophistication or material assets that its powerful neighbours, the Sassanian and Byzantine Empires, enjoyed. Though exhausted by prolonged and destructive wars, these neighbours were still academically, economically, and militarily more powerful. Hence the question is: what was it that led to a change in the quality of this bedouin society in such a way that it not only overcame its own handicaps but also brought about a revolutionary change in the societies that came under its influence?

A number of scholars, including Toynbee (1957), Hitti (1958), Hodgson (1977), Baeck (1994), and Lewis (1995), have argued that Islam played a positive trigger mechanism role in the rise of Muslim societies enabling them to use difficult challenges and to make rapid headway in all sectors of life. If it had not been for Islam, there would not have been, in the words of Toynbee, that "extraordinary deployment of latent spiritual forces by which Islam transfigured itself, and thereby transformed its mission, in the course of six centuries".[1] So how was Islam able to succeed in bringing about such revolutionary change in this society?

What Islam did was to activate all the developmental factors in a positive direction. It gave maximum attention to the people, who constitute the primary force behind a society's rise or fall. It tried to uplift them morally as well as materially, make them better human beings, and reform all the institutions that affected them. Its revolutionary worldview changed their outlook towards life by injecting a meaning and purpose into it. It made all individuals equal in their position as vicegerents (*khalīfahs*) of the Supreme Being Who created them as well as the whole universe. This gave dignity, equality and self-respect to all of them, irrespective of their race, sex, wealth or position. It also made this ideal an effective reality by firmly establishing positions of leadership on those who earlier had been oppressed and weakened (Qur'ān 26:56). It provided sanctity to life, property and individual honour and gave a prestigious place to knowledge by emphasizing its importance in the very first revelation of the Qur'ān (96:3-5). It accorded to women a respectable position in society by declaring them to be a "trust from God"[2] and sisters [not slaves] of men,[3] and enjoined men to treat them well (Qur'ān, 4:19). It made the proper care and upbringing of children one of the prominent goals of the Sharīʿah, so as to ensure that future generations were capable of effectively carrying forward the baton of development. It created a balance between the material and the spiritual aspects of life by declaring them both to be essential for human development and well-being. Accordingly, it gave a higher and more respectable status to the farmer, craftsman and merchant as compared with the position they enjoyed in the Mazdean or the then-prevailing Christian traditions. It replaced loyalty to the tribe by loyalty to God and, thereby, enlarged the individual's horizon to that of the *ummah*, all of whom profess the same faith, and to that of mankind, all of whom are brothers unto each other by virtue of their being *khalīfahs* of God and members of His family.

Since, as Cahen has rightly acknowledged, "the underlying tendency of the Qur'ānic legislation was to favour the underprivileged",[4] one of Islam's outstanding contributions was the uplifting of the weak and the downtrodden. It did not accomplish this by eliminating the rich and the powerful, or by abolishing private property and the market mechanism. Rather, it did it by ensuring justice, social solidarity and the well-being of all (including women and children) through moral and institutional reform that made the individual conscious of his obligations towards his fellow human beings while trying to serve his self-interest in the market place. All this helped deepen the loyalty of the people to their faith and created an inner urge in them to live up to its teachings. This may not, however, have been sufficient of itself. Islam, therefore, went further and provided an effective government to ensure the prevalence of not only law and order but also justice and socio-economic uplift. It guaranteed freedom to every individual within the bounds of its moral code and prevented corruption, arbitrariness and despotism.[5] It established a judicial system in which the law applied equally to the high and the low. The reason for the success of its political and judicial systems was essentially the moral revolution brought about by the Prophet (pbuh). Those people who occupied responsible positions were not only competent but also morally upright, well-meaning and incorruptible. Besley has rightly concluded in a recent article that, "The nature of the workings of government depends on the men who run it" and that "no society can run effective public institutions while ignoring the quality of who is recruited to public office and what they stand for".[6] In this way, the institutional requirements for development, recently emphasized by North, were satisfied.[7] Schatzmiller is, therefore, correct in stating that "all the factors which enabled Europe to succeed were available to Islam much earlier".[8]

The transformation of human beings and institutions

The transformation of human beings and their institutions through the "extraordinary deployment of latent spiritual forces" brought about by the rapid expansion of Islam provided positive externalities. Tribes who had been fighting for centuries were now tied together by bonds of brotherhood. This made it possible to establish a well-represented, strong, stable and 'good' government. In the beginning, the people supported it wholeheartedly because they realized that it was honest to the core and that it worked for the good of everyone and not just a few. This helped ensure law and order, security of life and property, and well-regulated markets, operating fairly and competitively along all the ancient Middle Eastern trade routes. This was previously vitiated by the long-prevailing tribal conflicts in Arabia and the destructive wars between the Sassanians and the Byzantines, who levied onerous taxes to finance these wars and, thus, retarded development.

The whole area under Muslim rule became an extended common market, with a growing monetization of economies, and the free and safe movement of goods, capital and human beings. This, along with low rates of taxation, contributed to all-round development, embracing agriculture, crafts and trade, and led to a substantial rise in the incomes of everyone. The benefits of development were shared by all, even though not as equitably as Islam would have desired.

The prevalence of justice strengthened the motivation for honesty, integrity, hard work, accumulation of capital and technological progress. The availability of educational and training facilities also led to improvement in human skills as also technological and intellectual development.

In keeping with Ibn Khaldūn's thesis, one may state that this invigoration of the people, which Islam brought about through its egalitarian values and institutions and their effective enforcement by political authority, ensured justice and the rule of law at all levels of society. This ensured not only solidarity (*'aṣabiyyah*) among the people but also played a vital role in the flourishing of Muslim civilization in all aspects of life, including the economic sphere. This does not mean that ideal conditions prevailed. It does, however, mean that the positive forces contributing to the advance of Muslim society were strong enough to offset the impact of negative forces.

Agricultural and rural advances

In the bedouin and rural societies of those days, agriculture was the first to benefit from Islam's externalities. The rapid growth of agriculture and the uplifting of rural society served as catalysts for development as has happened in practically all other societies.[9] This catalytic role played by agriculture was visualized very early on in Muslim society as is reflected in the writings of a number of scholars. The 'Abbāsid Caliph al-Mu'taṣim (d. 227/841), for example, said:

> Agriculture has many advantages. It develops the land and nourishes human beings. It enables an increase in taxes and an expansion in wealth. It feeds domestic animals, lowers prices, increases the sources of earning, and expands the economy.[10]

With the spread of Islam, sleeping agricultural and rural sectors suddenly became alive and robust because of the establishment of law and order, and the availability of a vast market without fear of the caravans being waylaid *en route* or subjected to extortionist taxes. This motivated all to do their best for their own advancement as well as that of their society.

In harmony with the emphasis on justice in the Islamic Message, the Prophet (pbuh) and the first four Caliphs (*Khulafā' al-Rāshidūn*) adopted the more humane practice of leaving agricultural land in conquered territories in the hands of original owners and tillers, in sharp contrast with the Byzantine and Sassanian practice of confiscating it from these owners and cultivators for distribution to their military elite and soldiers.[11] All *iqṭā'*s or land grants made by them were relatively smaller in size and were made from uncultivated and un-owned land. The Muslims were not even allowed to buy land from its original inhabitants.[12] This humanitarian policy not only prevented the Muslims from becoming feudal lords and helped maintain the continuity of administration and economic life in conquered territories, but also promoted intergenerational justice as well as Islam's egalitarian objectives.[13] The application of the principle of *fay'* to agricultural land in conquered territories implied the sharing of output (*muqāsamah*) between the state and the farmers. The farmers were required to pay the state's share in the form of a tax called *kharāj*. This share or tax was stipulated in the heyday of Islam at the relatively lenient rate of 5 to 10 percent of total output, as was the case with *'ushrī* lands.[14]

Since the tax was not a fixed amount, but rather a small proportion of the actual output, it did not break the back of farmers in bad crop years. In situations of natural disaster, such as flood, drought and the destruction of crops by unavoidable natural calamities (*āfāt*), *kharāj* was automatically remised in conformity with the teachings of the Prophet and the practice of the *Khulafā' al-Rāshidūn*.[15] Furthermore, this practice continued for a long period of time. So much so that even though tax rates had risen by the time the Saljūqids (447-590/1055-1194) came to power, "the taxes levied by the Saljūqid administration on the Christian population" may "conceivably have been lighter than those of the retreating Byzantine fiscal system".[16]

Even a small rate of taxation can become a burden if the proceeds do not bring a direct or indirect benefit to the taxpayer. Muslim jurisprudence has, therefore, made it a moral obligation of the state to construct and maintain dams and irrigation canals to improve the land productivity.[17] The *kharāj* proceeds were, therefore, used for promoting the well-being of the people through public expenditure, including the construction and maintenance of the physical and social infrastructure. The history of the Umayyads, the ʿAbbāsids, and other dynasties, down to the early Ottomans provides clear examples of the construction of large-scale irrigation schemes and their proper maintenance along the Tigris, Euphrates, Khabūr, Orontes (al-ʿĀsī) and Barada rivers.[18] Long underground water channels (*qanawāt*), sometimes hewn through rock, carried water from mountain sources far out over plateaus or the desert.[19] According to al-Maqrīzī (d. 845/1442), 120,000 labourers worked daily in the Nile Valley for the maintenance of dams and bridges.[20]

The just levy of taxes and use of the proceeds for development accounted for why farmers preferred Muslim to Byzantine and Sassanid rulers; the latter taxed heavily and in fixed amounts, and did not use the proceeds to enhance the people's well-being. Furthermore, fixed amounts forced the peasants to borrow in bad crop years, often on ruinous terms.[21] With a number of ups and downs the tax system continued to be lighter even in the early Ottoman period when the sultans tried to protect their subjects from all kinds of abuses and injustices.[22] It was perhaps for this reason that Martin Luther warned European rulers, in 1541, that the poor people oppressed by greedy princes, landlords and burghers might well prefer to live under the Turks than under Christians such as these.[23]

This humane policy was perhaps the most important cause of the agricultural revolution that took place in the Muslim world.[24] Peasants were thereby induced and enabled to use their land and tools more effectively. New techniques of growing were introduced and many new crops were grown. The use of water was highly developed. "So great", according to Watson, "were the increases in food production generated by the agricultural revolution that the countryside could feed not only much heavier rural populations but also large urban populations".[25] This may have been one of the important factors responsible for the "extraordinary stability in the price of Egyptian wheat from the sixth to the ninth century".[26]

Urban prosperity

Rural prosperity was transmitted to all other sectors of the economy and society. It led to a substantial expansion of urbanization and the development of urban crafts and industries, and, in turn, greater demand for agricultural as well as urban products: "The Islamic society accomplished a shift from agriculture to manufacturing, creating occupational dimensions which had not been visible before."[27] Transmission of prosperity from one sector to another over time constitutes one of the important building blocks of Ibn Khaldūn's circular causation and socio-economic and political dynamics. This vast common market, with free movement of goods, capital, labour, and entrepreneurs, led to the expansion of internal and external commerce. A vast network of trade relations was established both within the empire and with the outside world.[28] Commercial activities even expanded as far as China during the days of Hārūn al-Rashīd (170-193/786-809). In this way, then, the vast potential for development was optimally utilized and Iraq became a centre of world trade and finance.

Intellectual advances

Rural and urban prosperity promoted "a flourishing and diversified urban culture".[29] The availability of financial assistance to both students and scholars and the presence of proper facilities and an environment for rigorous intellectual activity, along with tolerance, the like of which was "at the time quite unknown in the rest of Europe", made the Muslim world a meeting place for scholars of all fields of learning and persuasions (Muslims, Christians, Jews, Zoroastrians and Sabians).[30] There was a free and unhindered discussion of all intellectual issues leading to an all-round intellectual advance. A "most momentous intellectual awakening"[31] was witnessed, particularly in the nearly quarter-century reign of Hārūn al-Rashīd (170-193/786-809), when Baghdād grew from nothingness to a world centre of wealth and learning. "This was the classic age of Islam, when a new, rich, and original civilization, born of the confluence of many races and traditions, came to maturity."[32] Qur'ānic, *Ḥadīth* and *Fiqh* literature developed and provided the bricks and mortar for a judicial system that fulfilled the legal and institutional needs of a rapidly growing society. In addition, original and path-breaking contributions were made to mathematics, science, medicine, philosophy, *kalām*, literature and art, leading to the supremacy of the Muslim world in these fields for almost four centuries from the middle of the eighth to the middle of the twelfth centuries.[33] Even after the Muslim world lost its number one spot, substantial contributions continued to be made for at least two further centuries.

If it had not been for the inspiration and boost provided by Islam, the Arab bedouin society would not have risen in the first place, and if it had, it would not have been able to survive the death of the Prophet in 11/632, or the end of Rightly-Guided Caliphate (*al-Khilāfah al-Rāshidah*) in 41/661. It not only did this, but was also able to withstand the overthrow of the Umayyad and 'Abbāsid Caliphates, thwart the repeated attacks by Crusaders (1095-1291), and convert the conquerors themselves from Central Asia and China to Islam.[34] George Sarton accordingly pays tribute to Islam in his *Introduction to the History of Science* by writing: "Religious faith dominated Muslim life to an unprecedented extent. No people ever took their religion as seriously as the Muslims, and this was undoubtedly the main cause of their cohesion and of their strength against their enemies who were divided and whose faith was weak and tepid."[35]

Notes

1. Toynbee, abridgement by Somervell, 1957, Volume 2, p. 30. Baeck emphasizes that, "it was with Islam that they [the Arabs] became a world power and the guiding light of a large part of the Mediterranean. In the transition from late Antiquity to the emergence of the Latin West in the twelfth century, Islam was at its apogee and played an eminent role as a maker of Mediterranean culture and history" (Baeck, 1994, p. 95).
2. Cited from Jābir ibn ʿAbdullāh by Muslim in his *Ṣaḥīḥ, Kitāb al-Manāsik, Bāb ḥajjat al-Nabiyy,* Volume 2, p. 889:147; Abū Dāwūd, *Kitāb al-Manāsik, Bāb ṣifat ḥajj al-Nabiyy* and Ibn Mājah and Aḥmad, *Musnad.*
3. Cited from ʿĀ'ishah by al-Suyūṭī in his *al-Jāmiʿ al-Ṣaghīr* on the authority of Aḥmad, Abū Dāwūd and al-Tirmidhī, Volume 1, p. 102.
4. Cahen, 1970, p. 542.
5. According to Lewis, 2007, "The Islamic tradition ... emphatically rejects despotic and arbitrary government. Living under justice is the nearest approach to what we would call freedom."
6. Besley, 2005, pp. 43 and 58.
7. North, 1973, pp. 2-3; and 1990, pp. 3-10.
8. Schatzmiller, 1994, p. 405.
9. The World Bank has rightly remarked: "In virtually all countries where agricultural development has been strong, economic growth has advanced at a rapid rate", and that: "While the role of agriculture in development has been debated for hundreds of years, the evidence, both historical and contemporary, is remarkably consistent. In Europe, Japan, and the United States, for example, a dynamic agriculture accompanied – and in some instances led – the process of industrialization and growth." IBRD, *World Development Report,* 1982, pp. iii and 39.
10. Cited by al-Masʿūdī (d. 346/957) in his *Murūj al-Dhahab*, 1988, Volume 4, p. 47. The actual word used by al-Muʿtaṣim is *ʿumrān,* which means development. However, the context, as well as the stage of Muslim development at that time, indicates that he was perhaps referring to agriculture.

11. See Hodgson, 1977, Volume 1, p. 242, and Ziaul Haque, 1977. See also Cahen, 1990, p. 1031 and Lambton, 1990, p. 1045.
12. See Abū Yūsuf, 1352 AH, pp. 24 ff; Yaḥyā ibn Ādam al-Qurashī, 1384 AH, pp. 41-42. See also Ziaul Haque, 1977, p. 171; and Cahen, 1970, p. 571.
13. Yaḥyā ibn Ādam al-Qurashī (d. 203/818), 1384/1965, p. 52, Numbers 157 and 158.
14. See Abū 'Ubayd (d. 224/839), 1968, pp. 59-66, see in particular, paras. 110, 114 and 118; Abū Yūsuf, 1352 AH, pp. 24 ff; and Yaḥyā ibn Ādam al-Qurashī, 1384 AH, pp. 41-42. See also Hitti, 1958, pp. 349 and 384-86; Cahen, 1990, p. 1031; Lambton, 1990, p. 1038 and Ziaul Haque, 1977, p. 171.
15. See Abū Yūsuf, 1352 AH. See also, Aghnides, 1916, p. 389.
16. Bosworth, 1995, p. 959.
17. This emphasis is clear from the writings of Abū Yūsuf (d. 182/798), al-Māwardī (d. 450/1058) and all prominent *fuqahā'*.
18. Al-Shihabi, 1965, p. 901.
19. Hodgson, 1977, Volume 1, p. 301.
20. Al-Maqrīzī *al-Khiṭaṭ*, Volume 1, p. 74.
21. See Watson, 1983 and Cahen, 1990, p. 1031.
22. See Inalcik, 1994, pp. 16 and 17.
23. Cited by Lewis, 1995, p. 128, from Luther's "Admonition to prayer against the Turks" (1541).
24. For the agricultural revolution, see Cahen, 1970, p. 512 and Watson, 1981 and 1983.
25. Watson, 1981, p. 45.
26. Cahen, 1970, p. 512.
27. Schatzmiller, 1994, pp. 399-400.
28. Cahen, 1970, p. 516.
29. Lewis, 1960.
30. Saunders, 1966, p. 24. See also Gibb, 1962, p. 20; Lewis, 1995, p. 72. Kennedy has also stated that "Tolerance of other races brought many a Greek, Jew and Gentile into the sultan's services" (Kennedy, 1987, p. 11).
31. Hitti, 1958, p. 306.
32. Lewis, 1960, p. 20.
33. See Sarton, 1927, particularly Volume 1 and Book 1 of Volume 2.
34. Buwahids, Saljūqids and Mongols.
35. Sarton, 1927, Volume 1, p. 503. According to Sorokin: "The Arabian civilization (whose dominant trait Toynbee does not stress) displayed an enormous scientific and technological *élan* in the centuries from the eight to the thirteenth – much more than the Western civilization during these centuries" (Sorokin, 1951, p. 238).

3

FACTORS RESPONSIBLE FOR MUSLIM DECLINE

If Islam was the factor that triggered the rise of Muslim civilization, then the question that inevitably arises is why did Muslim societies start declining after reaching such a zenith. Given the upward push that Islam provided to these societies, there would be little justification in blaming it for their later decline. Hence, a number of scholars have argued, as indicated earlier, that Islam was not the cause of Muslim decline. If it did deserve the blame, Muslims may have long abandoned it, in keeping with peoples' general tendency to abandon their fondness for something that has been a source of their problems and decline. The Qur'ān itself clearly asserts: "The scum is lost in vain, while that which is useful for people continues to exist on earth", (13:17). This has not happened so far to Islam. Rather, a fond longing for a return to it has persisted over the centuries and a revival is, in fact, now steadily gaining momentum.

Muslims continue to be inspired by the Islamic vision – the vision of a society where the individual is morally-charged and tied to others through strong bonds of human brotherhood; where justice prevails and the needs of all are fulfilled; where the family continues to be strong and children receive the love, affection and care of both parents; where crime, tension and anomie are minimized and social harmony prevails, and where the well-being of all is ensured. Hodgson has rightly indicated that "the vision has never vanished, the venture has never been abandoned; these hopes and efforts are still vitally alive in the modern world".[1] It is to the credit of Islam that, in spite of linguistic and ethnic differences, political upheavals, the disintegration of Muslim countries, and economic decline, Islam continues to inspire the people, and the Muslim world remains emotionally unified and "consciously and effectively, a single historical whole".[2]

Is Islam the cause of Muslim decline?

Nevertheless, there are some scholars who argue that even though Islam may have promoted development in the past, the Muslim world is poor and underdeveloped today as a result of certain Islamic institutions that were "designed to serve laudable economic objectives", but which nonetheless had the unintended effect of serving as "obstacles to economic development".[3] Noland has, however, concluded in a recent unpublished study that, "in general this is not borne out by econometric analysis either at the cross-country or within-country level" and that "Islam does not appear to be a drag on growth or an anchor on development as alleged. If anything, the opposite appears to be true".[4]

Nevertheless, it is worthwhile looking at the three Islamic institutions that are alleged, by Kuran, to be inimical to growth. These are:

1. Islam's egalitarian inheritance system, which did not allow primogeniture to take root in Muslim societies;
2. The absence of concepts of limited liability and juridical or legal personality in Islam, and
3. The Islamic institution of *waqf* (philanthropic trusts).[5]

It is claimed that the first two of these hindered the accumulation of capital and the formation of corporations, both of which are essential for accelerated development. The third institution is alleged to have blocked vast resources that were put into projects which became dysfunctional over time.[6]

The absence of primogeniture

There is no doubt that Islam stands for an egalitarian inheritance system in which there is absolutely no room for primogeniture. However, Kuran has not substantiated his contention that primogeniture contributed to the development of large enterprises in the West. Primogeniture primarily served the needs of feudalism by ensuring that the fief was not broken up among the many sons of the vassal or tenant and that only one person remained responsible for providing the required military and other services to the lord.[7] Feudalism, however, enabled the lords "to extract a rent by extra-economic coercion" as a result of which the peasant labourers had "no *economic* incentive to work diligently and efficiently for the lords". This "limited the agricultural economy's capacity to improve".[8] Consequently, feudalism was buried in Western Europe by 1500, "when capitalism as it is known today was not yet born and the Industrial Revolution was fully two-and-a-half centuries into the future".[9] The demise of feudalism weakened primogeniture except among ruling families. In America, it was swept away during the course of the American Revolution, while in Europe, it collapsed during the French Revolution, with the Napoleonic Code taking care to prevent its re-establishment.[10]

The onset of economic development in Europe depended rather on "the transformation of the feudal property relations into capitalistic property relations".[11] Hardly any scholar, therefore, mentions primogeniture among the causes of the Industrial Revolution. The causes that are rather emphasized include the enforcement of property rights by democratic governments and the boost that the spread of education, research and technology provided to development.[12] Arnold Toynbee, uncle of the great historian Arnold J. Toynbee, placed great emphasis on the inventions that helped provide the technology needed for the revolution in agriculture, manufacturing, and transport.[13] In the agricultural sector, the steam plough helped bring about the consolidation of small farms into large ones and also made possible the tillage of inferior soils through the enclosure system. In the manufacturing sector, the spinning jenny, steam engine and power loom facilitated the establishment of large factories. In the transport sector, the coming of the railroad, in 1830, brought about a substantial expansion in the market as well as trade.[14] "The new class of great capitalist employers made enormous fortunes."[15] It was this fortune, along with the technology, and not primogeniture, that made the establishment of large businesses possible, and thereby, created a need for the corporation.

However, even if it is assumed that primogeniture did play a role in the development of Europe and America, there is no reason to assume that it is indispensable for the development of all countries. Japan and the East Asian tigers have developed without primogeniture having played any role in their development. Some of the factors that did play a crucial role in their development were good governance, land reforms, social equality, and cultural values.[16] Of these, land reforms had an effect which was the opposite of primogeniture: in this respect, the average family holding in Japan was reduced to about 2.5 acres of arable land.[17] Even in 1985, the average farm size amounted to 1.2 acres in Japan, with only 4 percent of all farms operating on land of more than 3 hectares (7.41 acres).[18] According to Sachs, "land reforms in these countries were more extensive than in any other case in modern history".[19] While the extremely small size of land holdings has had the effect of making Japanese agriculture somewhat inefficient and dependent on state subsidies, it had the immediate salutary effect of destroying the power base of the feudal lords and virtually eliminating farm tenancy, which had been widespread before the reforms. This had the far-reaching effect of substantially reducing income and wealth inequalities. The higher income of small farmers plus the cultural values of simple living enabled them to save more. The high rate of saving kept inflation and interest rates at a relatively lower level and enabled rural as well as urban development without unduly large monetary and credit expansion and external borrowing.[20] Since concentration of wealth is a major obstacle in the realization of socio-economic justice in the Muslim world, the absence of primogeniture should have a salutary effect on justice and development.

Juridical entity and limited liability

Kuran is certainly right in asserting that a legal entity with limited liability of shareholders is indispensable for large-scale investment. However, the seeds of both these concepts existed in the classical discussions of Islamic jurisprudence. The closest approximation to the corporate legal entity were the *bayt al-māl* (public treasury), mosque property, and *waqf*.[21] Even the concept of limited liability existed in the *muḍārabah* (commenda) form of business organization,[22] and has been extended without any difficulty to the corporation in modern times.[23]

It is unrealistic to expect that everything necessary for development would be specified in the Qur'ān or the *Sunnah* (the Prophetic traditions). One of the most important and well-known principles of Islamic jurisprudence is that whatever is not specifically prohibited is allowed. Since very few things have been specifically prohibited, there is a great potential for the evolution of institutions needed for promoting development. This did take place in Muslim societies, as Kuran himself has acknowledged by stating that: "the distinguishing economic features of classical Islamic civilization evolved over the next three centuries".[24] Such evolution took place in accordance with need. This was in keeping with the natural evolutionary process in the development of institutions in human societies. There is hardly any society where all the institutions needed for development in the future evolved together in the very initial phase of development. This raises the question of why the need for corporate form did not arise earlier in Muslim societies.

The answer to this question needs to be found not in Islamic teachings but rather in authoritarian governments which did not effectively enforce the property rights enshrined in Islamic teachings. North has rightly argued that insecure property rights "result in using technologies that employ little fixed capital and do not entail long-term agreements. Firms will typically be small".[25] This is what happened in the Muslim world. If property rights had been secure, the momentum of development that had been built up from the eighth through the fourteenth centuries would have continued and created a need for the replacement of small firms by large business organizations.

There is no reason to assume that the increased need for finance that this would have created would not have led to the development of the corporation, the seeds for which, as indicated earlier, were already present in Islamic jurisprudence. In the twentieth century, when development started once again in the Muslim world, the need arose for large business establishments and jurists had no difficulty in approving the corporate form of business organization. If there had been anything in Islam against it, there would not have been such great unanimity in its acceptance. Lal has rightly observed that "it is not Islamic institutions themselves that have hindered development but dysfunctional etatism and dirigisme which, when reversed in the Muslim parts of Southeast Asia, have developed Promethean intensive growth".[26]

Even in medieval England, the earliest corporations were boroughs, guilds, churches and charities.[27] This is similar to what happened in Islam. These earlier corporations in medieval England did not, however, become the forerunners of today's corporations until they became fully private, which happened at the end of the seventeenth century,[28] long after the death of feudalism and the weakening of primogeniture. Nevertheless, it was not until the nineteenth century that the limited liability principle was established in both the US and the UK.[29]

The agricultural and scientific revolution that took place in early Islam could not transform itself into an industrial revolution because of a number of factors, the most important of which was political illegitimacy. Insecure property rights resulting from this forced people to hide their wealth to avoid its becoming subject to unjust taxation and outright confiscation. Hence, firms remained small. Furthermore, it was not possible for large business enterprises to develop in such an environment. If this had not been the case, the absence of primogeniture should in fact have had the effect of leading to the establishment of corporations by motivating people to put together their capital as shares to form larger and viable business enterprises.

Awqāf (*philanthropic trusts*)

As far as the institution of *waqf* is concerned, it developed in the Muslim world during the early days of Islam, long before it did in the West, and made a significant contribution to the development of Muslim societies. As Kuran himself has acknowledged, the *waqf* supplied a vast array of social services.[30] These included education, health, science laboratories, the construction and maintenance of mosques, orphanages, lodging for students, teachers and travellers, bridges, wells, roads and hospitals.[31] This happened when the *waqf* were properly regulated and supervised.[32] However, when effective regulation and supervision did not continue and led to corruption, loss of the original deeds, lack of proper maintenance, and misuse and misappropriation of *waqf* properties,[33] they became dysfunctional as Kuran has rightly pointed out.

The extent of corruption that existed can be judged from the advice given by Ibn ʿĀbidīn (d. 1258/1842), a prominent Ḥanafī jurist in the first half of the nineteenth century, to the people who wished to appoint a trustee for the maintenance of a mosque related *waqf*. One would expect such an appointment to take place normally through a court deed. Ibn ʿĀbidīn, nevertheless, advised them not to even inform the courts about the existence of this trust because the judges had become so corrupt that once they came to know about the existence of a *waqf* property they would try to usurp it.[34] If the courts were corrupt, then one can imagine the condition of the *waqf* property if the trustees also had bad intentions and there was no possibility of recourse to a court of law. In addition to corruption and misappropriation, the tax system also played a significant role in hindering the further development of the *waqf* system.

Given these adverse factors, it is unjust to blame Islam for what happened. Islam has always sought to prevent such corruption and not encourage it. It is the job of the government and the judiciary to enforce Islamic teachings. It is, however, refreshing to know that the *waqf* institution is once again receiving impetus in the Muslim world because of the recognition of the sanctity of property rights and renewed private initiatives along with government support, regulation and supervision.[35] It is hoped that the *waqf* system will once again start to play the same crucial role in the development of social and physical infrastructure through private philanthropy as it did in the past.

The gist of this whole analysis is that it is not Islam that has led to the relative poverty and underdevelopment of Muslim societies. It is rather the adverse effects of lack of political accountability, including the violation of property rights and decline in official support for education and technological research and development. Democratic governments in the West have promoted development through a number of measures, including the protection of property rights and the support of education and research. It is this development which created the need for the corporation. Illegitimate governments, which are not accountable before the people, are generally not under pressure to enforce property rights and serve the interests of the people. Development, therefore, suffers. Hardly anyone would agree with Kuran's contention that "such [authoritarian] governments were all governed at least until the nineteenth century, and in some cases until more recently, by Islamic law".[36]

Is moral degeneration the cause of Muslim decline?

If Islam is not the cause of Muslim decline, then one should ask the question of whether moral degeneration can be held responsible for such decline. Using the analytical framework of Ibn Khaldūn's socio-economic and political dynamics, the answer, here too, is negative. Even though the Muslims' moral decay has undoubtedly played a substantial role in sapping creativity, vitality and solidarity, and made them incapable of facing the challenges ahead, the *Muqaddimah* leads one to the conclusion that moral decay was, itself, an effect rather than a cause.

People of both sexes need an enabling environment, in terms of proper moral and technical education as well as political, legal, and socio-economic institutions to ensure justice, the development of their full human potential, and their full participation in the development of their society. The gradual disappearance of such an enabling environment is perhaps the dominant factor that has led to the moral decline of the Muslim peoples and the loss of their vitality and solidarity. Ibn Khaldūn, as quoted in Chapter 1, rightly pointed out that under despotic rulers, "the people become fearful and depressed and seek to protect themselves by means of lies, ruses and deception. This becomes their characteristic trait whereby perceptions and character become corrupted".[37]

While prevailing inequities have exerted a bad impact on character, even Islam's emphasis on nobleness of character (*khuluq ḥasan*), one of the key characteristics of its teachings, has become diluted. Parents are unable to instil this in their children because of their illiteracy and lack of Islamic education. Furthermore, modern secular schools do not care to do this. Even the mosques and *madrasahs* have failed here because of their limited perception of Islam. What is needed badly is greater justice along with proper education.

Did the start of political illegitimacy trigger the decline?

If Islam, as it was preached by the Prophet (pbuh), and if the moral degeneration of Muslims did not serve as the trigger mechanism for Muslim decline, then what was responsible for the loss of *élan*? It is difficult to do justice to this question by trying to answer it within the span of a small book. However, since the objective is not to write history in conformity with Ibn Khaldūn's model, but rather to draw some *'ibar* (lessons) for suggesting a proper strategy for future development, it will be helpful to highlight those aspects of Muslim history which played a major role in the decline. To avoid too much detail and repetition, the analysis confines itself to only those central Islamic lands ruled by the Umayyads, the 'Abbāsids, the Mamlūks and the Ottomans and avoids other areas like Spain, Africa, Central Asia, Iran, India and East Asia. The analysis may, nevertheless, be applicable to even these areas without significant change because nearly the same undercurrents affected them.

Ibn Khaldūn and a number of classical Muslim scholars, both before and after him, have held the view that Muslim history took a wrong turn when the *Khilāfah al-Rāshidah* was brought to an end by the accession of Mu'āwiyah in 41/661, the hereditary succession of his son, Yazīd, in 60/679, and the establishment of the Umayyad dynasty (41-132/663-750).[38] This sowed the seeds of political illegitimacy and gave birth to *mulk* or hereditary monarchy with absolute power and without adequate accountability, in clear violation of the moral imperative of *khilāfah* and *shūrā*, or the ideal political system enjoined by Islam for Muslims.[39] This violation generated much discontent in Muslim society, particularly among those of the Prophet's Companions who were still alive.[40] There were also revolts, particularly in Madīnah (the Battle of Ḥarrah), Makkah, and Karbalā' (Iraq). These were, however, mercilessly suppressed. As a result, Yazīd has gone down in Muslim history as one of the most disliked of people.

The time was perhaps then not ripe for the flourishing of a radical political reform of the nature of *khilāfah* and *shūrā* that Islam stood for and for which four of the Prophet's close Companions tried their best to live up to. The anchoring of political illegitimacy gradually set in motion over the next few centuries a vicious cycle of circular causation which has adversely affected all aspects of Muslim society as will hopefully become clear with the progress of this discussion. This raises the question of why efforts were not made later on to get rid of the illegitimacy and to establish the ideal Islamic form of government. A number of scholars have expressed the view that this was due to fear of creating disorder and anarchy,[41] which inevitably led to the perpetuation of the *status quo*.

Khilāfah and democracy

Khilāfah, as generally understood by Muslim scholars, is a form of government where the *khalīfah* (head of the state) is elected by the people and is accountable to them. His primary responsibility is to establish a just order and to cater to the well-being of the people by managing the affairs of the state in keeping with the teachings of the

Sharī'ah and the decisions of the *shūrā* (consultative council). Even though the term *shūrā* literally means a consultative council, most classical and modern scholars imply by it an elected autonomous body whose existence is imperative (3:159 and 42:38) and whose decisions are binding.[42] Resources of the public treasury are a trust – revenues must be derived justly and spent efficiently and equitably for serving the interests of the people. There has to be freedom of expression within the constraints of the Sharī'ah, and all citizens, including non-Muslims, must have equal rights.[43] It is the function of the *shūrā* to ensure that the *khalīfah* utilizes his powers and resources for the well-being of the people in conformity with the Sharī'ah. The *khalīfah* as well as the members of the *shūrā* hold their position as long as they enjoy the people's confidence.

The procedure to be adopted for the selection of the *khalīfah* and the *shūrā* is left open by the Sharī'ah. It is for the *ummah* to determine this in keeping with its own circumstances. What is absolutely clear from the election of the first four Caliphs is that acquisition by virtue of heredity or the use of force was in clear conflict with the Islamic imperative. In the pluralist societies of modern times, when means of communication are fast and it is possible to hold elections throughout the country, the most suitable procedure for electing the *khalīfah* and members of the *shūrā* would be elections through a secret ballot. However, it would simultaneously be imperative to introduce certain reforms in the election system so as to reduce the play of wealth, power and corruption in elections.

This makes democracy and the *khilāfah* very similar. However, while the people's choice of their leaders and the leaders' accountability before the people are common to both, the people themselves, as well as the leaders, are not absolutely free under the *khilāfah*. They are contractually bound by the goals, moral constraints, and institutions of the Sharī'ah, and are not allowed to deviate from them as long as they stand committed to Islam. Vaglieri has hence stated that the *khilāfah* was an institution "which had no equivalent and was destined never to have any outside the Muslim world".[44]

Vaglieri may be right if one were to assume the absence of moral constraints on democracy. This is, however, not true in spite of secularism. What secularism brought about in the West was freedom from the dictates of the Church. Moral constraints have continued all along. These are largely reflected in the constitutions, laws and other institutions of different democratic countries. This is one of the reasons why democracy has, in general, been able to uphold the supremacy of law and to promote justice and the well-being of people in Western societies to the extent it has within the framework of secularism.

Given the absence of a church in Islam to dictate to the government, and the moral constraints on democracy, there is no significant difference between democracy and *khilāfah*. Although it is theoretically possible for a democracy to violate the moral code of a society, this does not normally happen. If there is deviation, this would essentially reflect a change in society's values, which does not take place suddenly and often, but rather gradually over a long period of time. The legal blessing given to gambling, drinking, homosexualism, lesbianism, prostitution, and cohabitation of unmarried couples in some democratic societies may be an instance of change in values. Since this leads gradually to a number of ills, including the disintegration of the family, it may adversely affect the moral and material well-being of these societies and cast a shadow over their continued economic, technological and military supremacy in the future. Hence, the moral law is supreme everywhere and there can be no 'liberation' from it. This is what the Qur'ān implies when it says: "The word of your Lord has been completed in terms of both truth and justice, and no one can change it" (6:15). The adverse effects of violating it cannot be avoided by any nation, irrespective of whether it is Muslim or secular. It is not, therefore, realistic to exaggerate the differences between democracy and *khilāfah*.

The Prophet (pbuh) "gradually evolved a coherent set of policies and built up viable institutions" for establishing the Islamic system.[45] He could also have ensured a longer continuation of the *khilāfah* by eliminating all the pillars of the then-prevailing power structures of his society – structures that had tortured and persecuted the Muslims, forced them to migrate, and continually waged war against them. After the Conquest of Makkah in 8/629, he had the opportunity and the necessary power to accomplish this task. He did not, however, do so, for it would have set a bad example, which he did not wish to do. Instead, he forgave them all, even though he had an inkling, as some *aḥādīth* indicate, that the offspring of some of them might revive the old power structures in the future.[46] The Prophet (pbuh) might also have thought that power structures cannot be permanently destroyed. Instead, they change hands and try to assert and reassert themselves. He, therefore, wanted to make it clear that the morally superior way of undoing power structures is to follow his example of weakening them by educating the people, improving their socio-economic conditions, and establishing effective moral, legal and other institutional checks that blunt them so that they are unable to acquire, or exercise, absolute and unrestrained power.

The consolidation of illegitimacy

What the Prophet, peace and blessings of God be on him, had anticipated did take place. With the establishment of the Umayyad dynasty (41-132/661-750), *jāhiliyyah* (pre-Islamic) power structures resurfaced and Islamic teachings with respect to statecraft were no longer fully reflected in the political institutions of the Muslim world. There were revolts, but, as indicated earlier, these proved to be unsuccessful. "The trend was towards greater, not lesser, personal authority for the sovereign and his agents."[47] 'Umar ibn 'Abd al-'Azīz (d. 101/720), eighth among the twelve rulers of the

Umayyad dynasty, tried officially to undo this illegitimacy but was unsuccessful. He was poisoned by those with vested interests after a brief rule of about only two-and-a-half years. This has, in general, tended to be the fate of most reformers who have sought to reform political and economic structures in a way that hurts vested interests.

The ʿAbbāsids came to power in 132/750 after overthrowing the Umayyads. The rationale they provided for this was the reform of the ills that had been introduced into the body politic by the Umayyads. They did not, however, fulfil their promise. Why would they? There was nothing to compel them. A moral obligation has to be accompanied by a proper legal and institutional framework. They would have been obliged to fulfil their promise if they were accountable before the people and if their appointment as well as removal were in the people's hands. In a system of hereditary succession, the people do not enjoy this privilege and powerful rulers have nothing to fear if they do not fulfil their obligations towards the ruled. The people can, of course, revolt, but such revolts are usually crushed mercilessly.

The ʿAbbāsids reached their apogee during the reign of Hārūn al-Rashīd (170-193/786-809), there being a rapid slide thereafter into the unrestrained and arbitrary exercise of royal authority in step with their Sassanian and Byzantine predecessors. There was a war of succession between his sons, al-Amīn and al-Ma'mūn, revolts in different parts of the empire, and public unrest when al-Ma'mūn tried to impose some unacceptable *Muʿtazilah* views against the will of the Muslim community. Decline was further accentuated when the ʿAbbāsid caliphs became puppets in the hands of the Buwayhids (334-447/945-1055) and the Saljūqids (447-590/1055-1194) who, as well as their followers in later dynasties, did not have the inhibitions which the ʿAbbāsids had, because of the moral authority they sought by linking themselves to ʿAbbās, the Prophet's uncle, and their professed commitment to reform.

The Mongol (Ilkhānid) (656-758/1258-1355) and Tīmūrid (737-807/1336-1405) occupations, were perhaps the most ruthless, exploitative and destructive in Muslim history. When the Ilkhānid and Tīmūrid Empires broke up into a number of successor states, the Muslim world became fragmented and passed into the hands of several dynasties. The advantages of a vast common market that had previously been reaped and that had accelerated development, were thus lost to a great extent, if not fully. They were not realized again until the reunification of a substantial part of the Muslim world under the Ottomans with their conquest of Egypt and Syria in 923/1517 and of Baghdād and Tabrīz in 940/1534.

However, since the title of the *Khalīfah* carried a great deal of respect and charisma, the rulers of a number of dynasties, and in particular the Umayyads (41-132/661-750), the ʿAbbāsids (132-656/750-1258), and the Ottomans (699-1342/1299-1924) found it politically advantageous to refer to themselves as *Khalīfahs*. However, this could not remove the stigma of illegitimacy, one of the major bones of contention between the righteous *ʿulamāʾ* (religious scholars) and rulers throughout Muslim history. With the end of the titular *khilāfah,* use of the words *sulṭān* and *malik* became common. The institutions of *shūrā* and *bayʿah* were retained but were, for all practical purposes, mock replications of those that existed during the *Khilāfah al-Rāshidah*, and did not exercise the role they were expected to in restraining the arbitrariness of rulers.

Except for some rulers, at different times in practically all dynasties, who were pious and competent and who tried to perform at least some of the functions associated with the *khilāfah*, most rulers were absolute monarchs and their rule did not reflect the teachings of Islam. Gradually, equality before the law and freedom of expression began to decline, all in clear violation of the Sharīʿah. Competent people were not appointed to senior positions. Sycophants, who did not and could not make any worthwhile contribution to the country, often surrounded these sultans and scooped all the benefits by telling them what they wished to hear. There were court conspiracies, internecine wars of succession, and military *coups*, which drained the resources of the *ummah*, sapped its creative energies, and led to overall decline. Transfer of power even among members of the same family was not always without bloodshed and the army seems to have played a decisive role in such acquisition and transfer. Succession wars almost always heightened insecurity, which in turn adversely affected production and trade, particularly when taxes already paid to the previous regime had to be repaid to the new regime to help it solve its financial problems. Hodgson is, therefore, right in saying that the "civilization of Islam as it has existed is far from a clear expression of the Islamic faith".[48]

It is not the intention here to show that continuation of the institutions of *khilāfah* and *shūrā* would have been a panacea and eliminated all conflicts and problems. It would not. However, accountability of the political authority combined with the freedom of the people to criticize government policies and functionaries would have led to a more effective government, one that would have tried to ensure the prevalence of justice, law and order, and the effective use of available resources for all-round development.[49]

In spite of secularism, democratic governments in Western countries have done a great deal to promote justice, development and general well-being. This because the greater the accountability and freedom of expression, the higher the probability that the political authority will fulfil its obligations conscientiously towards the people. Free discussion of problems enables their correct diagnosis, and accountability motivates the political authority to adopt effective remedies for solving them before it is too late.

This does not necessarily imply that democracy can always provide honest and competent rulers and that illegitimate rulers cannot provide an effective government. Democracy has also led to the election of a number of incompetent and corrupt rulers around the world, while there have been a number of competent and incorruptible rulers throughout Muslim history in spite of political illegitimacy. This has, however, not been the result of an institutional imperative. It has, rather, been the result of their own volition, and has rarely continued after their death. The continuation of *khilāfah* would have helped arrive at some mechanism for the smooth and peaceful transfer of power, thereby helping avoid the wars of succession and bloodshed, destruction and insecurity that followed. It would also have ensured the rule of law and sanctity of life and property in accordance with Islamic teachings. Honest and competent people would perhaps have continued to be appointed to high positions as in earlier centuries, particularly to the positions of *qāḍīs* (judges), and thereby helped reduce injustice and corruption. Public pressure would have led to greater fairness in taxation. Prolonged deficits would also have been avoided as a result of decline in corruption, and a larger proportion of public resources may have been used for public good rather than private benefit. In short, the momentum provided by Islam to development would not have been lost.

The Muslim world has, until now, been unable to establish a procedure for orderly and peaceful transfer of the reins of power to the most upright and competent person in the eyes of the people, the efficient and equitable use of public resources in accordance with the Sharīʿah, and the free and fearless criticism of government policies. Acquisition of power by military *coups* or heredity transfer still continues in most countries of the Muslim world. Even where elections do take place, the socio-economic environment is such that it is possible for the army and a small oligarchy of landlords or industrialists to perpetuate their hold on the affairs of state. The use of public resources for private benefit therefore continues to a greater or lesser extent, depending on whether the ruler is inspired by the principles of *khilāfah* or *mulk.* Public criticism of government policies continues to be difficult. However, the needed correction of the political fault line in Muslim history, which has perhaps been the primary cause of this malaise, seems to now be gradually taking place because of circumstances indicated later on in Chapter 9.

The restraining influence of the Sharīʿah

Societies do not, however, go down very rapidly like a roller-coaster. Ibn Khaldūn visualized three generations or 120 years for the disintegration of dynasties. Since we are concerned with the whole Muslim civilization, the period indicated by him does not apply. If one sector of society malfunctions, other sectors try to take over some of its functions. The end of *khilāfah* did not bring to a total end the hold of the Sharīʿah; rather, it continued to influence the hearts and minds of the people in different walks of life and acted as a countervailing force against despotism and tyranny.[50] Therefore, in spite of illegitimacy, "the power wielded by the early caliphs was very far from despotism ... It was limited by the political ethics of Islam and by the anti-authoritarian habits and traditions of ancient Arabia".[51] If this had not been the case, and the influence of the Sharīʿah had not been asserted and reasserted, off and on, even though partly, the Muslim world would have been atrophied and marginalized much earlier than it actually was. Toynbee has rightly observed that a religion which had "succeeded in winning loyalty in virtue of its intrinsic merits, was not doomed to stand or fall with the political regimes which had successively sought to exploit it for non-religious purposes".[52]

The hold of the Sharīʿah has, in general, been so strong on the psyche of the people that even absolute monarchs could not afford to ignore it totally. They were under a moral constraint to ensure the continued performance of at least some of the religious and welfare functions associated with the *khilāfah*. There has been, and continues to be today, what Ibn Khaldūn calls a mixture of *khilāfah* and *mulk* or monarchy,[53] with a preponderance of one or the other, depending on the individual ruler's own personality and circumstances. Since the charismatic title of *khalīfah* also continued to be used for a long time, this helped strengthen the hands of a number of rulers, from the Umayyads to the Ottomans who, though illegitimate, were able and just and who helped decelerate the decline. Decline was not, therefore, precipitous. The judicial system also remained to a great extent fearlessly honest and above board for centuries. This helped maintain the rule of law, check arbitrary state action, ensure the fulfilment of contracts, and provide justice to the aggrieved. Production and trade continued to expand and the people prospered. Their honesty, integrity and willingness to work hard were affected only gradually. Hence, Schatzmiller seems to be right in stating that "Islamic society in the Middle Ages was in many respects, a much happier place to live than it is today."[54]

However, as Ibn Khaldūn's model implies, it was inevitable that the decline in the Sharī'ah's hold in the political field, unless reversed, would gradually weaken its command over other fields of life. Just as the market system cannot operate effectively without competition and orderly markets, and stands in need of the state to ensure these, so also the Islamic system cannot operate effectively without reforming the individual as well as the institutions that affect his behaviour. It is now, then, time to see how the introduction of political illegitimacy led over time, through the operation of circular causation, to the corruption of all other institutions and even to moral and economic decline.

Notes

1. Hodgson, 1977, Volume 1, p. 77.
2. Ibid., Volume 2, p. 3.
3. Kuran, 2004, pp. 71-72.
4. Noland, pp. 26-27.
5. Kuran, 2004, pp. 71-72.
6. Ibid.

7. Rheinstein and Glendon, 1994, p. 641.
8. Brenner, 1987, pp. 309 and 311, italics in the original.
9. North and Thomas, 1973, p. 102.
10. Rheinstein and Glendon, 1994, p. 642.
11. Brenner, 1987, p. 133; Dobb, 1946 and Hilton, 1969.
12. See North, 1990, pp. 130-40 and Checkland, 1987.
13. Toynbee, 1961.
14. Ibid., pp. 58-66.
15. Ibid., p. 65.
16. See Chapra, 1992, pp. 173-181.
17. Jansen, 1973-74, p. 88.
18. Australian Bureau of Agricultural and Research Economics, 1988.
19. Sachs, 1987, p. 301.
20. For details, see Chapra, 1992, pp. 173-81.
21. Al-Khafif, 1962, pp. 22-7; Udovitch, 1970, p. 99 and ʿAbdullāh, n.d., pp. 235-239.
22. Chapra, 1985, pp. 255-256; Cizakca, 1996, p. 14 and Usmani, 1998, pp. 221-228. According to Cizakca, the limited liability in *muḍārabah* (commenda) contracts was so universal and well understood that a merchant involved in international trade could easily defend his case in foreign courts.
23. ʿAbdullāh, n.d., p. 239.
24. Kuran, 2004, p. 72.
25. North, 1990, p. 65.
26. Lal, 1998, p. 66.
27. Hessen, 1987, p. 675.
28. Ibid., p. 678.
29. Oesterle, 1994, pp. 590-91.
30. Kuran, 2004, p. 754.
31. See for example Makdisi, 1981, pp. 35-74; Hodgson, 1977, Volume 2, p. 124; Kahf, 2004 and Ahmed, 2004.
32. Inalcik, 1970, p. 307.
33. Ahmed, 2004, pp. 42-44.
34. Ibn ʿĀbidīn, 1386/1966, Volume 4, p. 422. This reference was brought to my attention by Dr. Monzer Kahf.
35. Ahmed, 2004, pp. 42-44.
36. Kuran, 2004, p. 83.
37. M: pp. 88-2; R: I, p. 383.
38. See Osman, 1986. pp. 52-55.
39. See the article on *shūrā* in the *Mawsūʿah al-Fiqhiyyah* published by the Ministry of *Awqāf* and Islamic Affairs, Kuwait, Volume 26, pp. 279-285; *Tafsīr al-Qurṭubī*, 1957, Volume 4, pp. 249-252 and Volume 16, pp. 34-38 and al-Jaṣṣāṣ, 1347 AH, *Aḥkām al-Qur'ān,* Volume 2, pp. 48-50.
40. When Saʿd ibn Abī Waqqāṣ (d. 55/674), one of the Prophet's ten most prominent Companions, met Muʿāwiyah after the latter had installed himself illegitimately

as the first ruler of the Umayyad dynasty against the wishes of the community, he greeted the latter by saying: "*Assalāmu 'alayka ayyuhā al-malik* (peace be on you, O Monarch!)" instead of *Amīr al-Mu'minīn* (Leader of the Faithful), the expression used by Muslims for the *Khulafā' al-Rāshidūn*. (Ibn al-Athīr (d. 630/1233), *al-Kāmil*, 1965, Volume 3, p. 205.) Al-Jāḥiẓ (d. 255/869) wrote that the year in which Mu'āwiyah installed himself as the ruler, the *Khilāfah* changed into the kingdom of Chosroes and the tyranny of Caesar (Al-Jāḥiẓ, 1964-5, Volume 2, pp. 10-11. See also Lewis, 1995, p. 141). The historian al-Mas'ūdī also calls the Umayyad and 'Abbāsid Caliphs kings in his *Murūj al-Dhahab*. (See al-Mas'ūdī, 1988, Volume 3, p. 241, where he briefly discusses the causes of the Umayyad's downfall, and Volume 4, p. 387, where he recapitulates the major events narrated by him in his four volumes.)

41. Al-Ghazālī states that as long as the sultan has military power and the effort to remove him is expected to create anarchy and to add to the suffering of the people, then it is in the public interest to submit to the sultan even though he may be ignorant and unjust. (Al-Ghazālī, *Iḥyā'*, Volume 2, p. 140. See also Mumtaz Ahmad, 1986, p. 8 and Osman, 1986, pp. 72-74.)
42. Abū Fāris, 1988, p. 20; and also pp. 19-30. Sayyid Qutb in his commentary of verse 3:159 of the Qur'ān ("And consult with them in all matters [of public concern], and once you have taken a decision, then trust in God for God loves those who place their trust in Him", emphatically clarifies that "there is no room for wavering, double-mindedness, and changes of opinion after this decision of the *shūrā*, because such behaviour leads to unending indecisiveness, paralysis and negativism. The decision of the *shūrā* must be followed by determined (*'azm*) implementation (*maḍā'*) and trust in God, which He likes". (Sayyid Qutb, 1986, Volume 1, p. 497.) In his commentary of verse 42:38 ("And they take decisions in all affairs by mutual consultation"), he says that this verse applies not only to the affairs of the state but also to those of the family and society. (Volume 5, pp. 3165-66.) See also Muhammad Asad's comments 222 and 38 on pp. 92 and 746 respectively, in his translation and commentary. See also Mumtaz Ahmad (ed.), 1986, particularly the editor's 'Introduction' (pp. 1-22) as well as the paper by Fathi Osman (pp. 51-84).
43. See Mawdūdī, 1966, pp. 83-102 and 157-75. See also Lewis, 1995, pp. 72-73.
44. Vaglieri, in Holt, Lambton and Lewis, 1970, Volume 1, p. 57.
45. Watt, in Holt, Lambton and Lewis, 1970, Volume 1, p. 55.
46. The Prophet (pbuh) said: "After me there will come rulers (*a'immah*) who will not take guidance from me and will not follow my *Sunnah*. There will be among them people who will have the hearts of devils in the bodies of human beings." (Reported from Ḥudhayfah ibn al-Yamān by Muslim, Volume 3, p. 1476:52, *Kitāb al-imārah*, *bāb* 13.) There is also another *ḥadīth* which says: "The *khilāfah* in my *ummah* after me will last 30 years, after which there will be [hereditary] monarchy." (Reported from Abū Hurayrah as a strong (*ṣaḥīḥ*) *ḥadīth* by al-Suyūṭī

in his *al-Jāmiʿ al-Ṣaghīr*, Volume 1, p. 12, on the authority of *Musnad* of *Aḥmad*, al-Tirmidhī, *Musnad* of Abū Yaʿlā, and *Ṣaḥīḥ* of Ibn Ḥibbān.)

47. Lewis, 1995, p. 144.
48. Hodgson, 1977, Volume 1, p. 71.
49. The World Bank has rightly emphasized that: "Development requires an effective state, one that plays a catalytic, facilitating role, encouraging and complementing the activities of private businesses and individuals. Certainly, state-dominated development has failed. But so has stateless development.... History has repeatedly shown that good government is not a luxury but a vital necessity. Without an effective state, sustainable development, both economic and social, is impossible." (World Bank, *World Development Report*, 1997, p. 111.)
50. Bulliet, 2004.
51. Lewis, 1995, p. 140.
52. Toynbee, abridged by Somervell, 1957, Volume 2, p. 31.
53. After discussing the transformation of *khilāfah* into royal authority or kingship in a whole chapter (*Muqaddimah*: pp. 202-8; Rosenthal, Volume 1, pp. 414-28), Ibn Khaldūn concludes: "You have seen how the form of government was transformed into kingship. Nevertheless, there remained [in the beginning] the meaning of *khilāfah* which required the observance of religious teachings and adherence to the path of truth .... Then the characteristic traits of *khilāfah* disappeared and only its name remained. The form of government became kingship, pure and simple. Acquisition of power reached its extreme limit and force came to be used for serving self-interest through the arbitrary gratification of desires and pleasures" (M: 208; R: I, p. 427).
54. Schatzmiller, 1994, p. 1.

4

ECONOMIC DECLINE

Living beyond means: fiscal imbalances

One of the first things that resulted from the lack of political accountability was loss of control over public finances. This worked against the establishment of checks and balances on the use of public resources. Instead of treating state resources as a trust and using them for the well-being of the people, as required by the Sharīʿah, rulers committed the unforgivable crime of using them indiscriminately for financing military campaigns, leading a life of luxury and extravagance, and supporting a large retinue of unproductive hangers-on and sycophants.[1]

While it may not have been possible to avoid all military campaigns in those days when neighbours like the Habsburgs and the Safavids were over-anxious to expand their frontiers, and conventional wisdom required a country to overpower its enemies before it was itself overpowered by them, a number of campaigns may not have been necessary. This was particularly true in the fifteenth and sixteenth centuries when the highest priority of the Ottoman sultans seems to have been the pursuit of conquests.[2] Mehmed II, the Conqueror (1451-81), who established the distinctive character of the empire, "wished Istanbul to become the centre of the world in all respects" and devoted the full 30 years of his rule to the realization of this goal.[3]

These campaigns required an increasingly large standing army, which drained the resources of the empire. According to Ḥājjī Khalīfah (d. 1067/1657), the total number of paid troops in the army of Suleyman the Magnificent (1520-66) was 41,479 men in 970/1562, with an annual salary bill of 122.3 million akces (Table 1). By the end of his reign, in 974/1566, the number of troops had risen to 48,316 with a salary bill of 126.4 million akces. Expansion continued until the number of troops reached 91,202 with a salary bill of 310.8 million akces in 1018/1609, the year when the Celali Rebellion in Anatolia was ruthlessly suppressed after almost 13 years of struggle against it by the state. The rise of only around 2 percent per annum in both the number of troops as well as the salary bill over these 47 years from 1562-1609 may prompt one to ignore it, particularly because the rise in consumer prices over this period was also around 2.3 percent per annum.[4] However, one cannot do so if one takes into account the suggestion by Luṭfī Pāshā (d. 970/1563), the experienced and conscientious Ex-Grand *Wazīr* of Suleyman the Magnificent, that a paid standing army of 15,000 was quite sufficient.[5] At a time when the state was facing financial problems, the government should have cut its military and unproductive spending. The government did not, however, do this. Instead, it continued to expand its standing army and to offset the financial burden arising from this by raising taxes and reducing development spending. It was perhaps not realized that the economic difficulties faced by the people may have been one of the major reasons for the Celali Rebellion (1596-1609) as well as other revolts in the country both before and after it.

Table 1: Troops and Salary Bill

Year	Sultan	Troops	Annual pay (million akces)	Average annual pay
970/1562	Suleyman	41,479	123.3	2,972.5
974/1566	Suleyman	48,316	126.4	2,616.1
997/1588	Murad III	64,425	178.2	2,766.0
1004/1595	Mehmed III	81,870	251.2	3,068.3
1018/1609	Ahmed I	91,202	310.8	3,407.8
1027-31/1618-22	Osman II	100,000	n.a.	–
1031-32/1622-23	Mustafa I	100,000	n.a.	–

Source: The figures for troops and annual pay are from Ḥājjī Khalīfah (d. 1067/1657), *Dustūr al-ʿAmal li Iṣlāḥ al-Khalal*, cited by Lewis, 1962, p. 80.

Note: Akce (*Aqjah*) was a silver coin used by the Ottomans. For details about its varying silver content and exchange rates, see Sevket Pamuk's "Appendix" in Inalcik, 1994, pp. 947-80.

It would, however, be too much to expect authoritarian rulers, who had become secluded from the people and who were unaware of their problems, to reduce taxes and unproductive spending. Hence, there was a nearly total loss of control over spending. The empire's resources became severely drained and fiscal imbalances escalated. In 1006/1597, the budgetary deficit was 67 percent of total spending (Table 2). This may have been due to the long wars with the Habsburgs (1593-1606), the spending for which reached its peak in that year. It was, however, brought down to 22.5 percent of the total spending of 687.2 million akce in 1060/1650.

Table 2: Ottoman Empire Government Income, Expenditure and Deficit (Million akces)

Year	Income	Expenditure	Surplus or Deficit (-)	Surplus or deficit as per-cent of Expenditure
972/1564	183.0	189.6	- 6.6	- 3.5
1000/1591	293.4	363.4	- 70.0	- 19.3
1006/1597	300.0	900.0	- 600.0	- 66.7
1058/1648	361.8	500.5	- 138.7	- 27.7
1060/1650	532.9	687.2	- 154.3	- 22.5

Source: Revenue and expenditure figures from Ḥājjī Khalīfah (d. 1067/1657), *Dustūr al-ʿAmal li Iṣlāḥ al-Khalal*, cited by Lewis, 1962, p. 81. Cf. Oghli, 1989, p. 625 and Inalcik, 1994, p. 99.

Note: Revenue figures do not include *tīmār* revenues (for which see the next section).

These deficits were, nevertheless, excessively large, considering the fact that practically all scholars before and during Ottoman rule deplored excessive state spending and deficits in state budgets except during emergencies. But the Ottoman Empire was, either willfully or by force of circumstance, geared towards war and was always engaged in it. War spending, therefore, took the largest share of its total expenditure.[6]

Even though the Ottoman Empire was not unique in this respect and had parallels all over Europe, excessive war spending over a prolonged period sharply curtailed its ability to finance education, infrastructure construction and development, something that public pressure may not have allowed for such a long time in a democratic setting. Furthermore, rulers adopted a number of undesirable measures to finance their burgeoning deficits. Most of these measures were inimical to the justice and public well-being that had earlier been promoted by the Islamic revolution.

The grant of large *iqṭāʿs* and *tīmārs*

One of the measures that proved to be the most damaging for development was the gradual movement away from the principle of *fay'* with respect to conquered lands. Large *iqṭāʿs* (land grants) were first given by the Umayyads to members of the ruling family and its supporters in clear violation of the precedent set by the Prophet (pbuh) and the first four Caliphs. The ʿAbbāsids, who came to power in 132/750 with the promise of undoing the injustice and the moral decay that had set in,[7] did not live up to this promise except for a short period at the very outset. They also started to slide into a life of luxury and adopted the same policies for which they had condemned the Umayyads, particularly the policy of awarding large *iqṭāʿs*. The awarding of *iqṭāʿs* (*tīmārs* under the Ottomans) accelerated under the Fāṭimids (297-567/909-1171), the Buwayhids (334-447/945-1055), the Saljūqids (447-590/1055-1194) and the Ottomans (699-1342/1299-1924) until it ultimately led to near-feudalism during the sixteenth and seventeenth centuries with the difference that, while under feudalism the feudal lord had to provide military services to the king, the *iqṭāʿ* (*tīmār*) holders in the Muslim world did not necessarily have to do so.

The Mongol or Ilkhānid conquest in 656/1258, further accelerated the ongoing political and economic decline.[8] The first 37 years of pagan Mongol rule, before the accession of Ghazān Khān in 694/1295, were characterized by excessive ruthlessness and exploitation.[9] There was a near devastation of many cities, the massacre of thousands of their inhabitants, the raping of women, and the destruction of libraries. "Because of the sack of Baghdad in 1258, not one in a thousand of the books quoted in the *Fihrist* of Ibn al-Nadīm is extant."[10] The Mongols usurped large tracts of land from the local owners to give to their own people to satisfy their greed, and imposed onerous taxes on top of those that had already been levied by the Buwayhids and the Saljūqids. This forced a large number of peasants to abandon their lands and, thus, substantially increased the nomadic population.[11] Additionally, lack of maintenance of underground irrigation channels caused their near destruction. Agriculture was thus reduced to a very low ebb and rural economies were nearly ruined. Indeed, the agricultural economic base prevailing before the Mongols was probably never fully restored.[12] The ideal of the Mongols was "war and the pursuit of military arts whereas that of the society which they had supplanted was stability and peace".[13]

The spendthrift ways of the Mongols led to financial crises in spite of extortive taxes. To overcome these, Gaykhatu (690-4/1291-5), fifth ruler of the Ilkhānid dynasty, attempted to introduce paper money, which the people were unwilling to accept. There was a widespread breakdown of trade and commerce that inevitably caused considerable damage to the economy.[14] Even though Ghāzān Khān (694-703/1295-1304), the seventh Ilkhānid ruler, accepted Islam and introduced a number of reforms, the improvement was not significant. He could not change the character of his own people, and failed to inspire the confidence of the Muslim population in the justness of Mongol rule. The destruction caused by the Mongols was accentuated by the Tīmūrids (737-807/1336-1405). Tīmūr sacked Baghdād in 803/1401 and other Muslim lands over a period of almost three decades before his death in 807/1405, thereby dealing the already declining economy an almost fatal blow from which it could hardly recover. The Safavid takeover of Iraq (1508-34) provided some relief, though not as much as necessary, because their rule was characterized there, as elsewhere, by feeble central government and economic stagnation.

After Mongol occupation, the Muslim world became, and remained, splintered and disunited until it was reunified once again by the Ottomans in 923/1517. The Fāṭimids (297-567/909-1171), the Ayyūbids (564-647/1169-1250), the Mamlūks (648-922/1250-1517),[15] as well as the Ottomans (699-1342/1299-1924) were relatively humane rulers compared with the Mongols and the Tīmūrids. Nevertheless, they were far from the precedents set in earlier centuries. Although agriculture experienced some revival, the boost needed to restore the earlier development could not be provided, particularly because the practice of granting *iqṭā'ṣ* (*tīmārs*) to themselves, their officials, generals and soldiers continued.[16] Even though these were initially given in lieu of salaries to relieve the treasury of the trouble and expense of collecting land revenue and disbursing it to soldiers, they nevertheless led to a great deal of abuse and hurt agricultural production, as will be seen in the next section.

Almost all of the fourteenth and fifteenth century Ottoman conquests were distributed as *tīmārs* to military personnel and government officials. Initially these *tīmārs* constituted a trust in the holders' hands. They were not transferable. Their continuation was conditional on service and could be annulled or replaced by a pension.[17] However, with the weakening of the central government in the later Ottoman period, the *tīmārs* began to be treated as private property. Most of the conquered lands became princely estates whose taxes went entirely to their holders, depriving the state of their revenue as well as the military service that was originally a condition for the *tīmārs*. This whole process of feudalization took several centuries to complete. But completed it was, particularly after the occupation of Muslim countries by Western powers, who awarded large tracts of land to those who collaborated with them and helped in perpetuating the occupation. A substantial part of agricultural land in the Muslim world is now owned by powerful landlords who keep a preponderant part of the output for themselves, leaving very little for the peasant. They pay hardly any taxes but, nevertheless, wield a great deal of political influence.

Unjust taxation

Large landholdings resulting from *iqṭāʿs* or *tīmārs* may not by themselves have caused severe damage if the land tenure and tax systems had been humane. The Muslim law of succession and inheritance, which rejects primogeniture and requires distribution of the deceased person's estate to all male and female heirs, would have shared out the land and consequently rapidly weakened the power of land-owning families. Moreover, until Ottoman times, few dynasties lasted long enough to preserve an entrenched aristocracy. Most dynasties were overthrown by internal upheaval or foreign conquest, thereby destroying the existing aristocracies and power structures. Hence, in spite of the *iqṭāʿs* and *tīmārs*, smallholdings prevailed through the Ottoman lands and large estates did not become common except at the end of the Ottoman period, particularly in the Arab provinces.[18] It was smallholdings, and not large estates, which generated most of the marketed surplus throughout the Ottoman era.[19]

What made the *iqṭāʿs* or *tīmārs* inimical to continued prosperity, was the persistent rise in taxation that they brought for the peasants. Since the ruling families and their attendants hardly paid any taxes, a preponderant part of the tax burden was borne by the peasants who constituted the majority in medieval Muslim society and who drew most of their livelihood from the soil. This started with the introduction of tax-farming during the Buwayhid and Saljūqid periods. Governors and generals were appointed as tax-farmers because of the power they wielded to enforce obedience and ensure a specified lump-sum annual payment to the state. The system was characterized by great abuse because the tax-farmers collected far higher taxes than what they paid to the state, keeping the difference for themselves.[20] The system worsened under the Ilkhāns, who not only collected the taxes existing on the eve of their occupation, but added many more.

Reforms introduced by a number of rulers under the Ayyūbids (564-647/1169-1250), the Mamlūks (648-922/1250-1517), the Ottomans (699-1342/1299-1924) and other dynasties in different parts of the Muslim world at different times made the tax system relatively more humane and bearable down to the mid-ninth/fifteenth century under the Ottomans. However, the rise in war expenditure resulting from the military campaigns of Mehmed the Conqueror, Suleyman the Magnificent, and others made the tax system gradually more burdensome removing it far from the principles of justice in taxation emphasized by scholars like Abū Yūsuf, al-Māwardī, Ibn Khaldūn and a host of writers on the "Mirrors for Princes".[21] The tragedy is that, while *iqṭā'* and *tīmār* holders collected a substantial proportion of the produce from the peasants, they hardly paid any taxes to the government, the purpose for which *iqṭā's* and *tīmārs* were originally introduced. Therefore, while agriculture was hurt, government revenue also declined.

In addition to the oppressive taxes on the peasants, there were other taxes which broke the back of craftsmen and traders and contributed further to economic decline. These were the *mukūs* (sing, *maks*).[22] Six *aḥādīth* have been cited by Abū 'Ubayd (d. 224/839) against *maks,*[23] and the *fuqahā'* continuously called for the abolition of these by using terms like *ibṭāl al-mukūs, musāmaḥāt, isqāṭ, waḍ',* and *raf' al-mukūs.* Jalāl al-Dīn al-Suyūṭī (d. 911/1505) wrote a treatise entitled *Risālah fī Dhamm al-Maks* (Treatise on the Denunciation of *Maks*). Nevertheless, the *mukūs,* continued to increase until there was hardly anything left untaxed under the Mamlūks (648-792/1250-1390). A number of rulers like Ṣalāḥ al-Dīn al-Ayyūbī (d. 589/1193) abolished many of these, thereby reforming the tax system.[24] However, the persisting fiscal problems of the governments led to the eventual reinstatement of these taxes by his successors.[25]

This helps one understand the socio-political reasons behind the '*ulamā*'s opposition, over the centuries, to all forms of taxation by governments. Their fear being that if governments are allowed to tax, they tend to exceed limits and become unjust. This should leave no doubt in anybody's mind that a number of the *fiqhī* positions are the result of conditions prevailing in the times of the *fuqahā'*. Their strict position against taxation was a natural response to illegitimate governments who were not accountable before the people for how they raised and utilized their resources. It may not, however, be reasonable to stick to the same *fiqhī* positions in a democratic political environment when it is possible to restrain the taxing and spending authority of governments.

One would perhaps object to this analysis by saying that taxes in those days were perhaps not high as compared with those levied by a number of modern welfare states. This may be true. However, these taxes were raised primarily from the peasants, craftsmen and traders, while influential people paid hardly any taxes at all. Therefore, the burden on those who paid the taxes was unbearable. Worse still, the taxpayers received hardly any benefit in return. The proceeds were used not for providing them with education, medical treatment, infrastructure and other facilities, as is done under welfare states, but rather for the luxury of the royal court and for maintaining an expensive war machinery. If taxes had been paid by all and the proceeds been used effectively for the development and well-being of the people, opposition to the same may not have been so vehement.

Debasing the currency

Fiscal imbalances also led to currency debasing. In the commodity money standard that prevailed in those days, dīnārs (gold coins) and dirhams (silver coins) constituted the basis of the official Muslim monetary system. In addition, *fulūs* (copper coins) were also minted with varying sizes and weights to satisfy the need for small commercial transactions. To safeguard the integrity of the coinage and consequently the interests of the general public, the office of *nāẓir al-sikkah* (inspector of coinage) was set up during the reign of Hārūn al-Rashīd (d. 193/809) and all units of currency were subject to inspection. Consequently, the standard of the early dīnār was exceptionally high with respect to its weight, fineness and appearance. However, this office seems to have gradually become ineffective with the weakening of the administrative authority of the 'Abbāsids.[26] Nevertheless, the standard of the dīnār continued to be maintained in most parts of the Islamic world down to the fourth/tenth century.[27] Even in later dynasties, the standard differed very little from that of the Umayyads and the 'Abbāsids. Ibn Ba'ra, writing around 625/1228 about the dīnār issued by Ṣalāḥ al-Dīn's nephew, al-Kāmil (d. 635/1238) in the Ayyūbid period (1169-1250), says: "There existed neither in the West nor in the East, dīnārs of a standard excelling the standard al-Amīrī al-Kāmilī."[28]

The weight of the dirham also seems to have remained stable in the earlier periods. For convenience, several denominations of dirham coins were issued. However, as a result of fluctuations in the price of silver, the rate of exchange between the dīnār and the dirham fluctuated. The ratio prevailing between the two coins was 10 at the time of the Prophet (pbuh), and seems to have remained generally stable at that level during the period of the first four Caliphs (11-41/632-61).[29] Such stability did not, however, persist continually. The two metals faced different supply and demand conditions which destabilized their relative prices. For example, in the second half of the Umayyad period (41-132/661-750), the ratio was around 12, while in the 'Abbāsid period (132-656/750-1258) it reached 15 or less.[30] The ratio, however, fluctuated and at times rose to as high as 20, 30 and even 50.[31] This was not due to debasing but rather to a decline in the price of silver relative to gold. According to al-Maqrīzī (d. 845/1442) and his contemporary al-Asadī (d. 854/1450), this instability enabled bad coins to drive good coins out of circulation,[32] a phenomenon which became referred to in the sixteenth century as Gresham's Law. The widespread acceptability of Arab coins in commerce between Muslim lands and the rest of the known world at that time is well-established by the discovery of Arab coins in hoards found in Russia, Europe and the Far East.[33]

In modern times, governments tend to resort to the excessive issue of fiduciary paper money to tide them over their financial problems. Efforts were also made by the Mongols in 693/1294 to issue paper currency. This was, as indicated earlier, seriously resisted by the people and led to an immediate and widespread breakdown of trade and commerce.[34] It may perhaps be because of this sad experience that the *fuqahā'* opposed paper currency and later governments avoided their issue. Governments, however, did not desist from exploiting their mint prerogative by stealthily debasing the currency to extract additional seigniorage for the purpose of closing the growing gap between income and expenditure.[35] Consequently, irregularities in weight and purity of coins began to appear in spite of opposition from the *fuqahā'*. This happened in particular during the Burjī (Circassian) Mamlūk (784-922/1382-1517) and Ottoman (699-1342/1299-1924) periods.

The shortage of silver in Europe led to the replacement of silver coins by copper *fulūs* during the Mamlūk period.[36] However, the increasing fiscal difficulties faced by the government, resulting from the decline of agriculture as a result of the unjust taxation of farmers, led to an excessive issue of copper coins. This, in turn, led to a decline in their value, and to inflation and further decline in development.[37] During the Ottoman period as well, the official silver coin, akce, was debased several times and its silver content declined from 0.85 grammes in 1469-79 to a paltry 0.0073 grammes in 1830-39.[38] Since the decline in the price of silver as well as the silver content of akce had reduced its value to an extremely low level, it had to be discontinued as a basic unit of currency in the *Tanẓīmāt* period (1839-1876) even though its silver content had been stabilized at 0.0083 grammes after 1850.

Since currency debasement is in sheer violation of the Sharī'ah's emphasis on honesty and integrity in all measures of value, fraudulent practices in the issue of coins in the fourteenth century and afterwards elicited a great deal of literature on monetary theory and policy. The Muslims, according to Baeck, "should, therefore, be considered forerunners and critical incubators of the debasement literature of the fourteenth and fifteenth centuries".[39]

External borrowing

When even onerous taxation and currency debasement failed to satisfy the spendthrift ways of corrupt rulers, they started to rely extensively on external debt. Between 1854 and 1877, the Ottoman Empire had to borrow practically every year until the debt reached the sum of 200 million pounds sterling, the approximate value of which in 2004, after adjusting for decline in the purchasing power of the pound, comes to around £8,131 million.[40] Since Turkey was then regarded as a poor risk because of its financial problems, the loans were granted on relatively difficult terms. Unfortunately, the amount borrowed was not used for development, but rather for financing non-development spending, as is still being done in a number of Muslim countries. This led the government on 6 October 1875 to default on its payment of interest and amortization.

Consequently, a Council of the Debt was established by the creditors for the recovery of the loan with interest. This Council had a staff of 893, more than that of the Ottoman Ministry of Finance. The Council became a very powerful body with far-reaching influence on the financial, economic and political life of the Ottoman Empire. This indicates how excessive, and particularly unproductive, spending by governments leads to excessive reliance on external borrowing and ultimately to loss of independence. Foreign governments and institutions are then able to exert a powerful influence on all aspects of the country and make the government powerless to take independent decisions. As Inalcik has rightly remarked: "the leaders had perhaps failed to realize that economic and financial subjection to foreign powers was no less a threat to political independence than defeat on the battlefront".[41]

Corruption and the sale of political positions

> For officers of the state, corruption is a disease without remedy... beware, beware of corruption. O God! Save us from it.
>
> Luṭfī Pāshā (d. 970/1563)[42]

For a long time the civil and military administration of the Ottoman Empire was considered to be the most efficient in Europe.[43] The Grand *Wazīr* (Chief Minister) was appointed for his competence. Once appointed, not only was his tenure permanent but he was also free from all illicit influence or pressure and could not be removed from office except for severe dereliction of duty.[44] However, efficiency began to deteriorate in the sixteenth century when the sultans started to advance their personal favourites to this rank. Consequently, the Grand *Wazīr* was subject to all kinds of interferences and intrigues by palace favourites, and liable not only to summary dismissal at any moment but also to confiscation of his property and even execution. This adversely affected the morale and efficiency of both the civilian and military administration.

No society can maintain its developmental momentum if the quality of the government declines. Ibn Khaldūn was, therefore, right in laying considerable emphasis in his model on the moral and mental quality of the power elite. However, authoritarian regimes not accountable to the people may not be competent and conscientious unless the head of the state is himself so and tries to ensure a caring and clean administration. In the earlier period, the Ottoman sultans took a keen interest in the affairs of the state and were accessible to their subjects who came to them with their complaints and petitions. However, from the time of Suleyman the Magnificent, the sultans became so preoccupied with the pursuit of conquests and defending them that they hardly had any time to attend to the affairs of state. Inevitably, then, they started to withdraw from society and its needs, and the solidarity that existed earlier between the rulers and the people was adversely affected. Rulers did not even have the time to pursue the education of their own children. Therefore, after Suleyman's death, in 1566, there was a succession of 13 incompetent sultans who did not have the ability to exercise real power even when they wished to do so.

Most nation-building activities were left to the Grand *Wazīrs*. There may not have been anything wrong in this if the *wazīrs* were themselves honest, competent and accountable before the rulers (as was the case in earlier dynasties), and operated on the basis of clear goals and directives. This would have helped ensure a relatively clean and effective administration under their auspices. However, the recurring financial crises and the constant need for resources in the sixteenth and later centuries led to the appointment of *wazīrs* on the basis of political manoeuvrings and the payment of significant sums of money rather than competence. The sale of offices became such a widespread practice after the seventeenth century that they were given only to those who bid the highest amount.[45] Once in office, the *wazīrs* misused their authority for personal gain and tried to recover these sums from the sale of other major offices.[46] Even the appointment and promotion of the *'ulamā'* and judges began to be made without reference to merit or seniority, shattering the people's confidence in them. This led to inefficiency and near paralysis of the government machinery. It may have been for this reason that Ibn Khaldūn had earlier deplored, in his autobiography, the spread of bribery, irregularities in judicial procedures, and other corrupt practices in his own lifetime during the reign of the Burjī Mamlūks (784-922/1382-1517).[47]

Unchecked corruption damaged every aspect of the civil, military, economic, social, political, and even religious life of the empire.

The search for revenues combined with corruption gave immense authority to tax-farmers, who fleeced the peasants and even resorted to the outright seizure of properties and other assets. Loss of central government protection as a result of corruption forced the peasants to drift away from their lands. Some fled to urban areas while others became bandits.[48] Security of life and property, the rule of law, and incorruptible justice, which were the hallmarks of the earlier centuries of Islam, were no longer present. Moral as well as economic development were bound to suffer under such circumstances.

To eighteenth-century Europeans, the inefficiency and corruption of the Ottoman Empire was obvious. "Everyone in a public position seemed to be for sale."[49] Western powers naturally took advantage of this weakness to buy the allegiance of high office holders and to obtain their assistance in supporting breakaway movements and so further weakening the empire.

There was no dearth of scholars who felt unhappy about the prevailing conditions and wrote treatises expressing their dissatisfaction and giving valuable advice. The literature on the 'Mirrors for Princes', already referred to, was reflected in Turkey in the writings of a number of scholars from the time the empire was at its zenith. Because of the change in the behaviour of the ruling elite, they foresaw the difficulties that lay ahead. These scholars included Luṭfī Pāshā (d. 970/1563), Muṣṭafā ʿAlī Akhīsārī (d. 1025/1616), Kochu Bey (d. after 1058/1648), Ḥājjī Khalīfah (d. 1067/1657), Ḥuseyn Ḥazarfenn (d. 1089/1679) and Sārī Mehmed Pāshā (d. 1179/1767).[50] All of them emphasized the need to check the greed of the royalty and its courtiers because of the evil consequences that this ultimately leads to. They emphasized the need for justice, respect for property rights, appointments and promotions solely on the basis of merit, moderation in taxation, and reduction in expenditure by reducing the army and the bureaucracy. However, path dependence and self-reinforcing mechanisms had become so firmly entrenched in the Ottoman Empire by then that it became difficult to introduce any significant change.

Economic decline

The Islamic goal of brotherhood and social solidarity may have been difficult to realize if it had not been buttressed by moral uplift and justice as well as a perceptible improvement in the social and economic position of the people, particularly the poor and downtrodden. For this purpose, governments in the classical period played a crucial role by ensuring the prevalence of law and order, reducing taxes and tariffs, promoting education and research, and providing infrastructure and other facilities. Almost everyone seems to have shared the fruits of prosperity. Consequently, there was a phenomenal rise in the output of agriculture and crafts accompanied by a rapid rise in trade and commerce and the establishment of a vast common market. The commerce of the Muslim world during the Middle Ages, as has been rightly acknowledged by Lewis, "was in every way ahead of that in Europe – richer, larger, better organized, with more commodities to sell and more money to buy, and a vastly more sophisticated network of trading relations".[51]

However, by the twelfth/eighteenth century, this position was reversed. The reasons are not difficult to understand. Overindulgence in military campaigns and ostentatious living on the part of the political elite, along with an overextended and corrupt bureaucracy, left meagre resources for nation-building activities like education, medical facilities, infrastructure construction, and general well-being. This, along with high rates of taxation and insecurity of life and property, led to the inability of the Muslim world, in spite of its great potential, to transform the earlier agricultural and intellectual revolution into the kind of Industrial Revolution that took place in Europe, the United States and later on in Japan. The potential was hijacked by lack of political accountability, which made the government unable to play the role that it had played in earlier centuries. In essence, the sort of public pressure that generally forces democratic governments to be effective simply did not exist. This had grave consequences, the effects of which the Muslim world is still suffering from and will probably continue to do so for some time in the future.

Education, which is one of the essential locomotives for promoting development, received very low priority in the Ottoman Empire. Accordingly, the rate of literacy among the Turkish masses was only about 2 percent in 1868.[52] Even physical infrastructure, which is another essential locomotive for development, also seems to have been generally ignored. In 1850, there was hardly a single railroad track in Turkey or in the territories under Ottoman control.[53] The construction of railroads was undertaken long after 1860, the length of railway lines rising to 180 kilometres in 1870 and 5,438 kilometres in 1913 (Table 3). This was, however, far less than 21,500 and 32,623 kilometres respectively in those two years in the UK and 85,170 and 401,977 kilometres in the USA.

The lack of adequate social and economic infrastructure coupled with the oppressive tax system and the non-enforcement of property rights put the empire's economic machinery at a great disadvantage and ensured that productivity remained at a low level. The luxury of the aristocrats along with the low incomes of peasants and artisans contributed to low savings. Even the savings that did take place remained hidden because of the constant fear of harassment by the tax-farmers. They could not, thus, be utilized effectively for improving the tools and techniques of production.[54] The poverty of the rural sector also hurt the urban manufacturing sector. Lack of adequate demand along with the exploitative political atmosphere were not conducive to the establishment of large-scale industries and corporations. Firms remained typically small, using old-fashioned labour-intensive techniques that required little fixed capital. The agrarian as well as the manufacturing base of the economy, thus, failed to expand with the empire's needs. A viable industrial and commercial superstructure that could compete in the international market and help raise not only the empire's share in expanding international commerce but also the government's revenues,[55] could not, therefore, develop.

Table 3: Length of Railway Lines in Some Relevant Countries
(Kilometres)

	1870	1913
France	15,554	40,770
Germany	18,876	63,378
Greece	–	–
India	7,678	66,822
Italy	6,429	18,873
Russia	10,731	70,156
Turkey	180	5,438
UK	21,500	32,623
USA	85,170	401,977

Source: Maddison, 1995, Table 3.4, p. 64.

In the absence of relevant macroeconomic data, one is left with no other option but to use whatever data are available. These clearly indicate the weak economic position of the country. For example, wheat production in Turkey was only 50 million bushels in 1888 (Table 4), when it was 76 and 275 million bushels respectively in the UK and France, and 415 and 478 million bushels in the USA and India.[56] In the manufacturing sector there were, as late as 1913, only 269 establishments working with machines, employing about 17,000 workers in the whole of Ottoman Turkey.[57] The contribution of industry to GNP was only 13 percent in 1939.[58] While the

Ottoman Empire was in this fragile economic condition, Western powers were raising productivity and reducing production costs by placing substantial importance on improvement in the quality of their social and physical infrastructure, along with the mechanization and rationalization of both agriculture and industry.[59]

Table 4: Wheat Production in Some Relevant Countries
(Million bushels per annum)

	1831-40	1851-60	1871-80	1881-87	1888
France	190	223	275	290	275
Germany	50	70	94	98	103
Greece	2	2	3	4	6
India, etc.	108	187	282	375	478
Italy	60	75	115	105	141
Russia	110	130	224	250	258
Turkey, etc.	20	30	40	47	50
UK	120	121	85	78	76
USA	78	137	338	440	415

Source: Rostow, 1978, Table III. 19, p. 147, and Table III. 24, pp. 164-65.

To add fuel to the fire, the development of the steam engine, and faster and cheaper means of land and sea transport in the West reduced the cost of transportation, and worked against Ottoman agriculture and industry. Decline in the prices of imported food products and manufactured goods put Ottoman producers at a disadvantage not only in export markets but also in their own local markets. The Ottomans gradually became exporters of raw materials and importers of manufactured goods like other developing countries. The terms of trade also generally moved against them and in favour of industrial nations.[60] Turkey's merchandise exports amounted to only $49 million in 1870 compared with $541 million, $424 million and $971 million respectively for France, Germany and the UK, and $403 million for the USA (Table 5). The rate of growth of only 1.5 percent per annum in exports, over the 43 years 1870-1913 was the lowest as compared with Turkey's major competitors (see Table 5). Because of the low rate of growth in exports, Turkey continued to experience trade deficits,[61] which had to be financed by a reliance on credits.[62] The Ottoman Empire thus declined in relative global economic importance during the eighteenth and nineteenth centuries.

Table 5: Merchandise Exports

(Value in million Dollars at current exchange rates)

	1870	**1913**	**g**
France	541	1,328	2.1
Germany	424	2,454	4.2
Greece	7	23	2.8
India, etc.	255	785	2.7
Italy	208	485	2.0
Russia	216	783	3.0
Turkey, etc.	49	94	1.5
UK	971	2,555	2.3
USA	403	2,380	4.2

g = Compounded annual rate of growth in percent from 1870-1913.

Source: Maddison, 1995, Table 1.1, pp. 234-5 and 2001, Table F-1, pp. 359-60. It would have been more meaningful to show exports at constant prices, and Maddison's Table 1.2 does give data at constant prices. However, since Turkey is not included in that table, exports at constant prices are not shown here.

In the absence of real GDP data before 1913, the data on real wages can serve as a rough indicator of the people's living standard and the growth of the real economy. The index of real daily wages for unskilled and skilled construction workers in Istanbul rose, with substantial fluctuations, from 100 in 1489/90 to only 130 and 151 respectively on the eve of the First World War. This reflects a rise of only 30 and 51 percent over a long period of 423 years at the negligible compounded rate of less than one-tenth of 1 percent per annum.[63] Real GDP may have been rising at a somewhat higher rate, but the benefit of this was apparently not being shared by the common people through a rise in their real wages. As a result of this infinitesimally slow rate of growth, per capita GDP in 1990 international dollars was $979 in Turkey in 1913, the earliest year for which such data are available for Turkey, as against $3,452 and $5,032 in France and the UK, and $5,307 in the US (Table 6). The figures indicate that the US was the fastest growing economy at that time and its share of world GDP rose from 1.8 percent in 1820 to 8.9 percent in 1870 and 19.1 percent in 1913.[64] It was clearly on its way to becoming a superpower in the twentieth century. The role that the government played in this through its support to educational, technological, infrastructure and institutional development cannot be denied.

Corruption and high rates of taxation not only hurt the economy and the ability of the government to finance development, they also affect the solidarity between the government and the people. The flow of resources from the peasants, craftsmen and traders to the privileged few in urban areas created a gap in wealth and status that weakened the morale and character of the rest of the population. Inevitably, then, there developed a corollary tendency on the part of the people to find different ways of cheating the tax-farmer as well as others to offset the injustice inflicted on them. This must have gone a long way towards deteriorating their moral strength in keeping with al-Māwardī's observation that, "there is nothing that leads to a faster decay of the world and degeneration of people's conscience than injustice".[65] Social solidarity also declined and internal dissensions and disunity, which had to some extent existed all along, became aggravated, paving the way for the fragmentation of the sultan's authority. This led to disintegration of the empire. The reforms of the *Tanẓīmāt* period (1839-76) could not prevent this because lack of political accountability, the main cause of the decline, continued in full swing.

Table 6: Per Capita GDP in Some Relevant Countries
(In 1990 International Dollars)

	1870	**1913**	**g**
France	1,858	3,452	1.45
Germany	1,913	3,833	1.63
Greece	–	1,621	–
India	558	663	0.40
Italy	1,467	2,507	1.25
Russia	1,023	1,488	0.88
Turkey	–	979	–
UK	3,263	5,032	1.01
USA	2,457	5,307	1.81

g = compounded annual rate of growth in percent from 1870-1913.

Source: Data for 1870 and 1913 are from Maddison, 1995, p. 23, and pp. 194-206.

The large, energetic and innovative middle class that had emerged as a result of the revolution brought about by the Prophet (pbuh), gradually shrank, because of continuous contractions in the room for initiative and advancement.[66] National economic decay naturally resulted in the curtailment of intellectual development and the stifling of creative activity. Even *fiqh,* which had earlier fulfilled the legal needs of a growing society, became stagnant and unable to meet the new challenges, although this rigidity, as indicated earlier, may have saved it to a great extent from exploitation by the sultans and the feudal lords as a means to serve their own vested interests. The take-off that had taken place earlier, was, thus, now aborted. Without an enabling political authority to enforce justice and property rights and the rule of law as envisaged by the Sharīʿah, development suffered, and the people, in general, became incapable of showing initiative and enterprise.

The Muslim world lost the momentum of advance that had led the Ottoman Empire to its zenith under Mehmed II, the Conqueror (1451-81), and Suleyman, the Magnificent (1520-66). The conquests and magnificence of these rulers had clearly come at the expense of future development and prosperity. The zeal for conquests and expansion kept a large army engaged in central Europe, North Africa, the Aegean, Cyprus, the Red Sea and the Crimea, and an expensive navy operating in the Mediterranean. What made matters worse was the split in the Muslim world, with the Safavids aligning themselves with the Ottoman's enemies. It was but natural under such circumstances that positive forces needed for development were neglected. Negative forces, thereby, continued to gain strength until they reached a climax in the seventeenth century after the unsuccessful Siege of Vienna, in 1683, under Mehmed IV (1648-87). Furthermore, an overburdened rural economy was incapable of supporting the military superiority as well as the economic and technological advances that were necessary to face the challenge from the West. The Ottomans did not even have adequate resources to improve the technology and professionalism of their armed forces in which the West was rapidly advancing. The price for this neglect was paid through a number of defeats starting with Russia on the Danube in 1770.

Consequently, the empire fell more and more on the defensive, its frontiers vulnerable to superior military and naval power and its crafts to tough competition from the West. Furthermore, the empire lost most of the territorial gains it had made earlier. All those human and material resources spent on conquest, and the sacrifices made in terms of the people's education and well-being, came to nothing. These territorial losses not only led to a loss of revenues and to further decline in the government's ability to finance its spending without borrowing, but also shattered trade networks, profoundly affecting agricultural as well as manufacturing activities.[67] In spite of several efforts to initiate reforms and improve the situation, conditions did not improve significantly and Turkey descended from a position of 'magnificence' to that of 'the sick man of Europe'. By the time of the First World War, Turkey was exhausted economically as well as militarily. The crowning disaster was its decision, in November 1914, to enter the war on the side of the Central Powers. The resultant defeat led to the cutting of the empire into pieces shared as war booty among the victors. This was perhaps the lowest point in Muslim history. Ibn Khaldūn's model was, thus, fully vindicated.

Notes

1. For some glaring examples of such luxurious living during the 'Abbāsid period, see various books of history like al-Ṭabarī (d. 310/923), al-Mas'ūdī (d. 346/957), al-Aghānī (d. 356/967), al-Khaṭīb (d. 463/1071), Ibn Khallikān (d. 681/1382), and Hitti, 1958, pp. 302-4.
2. Faroghi, 1994, pp. 542-43.
3. Inalcik, 1970, Volume 1, p. 296.
4. The rate of growth in consumer prices is calculated from the consumer price index estimated by Pamuk, 2004, Table 1, p. 455.
5. See extracts from Luṭfī Pāshā's *Asafnāme,* cited by Lewis, 1962, p. 73.
6. Faroghi, 1994, p. 542.
7. See the address that Abū al-'Abbās, the father of the 'Abbāsid dynasty, gave in the mosque before receiving the allegiance (*bay'ah*) from the people, reported in Al-Ṭabarī, *Ta'rīkh*, 1979, Volume 9, pp. 125-27.

8. Baghdād fell to the Mongols on 10 February 1258.
9. See Morgan, 1993, pp. 230-35.
10. Sarton, 1927, Volume 1, p. 662.
11. Lambton, 1981, pp. 298 and 300.
12. Hodgson, 1977, Volume 2, p. 8.
13. Lambton, 1981, p. 299.
14. Spuler and Ettinghausen, 1986, p. 1121.
15. The Fāṭimids ruled North Africa and Egypt, the Ayyūbids ruled Egypt, Syria and Palestine, and the Mamlūks ruled Egypt.
16. Hitti, 1958, pp. 329-30; see also Rabie, 1970, pp. 129-38. According to al-Maqrīzī (d. 845/1442) "from the time of Ṣalāḥ al-Dīn Yūsuf ibn Ayyūb to the present day all the lands of Egypt have continued to be awarded as *iqṭā'* (land grants) to the sultan, his officials (*umarā'*) and soldiers (*ajnād*)" (al-Maqrīzī, *Al-Khiṭaṭ,* Volume 1, p. 97).
17. Cahen, 1986, p. 1090.
18. Quataert, 1994, p. 861.
19. Inalcik, 1994, p. 5.
20. The *fiqh* equivalent of tax-farming is *qabālah*, which a majority of the *fuqahā'* do not find permissible (*ghayr mashrū'ah* and *bāṭilah*) because it leads to oppression and injustice and harms the cultivators. (*Al-Mawsū'ah al-Fiqhiyyah*, Volume 32, p. 243; Abū Yūsuf (d. 182/798), *al-Kharāj*, 1352 AH, p. 105; Abū 'Ubayd (d. 224/839), *al-Amwāl,* 1968, pp. 99-100; al-Māwardī (d. 450/1058) *al-Aḥkām*, 1960, p. 176.) Ibn 'Abbās called the difference between what the tax-farmer receives from the farmer and what he pays to the government *ḥarām* while Ibn 'Umar equated it with *ribā* (Abū 'Ubayd, *al-Amwāl,* p. 100; al-Māwardī, *al-Aḥkām*, p. 176; and Ibn al-Athīr (d. 606/1210), *al-Nihāyah*, 1963, Volume 4, p. 10). See also *Qabālah* in Ibn Manẓūr, *Lisān*, Volume 11, p. 544 and Abū El-Fadl, 1992.
21. For a brief review of the literature on "Mirrors for Princes" by Ibn al-Muqaffa' (d. 139/756), al-Nu'mān (d. 363/974), al-Māwardī (d. 450/1058), al-Khaṭīb (d. 463/1071), Kai Kāus (d. after 475/1082), Niẓām al-Mulk (d. 485/1092), al-Ghazālī (d. 505/1111), and al-Ṭurṭūshī (d. 520/1126), see Essid, 1995, pp. 19-41.
22. *Mukūs* include all kinds of sales and excise taxes or customs duties (see the editor's note in Abū 'Ubayd, *Kitāb al-Amwāl,* 1968, p. 703. See also *maks* in *Lisān*).
23. Abū 'Ubayd, 1968, pp. 703-4, *Ḥadīth* numbers 1624-29.
24. Al-Maqrīzī (d. 845/1442) gives a long list of the *mukūs* abolished by Ṣalāḥ al-Dīn, (*Khiṭaṭ,* Volume 1, pp. 104-5). However, his son, Al-'Azīz 'Uthmān (d. 595/1198) not only re-imposed the *mukūs* which had been abolished by his father, but rather raised them (ibid., p. 105).
25. Some of the points cited in this paragraph are from Bjorkman, 1991, pp. 195-6.
26. Ehrenkreutz, 1991, p. 117.

27. Miles, 1992, p. 297.
28. Cited by Miles, 1992, p. 298. Ibn Ba'ra wrote between 615/1218 and 635/1238.
29. Al-Rayyis, 1961, p. 369; also al-Qaradawi, 1969, Volume 1, p. 264.
30. Al-Rayyis, 1961, p. 374; also al-Qaradawi, 1969, Volume 1, p. 264; and Miles, 1992, p. 320.
31. Al-Qaradawi, 1969, Volume 1, p. 264; Miles, 1992, p. 320.
32. Al-Misri, 1990, pp. 54 and 66.
33. See Miles, 1992, p. 320 and Kramer, 1952, p. 100.
34. Spuler and Ettinghausen, 1986, p. 1122.
35. Debasement of currency was not just a Mamlūk or Ottoman practice, it was also practised elsewhere. For the rates of debasement of various European currencies from the fifteenth to the eighteenth centuries, see Brandel and Spooner, 1967, figure 4, p. 458.
36. Since Ibn Khaldūn lived in a time of financial crisis, the impact of currency debasement on society and the economy received special attention in the *Muqaddimah* (pp. 261-264).
37. Al-Maqrīzī (d. 845/1442) *Ighāthah*, 1956, pp. 14-15, 32-38 and *al-Sulūk*, 1971, Volume 3, pp. 1130-34. See also Allouche, 1994, pp. 16-17.
38. For the silver content of the akce from 1469-1914, see Pamuk, 2004, Table 1, p. 455.
39. Baeck, 1994, p. 114.
40. The original unadjusted figure of £ 200 million is from Lewis, 1991, p. 677. The adjusted figure has been derived on the basis of data from the Bank of England and the IMF, *International Financial Statistics, Yearbook,* 2004. The Retail Price Index for England is estimated to have been 204.8 in 1874 and roughly around 8325.7 in 2004 (1694=100). It would have been more instructive to look at the debt in 1877 as a percent of GDP in that year. However, data on GDP are not available. Ozmucur and Pamuk have estimated an index of real wages (2002, p. 301). This does not, however, serve our purpose.
41. Inalcik, 1970, p. 369.
42. Luṭfī Pāshā, *Āsafnāme*, cited by Lewis, 1962, p. 72.
43. Saunders, 1966, p. 15.
44. Cited from Kochu Bey's *Risāle,* by Lewis, 1962, p. 75.
45. Inalcik, 1994, p. 74.
46. Ibid.
47. Ibn Khaldūn, *Kitāb al-Ta'rīf…,* 1951, pp. 257-58; see also, Khadduri, 1984, p. 189.
48. Inalcik, 1970, p. 342.
49. Hodgson, 1977, Volume 3, p. 158.
50. For the views of Akhīsārī see Meyer (1989), p. 313, and for those of others, see Lewis, 1962.
51. Lewis, 1995, p. 177.
52. Cited by Inalcik, in Holt, Lambton and Lewis, 1970, Volume 2, p. 369, from a quotation cited by Ziyā Pāshā from an article in *Tanẓīmāt,* I (Istanbul 1940), p. 841.

53. See Table III. 21, in Rostow, 1978, p. 152; see also Quataert, 1994, p. 804.
54. Faroghi, 1994, p. 207.
55. Inalcik, 1994, pp. 51-52.
56. Low wheat production in the UK may have been the result of imports from India. After suppression of the 1857 War of Independence, England had, by 1888, successfully de-industrialized India and transformed it into a colony exporting raw materials at the expense of its industries. By 1890, India's imports of cotton fabrics had risen to 2050 million yards from only 1 million yards in 1814. (Desai, 1971; see also Bairoch, 1982.)
57. Rostow, 1978, p. 475.
58. Ibid., p. 476.
59. Inalcik, 1994, p. 888.
60. Pamuk, 1987, p. 48 and Quataert, 1994, p. 830.
61. See Pamuk, ibid., p. 149. See also Quataert, ibid., p. 829.
62. See McGowan in Inalcik, 1994, pp. 724-29. See also Quataert, ibid., p. 762 and Faroghi, p. 467.
63. Based on the index of real wages for unskilled and skilled workers given in Ozmucur and Pamuk, 2002, Table 1, p. 301. The compounded rates of growth are 0.06 and 0.1 percent per annum respectively for unskilled and skilled workers over these 423 years. The table also clearly indicates the fluctuations in real wages over the years from the low of 51 and 50 in 1590-1599 and 52 and 51 in 1770-1779 respectively to a high of 130 and 151 in 1910-1914.
64. Maddison, 2001, Table B.20, p. 263. The US share rose to a high of 27.3 percent in 1950. It has, however, declined since then.
65. Al-Māwardī, *Adab*, 1955, p. 125.
66. See Ashraf, in Cook, 1970, pp. 308-12; see also Issawi, in Cook, 1970, p. 409.
67. Inalcik, 1994, p. 7.

5

DECLINE IN EDUCATION, SCIENCE AND TECHNOLOGY

The flowering of education, science and technology

As discussed in Chapter 2, one of the principal reasons for the success of Islam in the earlier centuries was its emphasis on the moral and socio-economic uplift of human beings. Education was considered to be of crucial importance in the realization of this objective. No wonder the very first revelation of the Qur'ān to the Prophet (pbuh) required him to: "Read in the name of the Lord ... Who taught man through the use of the pen what he did not know" (96:1-5). This accorded a high place to reading and writing in order to learn what one did not know. Accordingly, the Prophet (pbuh) also gave a high place to learning in the Islamic worldview by making it obligatory for every Muslim man or woman to seek knowledge, and equating the superiority of a learned person over a mystic to that of the full moon over all other stars.[1] This is but natural because it is only through education that a proper grounding can be provided to people in the values of their society, their skills can be raised to enable them to earn their livelihood in a morally lawful (*ḥalāl*) way, and they can be enabled to contribute fully to the realization of the *maqāṣid*. In keeping with this emphasis on education in the Qur'ān and *Ḥadīth*, *Fiqh* literature has also placed a great deal of similar emphasis. Abū Zahrah, one of the outstanding jurists of the twentieth century, says that it is necessary "to educate a person so that he is a source of benefit, and not of harm, to his society".[2]

The Prophet (pbuh) did everything possible to spread education. He did not fail to seize any opportunity that became available for this purpose, including the teaching of Muslims by prisoners of war as ransom for their freedom. The Prophet's example was followed by the *Khulafā' al-Rāshidūn*. There was, therefore, a "broad-based social and cultural support for education"[3] in Muslim societies, and almost all dynasties vied with each other over the first few centuries to promote learning and research and to patronize private sector efforts directed towards this end. Data are not available to show the impact of this support to education on the spread of literacy and education except in the case of Spain. During the reign of Ḥakam II (d. 366/976), the second Umayyad Caliph of Spain and son of 'Abd al-Raḥmān III, almost everyone could read and write when only the rudiments of learning were known in the rest of Europe and that too primarily among the clergy.[4] There is no reason to believe that the same situation did not prevail elsewhere in the Middle East, particularly because education was free and almost everyone was strongly motivated to have, at least, an ability to read the Qur'ān. However, literacy and education are by themselves not sufficient. They need to be pursued in such a way that there is also an advance in science and technology.

A number of science academies called *Dār al-'Ulūm* (Academy of Sciences), *Dār al-Ḥikmah* (Academy of Wisdom) and *Bayt al-Ḥikmah* (House of Wisdom) were, therefore, established.[5] These provided free education on all science subjects (*'ulūm 'aqliyyah*) such as agriculture, astronomy, botany, chemistry, logic, mathematics, medicine, philosophy, physics and zoology. Attached to each of them was an observatory, an extensive library and reading room, a translation bureau, and a place for copying manuscripts. Paper, ink and pens were supplied free of charge for this purpose. Stipends were provided along with hostel accommodation to full-time students, and generous financial rewards along with living quarters to scholars. There was a remarkable tradition for higher education and scholarly activity in the earlier centuries in the Muslim world.[6] Seminars were also organized on different subjects.

A significant part of the Muslim contribution to knowledge, research and technology was the result of these academies, the official support they received, and the push that the Islamic worldview had itself provided to observation, experiment and research. Muslims were, thus, able to not only benefit from the intellectual contributions made previously by the Byzantine, Sassanian, Indian and Chinese civilizations, but also make rich and path-breaking contributions themselves in a number of science fields like mathematics, physics, chemistry, astronomy, biology and medicine. They, thus, came to occupy the top place in these fields over a long period of almost four centuries, from the middle of the eighth century to the middle of the twelfth century. Even after losing their supremacy, they continued to make substantial contributions for at least two more centuries.[7]

Education and development thus went hand in hand in the Muslim world as has also been the case elsewhere. Education promoted improvement in the quality of human beings as well as technological advance, and led to accelerated development. This provided increased resources to governments as well as private philanthropists to finance education. As a result, the Muslim world became one of the most advanced economically because it was at the forefront of scientific and technological progress.

Stagnation and its causes

This raises the question of what it was that dimmed the flame of Islam's rationalist spirit in the earlier centuries and led to the stagnation of science and technology. It may not be possible to answer this question without looking back into history and examining the various undercurrents that led to this tragedy. Three important factors seem to have played a key role in contributing to this decline. These were: (i) Decline in state financial support; (ii) the inability of the private sector to shoulder the entire burden, and (iii) the use of force by the rationalists to impose unacceptable views on the public, coupled with adverse reactions to this, leading to a divorce of science subjects from religious schools.

Decline in state financial support

Lack of political accountability was perhaps the most important reason for the near-drying up of state financial support that had previously been generously available. The luxury of the royal courts combined with corruption and excessive spending on military campaigns drained government resources and reduced its ability to finance education, science and technology, infrastructure construction and economic development. The Ottomans, in general, tended to give low priority to education and other nation-building activities.[8] Therefore, the Islamic creative spark, which had dimmed by the time the Ottomans came to power in the beginning of the eighth/fourteenth century, was nearly eclipsed in later centuries. This may perhaps have been one of the primary reasons why the earlier push for development did not translate into an industrial revolution.

The inability of the private sector to play an effective role

Decline in the state's role left the major burden of education on the private sector. This it performed initially through primarily the medium of *waqf* (charitable foundations), which were established to support *madrasahs* and other institutions of higher learning, just as they were for the provision of a variety of public services, including the construction and maintenance of mosques, lodgings for students and travellers, bridges, wells, roads and hospitals.[9] The *waqf* received great impetus during the early Ottoman period. They were properly regulated and operated under close official supervision.[10] Shops and bazaars were also built by the *waqf* to serve as a source of income for religious, educational and other charitable activities.[11]

However, as will be discussed later below, the force used by the rationalists, with the help of political authority, to impose their unacceptable philosophical views on the public generated a severe reaction against philosophy. Since all practical sciences were bracketed in those days with philosophy, not just in the Muslim world but also elsewhere, religious institutions ceased to teach philosophy. This inevitability inflicted a stunning blow to all the practical sciences that philosophy incorporated. Privately supported education in the Muslim world through *waqf* and other charitable contributions primarily, therefore, came to be confined to religious activities on the basis of the false premise that science education was less meritorious than religious education in terms of earning reward.[12] This premise was absolutely unfounded because, according to the Prophet (pbuh), any human act which helps other people fulfil a need is an act of charity and earns a reward in the Hereafter, irrespective of whether this need is material or spiritual.[13] Accordingly, contributions to even science education and research were considered in the earlier centuries a way of earning reward in the Hereafter. Nevertheless, this false premise persisted and became even more deeply embedded as a result of the seclusion of the pious *'ulamā'* from the affairs of state and the real world (see Chapter 6). Little need was, therefore, felt for teaching sciences in religious schools and building students' analytical abilities. This unhealthy atmosphere continues to prevail in most *madrasahs* to this day.

The tempo of the private sector even for religious education did not rise with accelerating need. Furthermore, the continuous swell in the numbers of Muslims meant that a massive educational campaign needed to be carried out to make people aware of Islamic values. The economic problems that the private sector faced, the lack of government support, and the misappropriation of even *waqf* income by the trustees for private benefit,[14] did not, however, permit an increase in funds for this purpose. The private sector was unable to generate enough resources to spread even literacy and general religious education among the people, let alone build universities and research centres badly needed by the Muslim world. There was, thus, a loss in terms of both moral upbringing and scientific education. The moral flame, which had been ignited by the Prophet (pbuh), and the technological charge that was necessary to sustain Muslim superiority, were, thus, dimmed. In this way the Muslim world suffered a decline in both the moral as well as technological fields.

Meanwhile, effective democratic processes ensured the use of public resources for development in the Western world. Development in turn led to a rise in demand for education. While the population in the USA increased twelve-fold between 1840 and 1970, college enrolments rose 417 times.[15] Government support plus private initiatives led to unprecedented advances in science and technology, thus giving a further boost to development, and thereby creating a vast gap between the Western and Muslim worlds. Democracy, education and development thus reinforced each other in the Western world. When the encounter came between the Western and Muslim worlds, there was little chance for the Muslims with their lack of education and their outmoded military and manufacturing technology.

The use of force by the rationalists

CONFLICT BETWEEN THE RATIONALISTS AND THE CONSERVATIVES

The factor that hurt the continued flowering of science and technology most in the Muslim world was the conflict that arose between the rationalists and the conservatives as a result of the former's use of coercive state power to impose some unacceptable views on the population. The rationalist movement had arisen in the Muslim world in the second/eighth century, several centuries before it did in the West. This had become imperative as a result of the rapid spread of Islam in territories which were previously under the influence of the materially more advanced and intellectually more sophisticated Sassanian and Byzantine civilizations. Without the adoption of a rationalist approach, it may have been difficult to gain educated and intellectually sophisticated converts to Islam or even to save the common man from the adverse influence of heretics or *zanādiqah* (singular, *zindīq*).

The rationalists, however, did more than this. They also tried to determine the cause and effect relationship between different phenomena in human life and the universe around them. Their objective was to show that God does not operate in an arbitrary manner. He is rather systematic and methodical and operates on the basis of certain principles, which it is possible for human beings to discover. They were thereby trying to lay down a solid foundation for science within the religious paradigm. Both of these objectives (providing a rational defence of Islamic teachings and trying to understand how God operates in nature) were perfectly in keeping with the ethos of Islam, which calls upon human beings to use their intellect to understand the mysteries of the universe (Qur'ān, 3:190-91).

Who, then, were these rationalists? They were scholars from different intellectual backgrounds and may be classified into two groups: the *Mu'tazilites* and the *Falāsifah* (philosophers, singular *faylasūf*). There is no historical evidence to show that they were inimical to Islam.

The *Mu'tazilites*[16] were basically religious scholars and not philosophers. They wanted to provide convincing rational arguments for religious beliefs. This was necessary to create and strengthen conviction among the people. The stronger the conviction, the more steadfast the person would be in his/her beliefs and the more motivated they would be to act upon the teachings of Islam. In contrast with this, extreme conservatives did not believe in the need for rational arguments. They wanted people to accept religious beliefs on the basis of blind faith.

To help them in their task, the *Mu'tazilites* acquired expertise in philosophy, logic, the sciences and the scientific method, and developed a systematic method of logical reasoning called *'Ilm al-Kalām*.[17] Those who applied this method were called *mutakallimūn*, which literally means 'reasoners'. This method was original to the Muslims and, as Gardet has put it, was "certainly not an Arab adaptation of Mazdean or Christian theology".[18] In essence there was little difference between the *mutakallimūn* and the *Mu'tazilites* and the two terms were sometimes used synonymously. They attracted scholars from all shades of the Muslim spectrum. While some of them like Ja'far ibn al-Bishr (d. 226/841) and Abū Mūsā al-Murdār (d. 226/841) were renowned for their piety, others had the reputation of being lax in their religious observances.[19]

The *Falāsifah*, influenced by Greek philosophy, were primarily intellectuals and not religious scholars.[20] Since philosophy and science were closely related disciplines in those days, most of the philosophers were well recognized authorities in sciences like mathematics, physics, chemistry, astronomy, and medicine. They also performed experiments to the extent they could, in keeping with the practice of Muslim scholars in those days. They generally received government patronage and made substantial contributions to the development of these sciences. Moreover, since knowledge was not then compartmentalized, they were also quite well versed in the religious sciences, and some, like Ibn Rushd were even considered authorities in these. While the extremists among them like Ibn al-Rāwandī (d. 250/864) and Abū Bakr al-Rāzī (Rhazes, d. 313/925) held views that conflicted with some fundamental Islamic beliefs, most of them, including al-Kindī (d. 252/866), al-Fārābī (d. 339/950), Ibn Sīnā (Avicenna, d. 428/1037) and Ibn Rushd

(Averroes, d. 595/1198), were relatively moderate. They did not find any incompatibility between reason and Revelation. In fact, they tried to show the harmony between the two and rationally argued in favour of Revelation and Prophethood, life after death, and other Islamic beliefs and practices. They quoted profusely from the Qur'ān and the *Sunnah* to support their views.

THE NATURE OF THE DEBATE

This free and rational discussion of Islamic beliefs and practices raised a lively and extremely sophisticated intellectual debate on a number of epistemological issues, some of which were:

- What is the nature of God? Does He have a body with eyes, ears, hands and legs? If not, how does He see, hear, hold and move, and is it possible for human beings to see Him? What are His attributes (*ṣifāt*)? Are these attributes an integral part of His Being or separate from Him? Can reason help human beings know Him and His attributes, or are they totally dependent on Revelation for this purpose? Does He know everything that will happen in the future, even what human beings are going to do?
- If God is Eternal, is His creation also eternal? If not, was there a period when He was not a Creator? Is this conceivable?
- To what extent are human beings free or predestined? If their life is predestined, then would it be just for God to hold them accountable for their deeds and to reward or punish them?
- Is faith alone sufficient to be a believer or is it also necessary to reinforce it by deeds? Is a sinful Muslim a believer (*mu'min*), an unbeliever (*kāfir*) or something in between (*fāsiq*)?
- Will the resurrection of human beings in the Hereafter be only of the soul or also of the body? If there is bodily resurrection, will the body be the same as it is in this world or will it be different?

- If the Qur'ān is a part of God's speech (*kalām*), then is it to be considered created and transitory like this world or uncreated and eternal like other Divine attributes?
- To what extent is it possible for human beings to know what is right from what is wrong by means of reason and to what extent is Revelation necessary for this purpose? Is it conceivable that a just God would hold human beings accountable for their deeds without creating in them an innate ability to recognize right from wrong?

It is evident that hardly any of these questions had anything to do with science. The answers were bound to be speculative and could not have been given with precision. It was, therefore, not possible to have a single answer. There were differing opinions and neither the rationalists nor the conservatives constituted a homogenous whole.[21] The real bone of contention was the extent to which reason and logic could effectively help answer these epistemological questions. It seems, however, that the moderates among both the rationalists and the conservatives, who constituted the majority, appreciated the need for both reason and Revelation in different degrees. However, it was the extremists on both sides who succeeded in getting greater attention and who, therefore, set the tone of the debate.

The moderate rationalists, who stressed a greater reliance on reason, developed a set of five axioms (*al-uṣūl al-khamsah*) to help them argue their case more effectively. Two of the most important of these axioms were *Tawḥīd* (Unity) and God's *'adl* (justice), which are accepted by all Muslims without exception.[22] There would be no point in relying on axioms that did not command a consensus. Differences, nevertheless, arose in the deduction of their implications.

With respect to *Tawḥīd,* which is the most fundamental of all Islamic beliefs and stands for the absolute Oneness and Uniqueness of God, the general Muslim understanding is that human beings cannot comprehend Him fully because of their limited capabilities and perceptions. The Qur'ān itself makes this crystal clear by saying that "there is nothing like Him" (42:11),[23] and that human "eyes cannot encompass Him" (6:103). Therefore, in keeping with a Qur'ānic injunction (3:7), the general Muslim attitude has been to accept on faith those unseen metaphysical realities which are beyond the reach of reason and sense perception. They do not, therefore, try to probe into them too deeply. This would be a fruitless exercise because, while the existence of God can be established through observation and logical reasoning, His nature cannot be understood fully except through His attributes (*ṣifāt*) as revealed in the Qur'ān and the *Sunnah.* Extreme rationalists, however, insisted that reason was by itself capable of enabling human beings to know His nature. Their effort to do so inevitably embroiled them in sterile and divisive controversies on a number of metaphysical questions such as Divine attributes, Resurrection and Life after Death, angels, Revelation and Prophethood, the eternity of the world, the creation of the Qur'ān, Divine knowledge of particulars, and the ability of human beings to see God in the Hereafter. These extreme rationalists adopted such hard line positions, which were in clear conflict with the Qur'ān and the *Sunnah* that even moderate rationalists had difficulty accepting their views.

With respect to the concept of *'adl,* the debate was more practical and relevant to the human condition even though it also raised a great deal of controversy. Some of the conclusions that the moderate rationalists derived were as follows:

- God subjects Himself to the same moral principles which He applies to human beings. He does only that which is just and morally right. It is inconceivable that He would do something that is unjust or morally wrong.
- Goodness or evil are innate in the nature of things themselves and not necessarily because God arbitrarily declares them to be so. It is, therefore, possible for human beings to recognize

what is right or wrong through their own reasoning even though they need the help of Revelation to guide them and to confirm their conclusions.

- Since God is just, there is absolutely no room for the concept of predestination. Human beings are the authors of their own deeds, good or evil, and, therefore, rewarding or punishing them is a reflection of God's justice.

To a modern rationalist thinker there may be much appeal in a number of these views. Such appeal existed even in those days, and the initial objective, method and concepts of the moderate rationalists did not generate tension even among those members of the Muslim orthodoxy who did not accept the need for rational explanations for religious beliefs and practices. The differences of opinion that existed could have been resolved to a great extent over time in the light of the Qur'ān and the *Sunnah* and through rational debate. The question is, why did this not take place?

EXTREMISTS ON BOTH SIDES

It was the extremists on both the conservative and rationalist sides who generated a great deal of heat and changed the texture of the whole debate, creating an atmosphere of confrontation. On the conservative side, extremists like the *Ḥashawiyyah* insisted that faith is based entirely on the Qur'ān and the *Sunnah* and that there is absolutely no room for reason. In sharp contrast with this, extreme rationalists like Ibn al-Rāwandī and Abū Bakr al-Rāzī[24] insisted that reason and Revelation were incompatible and that all matters, including right and wrong, should be judged by reason alone. They belittled all attempts at reconciling philosophy and religion. They insisted on formulating a theology solely on the basis of reason, independent of Revelation, and approached what became known later on in the West as Natural Theology.[25] They tended to reject, just like the Western Enlightenment movement later on, all those metaphysical truths that could not be established by means of reason and experience. Acceptance of their views would have pushed Revelation into the background and made reason the sole determinant of faith instead of being a tool for its explanation and defence, as was the original aim of the *Muʿtazilites*.

Does this mean that there is no room for extreme views in human society? Not necessarily. Some of the views which have initially appeared to be extreme and unacceptable have at a later stage turned out to be ingenious and have ended up making substantial contributions to human development. However, social peace may, in certain circumstances, be served better if extremes are avoided, at least in religious and social matters. Nevertheless, if such views are put forward, then one would expect that people give them a patient and tolerant hearing. If extreme views are unable to establish their worthiness and to gain general acceptance, they will die their own natural death. Why then is it that such extreme views created a problem in Muslim society? Was there a lack of tolerance?

There seems to be little evidence of this in the early Muslim society where tolerance generally prevailed and the debate between conservatives and rationalists progressed relatively freely and smoothly. Even a heretic like Ibn al-Rāwandī received a patient hearing and his arguments were logically refuted by several generations of eminent religious scholars.[26] Given the spirit of the age, the prevailing intellectual controversies may perhaps have been resolved through free discussion, particularly because the differences of opinion between the moderates among the rationalists and the conservatives, who constituted a preponderant majority of intellectuals, were not irreconcilable. What then was it that polarized the then Muslim society into two belligerent groups, when in the same society different *fiqhī* schools were mutually tolerant and generally coexisted peacefully in spite of substantial differences of opinion among them?

THE *MIḤNAH* (INQUISITION)

The answer may perhaps lie in the use of force by an illegitimate political authority that did not enjoy the trust of the people. The normal tendency in human societies is that if one group uses force to impose its views on another, the reaction of the suppressed group tends to be severe, particularly if the latter happens to be in the majority. The *Mu'tazilites* exploited the political patronage and financial backing that they received from the government during a substantial part of the 'Abbāsid dynasty (132/750-656/1258), and particularly during the reigns of Ma'mūn al-Rashīd (d. 218/833), al-Mu'taṣim (d. 227/841) and al-Wāthiq (d. 232/846) to impose their radical views forcefully on all. They became aggressive and intolerant in clear violation of Islamic teachings and introduced the *Miḥnah* or testing (Inquisition) into the Muslim world. They went around questioning people about their beliefs and threatened to punish those who held different views: "No *faqīh* (فقية), *muḥaddith* (محدث), *mu'adhdhin* (مؤذن) or *mu'allim* (معلم) was left untested."[27] Freedom of expression, which had been an important characteristic of the Muslim society before this, almost disappeared.[28]

Furthermore, they jailed and tortured their opponents so as to impose their unacceptable views: "The prisons were full of those who had denied the *Miḥnah*."[29] Some prisoners like Muḥammad ibn Nūḥ (d. 218/833), Na'īm ibn Ḥammād (d. 228/842), Yūsuf al-Buwayṭī (d. 231/845) and Aḥmad al-Khuzā'ī (d. 231/845) even died in prison as a result of torturing.[30] Aḥmad al-Khuzā'ī's head was "placed on public view in Baghdād as a grisly warning to potential nonconformists, while his cadaver stayed in Samarrā', also on display".[31] Even prominent jurists like Aḥmad ibn Ḥanbal (d. 241/855), who were held in high esteem by the masses for their piety and scholarship, were not spared. He was flogged on the orders of al-Mu'taṣim until he became unconscious.[32] All this, because he was not willing to accept the *Mu'tazilite* view that the Qur'ān was created. The extremists even went to the extent of inscribing on the mosques of Fusṭāṭ that "There is no god but God, the Lord of the created Qur'ān",[33] thereby making the concept of the 'created Qur'ān' an incontestable part of Islamic belief.

The question is why were the *'ulamā'* so aggravated over an issue that would not be of great significance to a number of people now? The answer being that the use of force and persecution had the effect of creating bitterness and giving a hostile tone to an otherwise intellectual debate. It created suspicion among the *'ulamā'* about the motives of the government, making them feel, rightly or wrongly, that the state was trying to have a say in the definition of Islam.[34] The concept of the 'created Qur'ān' made them afraid that its acceptance would imply that the Qur'ān was not eternally true and could be changed or overridden by illegitimate and corrupt rulers. This they could not stand and steadfastly defended their position without being deterred by imprisonment or merciless flogging.

The *Miḥnah* and the resultant bitterness it generated among the *'ulamā'* against the government led to rising unrest and discontent among the population, particularly in Baghdād. This made even the illegitimate political leadership of that time realize, though belatedly and after the damage had been done, that the *Miḥnah* was unpopular and incapable of working. Al-Mutawakkil (d. 247/861), therefore, put an end to it in 234/849. Aḥmad ibn Abī Du'ād, the Chief *Qāḍī*, who was perhaps the most instrumental in its harsh implementation, was disgraced, became paralyzed, and died unsung in 240/854.

Although the *Miḥnah* was now over, it left two indelible marks on Muslim society. One of these healthy and the other unhealthy. That which has been good saw the distancing of the state from any role in the definition of Islam. Islam stands defined by the consensus (*ijmā'*) of the *ummah* in conformity with the Qur'ān and the *Sunnah*. That which has been unhealthy ensured the alienation of a majority of the *'ulamā'* from philosophy and science. This has had the effect of driving them towards greater conservatism, as will become clear with the progress of this chapter.

Al-Ghazālī (d. 505/1111)

In spite of the use of force, debate on the subject continued between the rationalists and the conservatives and, as a consequence, the extreme rationalists gradually started to lose ground. Essentially, their questionable views could not stand the onslaught from a new school, now generally known as the Ashʿarite. It provided a logical and convincing defence of Islamic beliefs and practices. The leaders of this school were Abū al-Ḥasan al-Ashʿarī (d. 332/943) in Iraq and Abū Manṣūr al-Māturīdī (d. 333/945) in Central Asia, followed by a number of other stalwarts like al-Bāqillānī (d. 403/1012), al-Juwaynī (d. 478/1085), and al-Qushayrī (d. 465/1072). All were extremely well-versed in religious sciences as well as in *ʿIlm al-Kalām* and philosophy. However, they were generally conservative, although to different degrees; al-Māturīdī being significantly less conservative than al-Ashʿarī.[35]

It was, however, al-Ghazālī (d. 505/1111) who inflicted the most stunning and fatal blow to the extreme rationalists. In his book, *Tahāfut al-Falāsifah* (Incoherence of the Philosophers), completed in 488/1095,[36] he logically exposed the "inconsistency of their metaphysical beliefs and self-contradiction of their theories".[37] He succeeded because he attacked philosophy "with full knowledge of its contents and all the force and clarity of his vigorous mind".[38] However, he did not believe in rejecting everything that the rationalists stood for. He clearly stated: "If what they [the philosophers] say is sensible in itself, supported by evidence, and not in conflict with the Qur'ān and the *Sunnah*, then it is not becoming of us to reject it. If we open the door to rejecting every truth that a heretic has arrived at, we will be constrained to reject a great deal of truth."[39] He took from them whatever appeared to him to be useful and tried to create a synthesis of philosophy, *'Ilm al-Kalām* and the Islamic sciences, and was thereby able to rationally resolve a number of the existential disputes prevailing in his time. In the words of Arnaldez, he created "the richest, widest and most open system".[40]

Of the 20 theories of the rationalists that al-Ghazālī found objectionable, only three were considered by him to be heretical and totally unacceptable. These were the eternity of the world, the impossibility of bodily resurrection, and Divine ignorance of particulars.[41] He argued that these theories, for which the philosophers claimed the same degree of certainty and incontestability as mathematics and logic, were essentially based on unproven assumptions and conjectures that could not be established by reason.[42] He had no qualms about accepting other theories that he did not find therein conflict with the Sharīʿah and which had a scientific basis behind them. In particular, he supported the rationalists' explanations for a number of natural phenomena, like lunar and solar eclipses, because rejection of such explanations would do harm to religion.[43] Physics, chemistry, astronomy, mathematics and other such physical sciences were upheld without any grudge. Al-Ghazālī boldly stated: "He who considers that Islam will be helped by the rejection of these sciences, has committed a grave crime against religion (*dīn*)".[44] He did not question the role of reason in human affairs. In fact he emphasized that: "Intellect is the fountainhead, starting point, and foundation of knowledge. Knowledge proceeds from it just like fruit from the tree, light from the sun, and vision from the eye."[45] He did, however, question reliance on reason alone to establish metaphysical truths and to distinguish right from wrong. Reason and Revelation must both play a complementary role in human life.

What provided further strength to al-Ghazālī's rational defence of Islamic beliefs and practices was his eloquence, his vast knowledge of the Sharīʿah, and his piety and high moral calibre. These earned him great respect and admiration. He came to wield considerable influence in the then Muslim world and continues to be widely read and quoted even to this day. It is because of him that *'Ilm al-Kalām*, which was introduced by the *Mu'tazilites* and incorporates somewhat extensively the vocabulary and arguments of the *Falāsifah*, became an officially recognized religious science and an essential part of the religious syllabi.

However, while al-Ghazālī rendered a great service to Islam by defending its beliefs and practices against attacks from heretics and extreme rationalists, he went off at a tangent by insisting that the only cause of every phenomenon is God, thereby de-emphasizing the role of efficient (or immediate) causes. He said that "the relationship between what is normally considered to be the cause and what is considered to be the effect is not necessary".[46] To prove this point, he argued that the relationship between quenching one's thirst and drinking, satisfaction of hunger and eating, burning and contact with fire, and healing and use of medicine is as previously destined by God.[47] It was a little odd for him to deny the role of efficient causes and yet recognize the importance of physical sciences, one of the central pillars of which is the establishment of cause and effect relationships. Even though he did not seem to place much emphasis on this point, he ended up strengthening the forces of extreme conservatism which, in turn, have been responsible for weakening the strength of rationalism and scientific inquiry in the Muslim world.

One, therefore, wonders why a scholar of his calibre decided to toe the Ash'arī line of denying the obvious relationship between cause and effect. It may probably have been an unconscious outcome of the prevailing climate of confrontation and suspicion created by the denial of fundamental epistemological realities by the extreme rationalists. He may even have been afraid that acceptance of the crucial role of efficient causes in various phenomena in human life might indirectly imply the irrelevance of God in human affairs and, thereby, His relegation to the role of a clock-maker deity. Though such a fear now seems to have been unfounded, it could, nevertheless, have been real in the intellectual climate confronting al-Ghazālī.

Ibn Rushd (d. 595/1198)

Ibn Rushd made a last gigantic effort to save the rationalist movement from collapse nearly 85 years after al-Ghazālī's fatal blow. He prepared a rejoinder which was completed in 576/1180 and published under the title *Tahāfut al-Tahāfut* (Incoherence of the Incoherence).[48] The two *Tahāfuts* of al-Ghazālī and Ibn Rushd clearly reflect the essence of the conflict of ideas about reason and Revelation that prevailed in the Muslim world from the second/eighth to the seventh/thirteenth centuries: the same conflict that arose in the West five centuries later.

A number of the charges that al-Ghazālī levelled against philosophers did not apply to moderate philosophers like Ibn Rushd, whose thinking on Islamic beliefs and practices was in conformity with that of the orthodoxy. Ibn Rushd realized the weak position of the extreme rationalists on a number of points and, therefore, adopted a conciliatory approach, stressing the role of both Revelation and reason in religion. He stated: "Every religion is based on Revelation (*waḥy*) but reason (*ʿaql*) is blended with it. He who holds that there can be a religion based only on reason concedes that this religion will necessarily be less perfect than those based on both reason and Revelation."[49] He also stressed that "to walk on the path of religious virtues is indispensable"[50] and that "it is the duty of every person to select the best religion of his time".[51] Having admitted the need for religion, he went on to defend the moderate philosophers by clarifying that "the wise among the philosophers do not permit discussion or disputation of the principles of religion".[52] He even went to the extent of asserting that "those who have doubts about these matters [religious truths] and are eloquent in disputing them are the ones who wish to destroy the religions and to undo the virtues.

They are undoubtedly the heretics who believe that the end of man is nothing but sensual enjoyment… What al-Ghazālī says against them is right."[53] In his *Faṣl al-Maqāl,* he makes a strong case for the mutual compatibility of both reason and the Sharīʿah.

However, Ibn Rushd tried to rectify al-Ghazālī's error with respect to efficient causes. He argued forcefully that even though the ultimate cause of every phenomenon is God, He has Himself established a secondary cause for every phenomenon. While He is capable of bringing about satiety without eating, quenching thirst without drinking, and burning without contact with fire, He does not normally do so. When He does do so, it becomes a miracle, which is among "Divine acts and beyond the reach of human intellect".[54] Because of this, "none of the previous philosophers discussed miracles in spite of their existence in the world".[55] Therefore, "to deny the existence of efficient causes observed in phenomena perceptible through the senses is sophistry".[56] Knowledge, according to Ibn Rushd, progresses through the establishment of cause and effect relationships: "Denial of causes implies the denial of knowledge, and denial of knowledge implies that nothing in this world can be truly known and that there can be only unlimited assumptions without evidence."[57]

In spite of his brilliance and profound scholarship, Ibn Rushd could not swing the prevailing opinion in favour of the philosophers. Hence, even though he played an important role in the history of the Latin Middle Ages,[58] he had little influence on Muslim thought and has the distinction of being perhaps the last of the great philosophers in the Muslim world.[59] "He had no disciples or followers."[60] This was undoubtedly a great misfortune for the Muslim world, not only in the realm of rationalism but also in the field of *Fiqh* where his treatise *Bidāyat al-Mujtahid* continues to be a respectable source of reference for scholars even today.[61] He believed in creating a balanced fusion of reason and Revelation (*al-jamʿ bayn al-maʿqūl wa'l-manqūl*) by giving reason and experiment (*al-qiyās wa'l tajribah*) a rightful place in the Sharīʿah, and was critical of those who rigidly and uncritically followed the opinions of their predecessors.[62] His scientific approach to problems, his depth of vision, and his liberal and tolerant attitude could have been a great asset in moulding the course of intellectual activity in the future.

Even the government patronage that the rationalists enjoyed could not continue when the caliphs became weaker and needed public support. They could not, therefore, afford to persist in alienating the masses by ignoring the Islamic basis of society. They were left with no other option but to return to the consensus view.[63] So, while scholars like Ibn Rushd fell into disgrace, the rationalist movement itself also lost its momentum, and became considerably weakened. With hardly anyone left to challenge it, the Ashʿarite movement had a field day. It became the dominant school in the Muslim world and has continued to be so until today, thanks to prominent defenders like al-Shahrastānī (d. 548/1153), Fakhr al-Dīn al-Rāzī (d. 606/1209), al-Ījī (d. 756/1355) and al-Jurjānī (d. 816/1413).

Ibn Taymiyyah, Ibn Khaldūn and Al-Maqrīzī

By the time Ibn Taymiyyah (d. 728/1328) wrote his *Kitāb al-Manṭiq* (The Book on Logic), the philosophical movement was totally discredited. He, therefore, goes to the extent of saying that "there is no philosophy in Islam" and that "the philosophers are not Muslims".[64] The reason for this was not their cause and effect analysis but rather their wild speculative philosophy. He, however, upheld the quest to establish cause and effect relationships and attacked the Ashʿarites for their denial of efficient causes, saying that "people know through their sense perceptions and intellect that some things are the causes of others".[65] According to him, those who deny efficient causes are violating the Qur'ān, the *Sunnah*, and the *ijmāʿ* (consensus) of the pious predecessors (*salaf*).[66]

Ibn Khaldūn (d. 808/1406), who was himself a great rationalist and supporter of reason and cause and effect analysis, was more careful in his characterization of the philosophers, but even he places philosophy among the discredited sciences like magic, astrology and alchemy. In this respect, see his Chapter on the 'Refutation of Philosophy' (*Ibṭāl al-Falsafah*) in his *Muqaddimah*.[67] His rationale was that philosophers neither acknowledged their limitations nor realized that the universe was too vast and complex to be comprehended in its entirety by human reason and sense perception. It was nothing but philosophers' vain pretention to assume that they could reach the ultimate truth by merely applying the rules of logic.[68]

Al-Maqrīzī (d. 846/1442), who was not as careful as Ibn Khaldūn in his characterization of philosophers, went even farther than Ibn Taymiyyah by placing the philosophers in the category of those who were opposed to Islam (*mukhālifūn*).[69] Such a charge may not be true except for a few heretics, among them Ibn al-Rāwandī. Most of them remained truly Muslims, and were generally considered to be within the pale of Islam. However, as indicated earlier, it was their extremism, intolerance and use of force which set the image and drew the response. Al-Maqrīzī's characterization reflects this negative image of the rationalist movement.

The move towards greater conservatism

This negative image proved to be tragic for the Muslim world. It not only weakened the rationalist movement but also drove the Muslim world gradually towards greater conservatism through the operation of path dependence and self-reinforcing mechanisms. The vigour and dynamism that characterized Muslim scholarship during the late Umayyad and early 'Abbāsid periods, when no discussion was considered a taboo, was substantially diluted. Unfortunately, it was not just philosophy but also the associated physical sciences that became excluded from the syllabi of religious schools. Additionally, since governments did not pay much attention to science education and research, as they had in earlier centuries, the stage was set for the intellectual and technological backwardness of the Muslim world.

If the Muslim scholars of that period were to be classified according to their commitment to rationalism or conservatism, they would fall into the following four groups: (a) extreme rationalists like Ibn al-Rāwandī and Abū Bakr al-Rāzī who aspired to attain all metaphysical truths by means of reason alone without the help of Revelation; (b) moderate rationalists like Ibn Rushd who accepted the need for both Revelation and reason; (c) moderate conservatives like al-Ash'arī, al-Māturīdī (d. 333/945) and al-Ghazālī, who recognized the role of reason but less than what would be acceptable to moderate rationalists, and (d) extreme conservatives, like the *Ḥashawiyyah*, who insisted on blind faith in the acceptance of religious beliefs and denied any role for reason even in the elucidation and defence of faith. Of these four groups, the extreme rationalists lost ground just like the extreme conservatives. The moderate conservatives, however, carried the day due to "a fault line in history".[70]

The tragedy, however, is that over the next few centuries the moderate conservatives moved gradually towards greater conservatism and rigidity, making it more and more difficult for even moderate rationalists to breathe freely. While it was possible in the earlier centuries for scholars like al-Ash'arī, al-Ghazālī, Ibn Rushd, and countless others to gain a solid grounding in both the religious and mundane sciences if they so desired, it became more and more difficult for them to do so with the passage of time. Science education did not return to the Muslim world in a significant way until after its colonization. However, a combination of the two, which was normal and relatively easy in earlier centuries, is still difficult. This became one of the crucial factors in the circular causation of decline.

Contrast between the Muslim and Western Enlightenment movements

In short, what hurt the rationalist movement was the failure of its extreme elements to appreciate the limits of reason, their intolerance of opponents, and their use of coercive state power to impose their views on the majority of the population. This led to the politicization of an otherwise intellectual debate, raised tempers and hardened attitudes. What was particularly offensive was that the views being imposed were in conflict with some of the fundamental, well accepted and rationally defensible Islamic beliefs.[71] The greatest damage in this respect was caused by the doctrine of the 'created Qur'ān'. The confrontation that had artificially been provoked in this way kept some of the best minds of the then Muslim world occupied, unproductively, in hair-splitting debates for centuries. If force had not been used, the fear may perhaps not have been so accentuated, confrontation may not have resulted, attitudes may not have hardened, and an unbridgeable rift between the government and the *'ulamā'* and between philosophy and religion may not have ensued. This rift proved to be tragic for the development of both *Fiqh* and physical sciences in the Muslim world.

The reasons for the downfall of the 'Enlightenment' movement in the Muslim world were thus the reverse of what led to its success in the West. First, in the West it was the corruption and despotism of the Church that led to the success of Voltaire's call to 'crush the infamous thing' and which shook confidence in the metaphysical beliefs that the Church stood for.[72] Voltaire wrote in his *Treatise on Toleration* that he would have borne with the absurdities of dogma had the clergy lived up to their sermons and tolerated the differences. However, the "subtleties of which not a trace can be found in the gospels are the source of the bloody quarrels of Christian history".[73] Durant in fact asserts that "the Church might have sustained the supernatural sanctions provided by the Hebraic Scriptures and the Christian tradition if her personnel had led lives of decency and devotion".[74] In contrast with this, most, if not all, of the great religious scholars in the Muslim world like Abū Ḥanīfah (d. 150/767), Mālik (d. 179/795), Shāfiʿī (d. 204/820), and Aḥmad ibn Ḥanbal (d. 241/855) were individuals of great piety and integrity, and commanded the respect and confidence of the people. They were not men of great wealth and, in general, refused to accept political appointments, even though these were offered to them to silence their criticism of corrupt and un-Islamic practices.

Secondly, as Hourani has rightly pointed out, "orthodoxy in Islam has never been defined by ecclesiastical councils, as in Christianity. No such councils have been held, due to the absence of ordained priesthood in Islam".[75] Orthodoxy has rather been defined by the Qur'ān and the *Sunnah* and the *ijmāʿ* or consensus of the Muslim *ummah,* reached through the free discussion of the *ʿulamā'* (religious scholars) who, according to a widely quoted and authentic *ḥadīth*, are the legatees of the Prophets (*warathat al-Anbiyā'*). The efforts of the state to define the contents of the Sharīʿah came to an end with the termination of the *Miḥnah.*[76] While Western scholars have challenged the authenticity of the Bible, Muslims have, as Ansari has rightly put it, "recognized the paramount authority of the Qur'ān and the *Sunnah* of the Prophet"[77] from an early period. All beliefs and religious and legal doctrines have been derived from these. The *ʿulamā'* around whose opinions the consensus was built up, did not impose their views on the people. The people, in fact, accepted their views because of their harmony with the Qur'ān and *Sunnah* as well as the force of their logic and confidence in their piety, integrity and scholarship.

Thirdly, while it was the Church which resorted to the Inquisition in the West, it was the rationalists who resorted to it in the Muslim world, though never as harshly as the Church. The burning of live human beings as resorted to by the Church never took place in Islam. Nevertheless, the *Miḥnah* left an unhealthy mark. This because repression generally tends to create a severe reaction and leads the repressed to extremism. Its use by the Church hurt religion in the West, and its use by the *Muʿtazilites* hurt rationalism in the Muslim world. If the debate between the *Muʿtazilites*, many of whom were respected religious scholars, and the conservatives had been allowed to progress freely without the use of force, rationalism and orthodoxy may both have been enriched and more balanced views established.[78]

Fourthly, while the Church stood for a number of beliefs, which could not be defended rationally and for which there was no basis in the Gospels, some of the extreme views of the philosophers and the *Muʿtazilites* had no basis in the Qur'ān or the *Sunnah* and could not even be defended rationally. By comparison, the beliefs held by the *ʿulamā'* as well as the people had their footing in the Qur'ān and the *Sunnah* and were relatively simple and easy to understand.

The future of rationalism in the Muslim world

We now come to the crucial question about whether the re-emergence of scientific inquiry in the Muslim world will give rise to a conflict between reason and Revelation and necessitate a change in the paradigm, in the same way as it did in the West. Note, however, that the Islamic paradigm does not itself necessitate a conflict between reason and Revelation.

During the first two centuries of Islam there was a free debate on all issues where there was a difference of opinion. According to Ibn Taymiyyah, no jurist, irrespective of who he may be, was considered at that time to have the right to impose his opinion on others and to force them to adopt his *madhhab* or juristic school.[79] Even a ruler did not enjoy this privilege. He was like one of the Muslims. All he could do was to argue logically and intellectually in favour of his opinion.[80] Perhaps this is why, when the Caliph Hārūn al-Rashīd (d. 193/809) thought of making all his subjects follow Imām Mālik's *al-Muwaṭṭa',* Mālik himself advised him against doing so.[81] This would have been against the spirit of freedom of opinion in Islam. It was during this period that Islamic jurisprudence witnessed its maximum development.[82] If the *Mu'tazilites* had abided by this precedent in Muslim society, they may not have aroused the tempers and the heat that they did. The conflict between the rationalists and the conservatives may not then have taken such a hostile and belligerent turn. There would have been no justification for this by virtue of two important reasons.

First, the Qur'ān itself strongly asserts the use of reason and observation. This emphasis has generally been reflected in the writings of Muslims throughout history. For example, Ibn Taymiyyah clearly stressed that the derivation by Muslims of their beliefs, prayers and values from the Qur'ān, the *Sunnah,* and the consensus of the *ummah,* "is not in conflict with reason, because whatever clearly contradicts reason stands rejected (*bāṭil*)".[83] He further argued that people do not perhaps appreciate that the texts of the Qur'ān and the *Sunnah* consist of words and that it is possible for them to understand these words incorrectly or to interpret them wrongly. So the problem lies with the interpreters and not the Qur'ān and the *Sunnah.*[84] The late Muṣṭafā al-Zarqā, a prominent and highly respected religious scholar, clearly declared that "whatever is against reason has no place in Islam".[85] Moreover, there is nothing in the Qur'ān or the *Sunnah* that has so far been found to be in conflict with an established fact or scientific theory.

Secondly, as stated earlier, the *Mu'tazilites* did a great deal to defend Islam against the heretics, and many of their views were rational and in harmony with the Qur'ān and the *Sunnah.*[86] If discord had not been created by excesses and inquisition, all issues might perhaps have been discussed relatively freely, and it is most likely that even the relatively moderate rationalists like Ibn Rushd would also have survived along with the moderate conservatives or Ash'arites like al-Ghazālī. The presence of a lively discussion between them may have, over time, helped resolve the prevailing controversies in a rational manner. This would have made it difficult for the Ash'arites to tilt later on towards increasing conservatism and rigidity and to use force in the same way as the *Mu'tazilites* did to uphold and spread their views.[87] The dual survival of both moderate rationalists and moderate conservatives could have served as a balancing force to exert a healthier influence on Muslim society. Science and religious education could have become integrated and encouraged the promotion of a relatively more liberal development of *Fiqh* and other religious and mundane sciences in the Muslim world.

What the *Mu'tazilite* excesses did, therefore, was to bedevil the atmosphere of intellectual freedom that had prevailed in earlier centuries. This pushed the pendulum in the opposite direction. All free thinking, became suspect and advanced an attitude of extreme caution and conservatism in the expression of opinions on religious issues. Consequently *ijtihād* suffered. It did not, fortunately, stop completely.[88] Voices were always raised in its favour and it continued to be exercized by some highly competent, respected and creative scholars, though not as frequently as in earlier centuries.[89]

In addition to the *Mu'tazilite* excesses, there were additional factors which strengthened this tendency towards rigidity and conservatism. One was the desire of the illegitimate and corrupt political elite to extract juristic verdicts to help them justify their illegitimacy and oppressive taxes. Therefore, as Muhammad Iqbal (d. 1357/1938), the renowned philosopher/poet of the Indo-Pakistan subcontinent, has rightly indicated: "For fear of further disintegration, which is only natural in such a period of political decay, the conservative thinkers of Islam focused all their efforts on the one point of preserving a uniform social life for the people by a jealous exclusion of all innovations in the law of the Sharī'ah as expounded by the early doctors of Islam. Their leading idea was social order and there is no doubt that they were partly right, because organization does to a certain extent counteract the forces of decay."[90]

A second factor which reinforced conservatism was foreign domination, starting with the Mongols. This raised the fear that foreign occupiers would try to use some of the jurists to achieve verdicts which would serve their vested interest and change the texture of the Sharīʿah.

A third factor was the overall decline of the Muslim world. Intellectual development, as Ibn Khaldūn rightly observed, takes place in a society only if the society itself is developing.[91] Jurisprudence is no exception. It was also bound to be in a state of limbo when the Muslim society was in a process of decline. Not only did an enabling environment for intellectual creativity not exist, but rather there was hostility towards any change, irrespective of whether it was, or was not, in harmony with the Sharīʿah. Ibn Taymiyyah and Shāh Walīullāh (d. 1176/1762) who were both creative and relatively liberal scholars, as compared with the rigid and fossilized schools of *fiqh* prevailing in their times, encountered considerable opposition for their independent, non-conformist views. Shāh Walīullāh even experienced serious opposition for his translation of the Qur'ān into Persian as did his sons when they translated it into Urdu.[92] However, since the government did not intervene either in favour or against, the more rational view ultimately prevailed and has become generally accepted to the point that no one now considers anything wrong, in principle, in the translation of the Qur'ān into any language.

Reason can, thus, play a considerable role in the restructuring of Muslim society without coming into conflict with Revelation, provided that the state, the rationalists and the conservatives do not try to step on each other's toes, and avoid confrontation and use of force. In spite of a substantial decline in the position of the *ʿulamā'* as a result of their low socio-economic status and their lack of a modern education, their upper hand in defining Islam, nevertheless, continues in the Muslim world, as Gibb rightly recognized in 1947:

"The future of Islam rests where it rested in the past on the insight of the orthodox leaders and their capacity to resolve the new tensions as they arise by a positive doctrine which will face and master the forces making for disintegration."[93] Historical experience suggests that if political leadership tries to impose, in the same way as the 'Abbāsid Caliphs did,[94] views which the *'ulamā'* consider to be in clear conflict with the ethos of Islam, they may end up raising tempers, hardening attitudes, and creating a conflict and polarization in the same way as happened in the past.[95] Such a conflict would almost certainly slow down the process of change and liberalization in the Muslim world.

Seventy years of forced secularism in Turkey has not succeeded in shaking the people's faith in Islam, and there is now a revival. Some other dictatorial regimes in Muslim countries are also trying to impose their own version of Islam on the people, and this may also not work. Free and amicable discussion, without attacking the Islamic basis of society, is necessary for resolving various issues. The Qur'ān and the *Sunnah* are both an integral part of the Islamic paradigm, and anyone who suggests the setting aside of both, or even the *Sunnah,* in the reconstruction of Muslim societies, is bound to generate extreme reaction. So much flexibility of interpretation seems to be possible within the Sharī'ah itself that an extreme attitude of this kind would be unrealistic and uncalled for. What the state should do is to facilitate a free and open discussion between the various rationalists and conservatives. Those whose views are more convincing would ultimately prevail.

The caveat, however, is that if the *'ulamā'* become intolerant and, instead of being prepared to end their stagnation and inflexibility, react aggressively and harshly to even moderate forms of rationalist thinking, which are necessary for enabling *Fiqh* to meet the challenges faced by the Muslim *ummah,* then an adverse reaction might occur. This could swing the pendulum in the direction of extreme rationalism, as it did in the West, and, thus, damage not only Islam but also the position of the *'ulamā'* themselves. To prevent this from happening, it may be helpful if modern sciences as well as at least one Western language, especially English, are introduced as compulsory subjects in the syllabi of all institutions of Islamic learning, and if religious education is also made an integral part of modern education. This may help create a better and more congenial atmosphere for dialogue between the graduates of Western and religious institutions and, thereby, lead to greater mutual understanding and meaningful discussion of various issues.

Fortunately, however, the rigidity of the *'ulamā'* seems to have steadily declined over the years as a result of the efforts initiated by people like Jamāl al-Dīn al-Afghānī (d. 1315/1897), Muḥammad 'Abduh (d. 1323/1905), Muhammad Iqbal (d. 1357/1938), and a number of other learned and well respected scholars and reformers. The *'ulamā'* are no longer involved in the same hair-splitting debates that they were in the past. The institution of *ijtihād* has also been gradually revived, and liberal thinking within the limits of the Sharī'ah does not raise eyebrows or create the same kind of adverse reaction as it did, say, in the eighteenth century during the lifetime of Shāh Walīullāh. The *'ulamā'* seem to have realized, though not adequately, that the world has moved forward substantially since the days of classical *fiqh* compendiums. Accordingly, the rigid juristic positions adopted on a number of issues seem to be losing ground in favour of relatively more liberal views, which are not only possible without coming into conflict with the Qur'ān and the *Sunnah,* but also necessary in view of changing circumstances.

The absence of a monolithic Church or an ecclesiastical council has also proved to be a great advantage. It has enabled liberal as well as conservative shades of opinion on various juristic issues to interact with each other. The independence of almost all Muslim countries from foreign domination, and the pressing need that this has created for finding solutions to the various problems encountered in the political, social, economic and educational fields, seems to be giving an edge to the relatively more liberal jurists. The *fiqh* committees of the OIC, the *Rābiṭah*, and the individual member countries, are doing valuable work at international and national levels. The revival of the institution of *shūrā* in a number of important Muslim countries may add further strength to the liberalization process.

It seems that the thrust of the Qur'ān and the *Sunnah* in favour of creating greater flexibility and ease is being increasingly realized. The Qur'ān states that "God intends ease for you and not hardship" (2:185; see also 5:6). The Prophet (pbuh) said: "The Islamic way of life (*al-Dīn*) is easy; whoever tries to make it hard is himself overpowered by it [he is unable to practice it]."[96] The increasing volume of literature on the *maqāṣid al-Sharīʿah* is also a reflection of the realization that the taking of these *maqāṣid* into account in the interpretation of texts is at least as important as the letter of the text. It is hoped that this development may continue steadily until it has led to the consolidation of all schools of jurisprudence in such a way that their different verdicts on various issues acquire the nature of different possible alternatives from which an individual, group, or nation may select the most suitable for its specific circumstances.

The problem, however, is that modern rationalists are, like their counterparts in the past, not a homogeneous group. There are those, for example, who are moderate. They are positive with respect to Islam and its values and are doing what they can to present a convincing case for breaking the thick crust of rigidity, which is necessary if Islam is to meet the challenges it faces in a world where secularism is still the dominant paradigm. They are not only not creating any problems but seem to be gradually making headway.

There is, however, another group, consisting of extreme secularists who would like to push aside the Qur'ān and the *Sunnah* and reconstruct Muslim societies in the image of the West. However, even the West is not a homogenous whole. It has religious as well as anti-religious and hedonistic elements. The extreme secularists wish the Muslim world to follow the path of the latter. They are generating conflict and tension, and using force to impose their views, just like the *Mu'tazilites*, by virtue of the political power that some of them now have at their command. Force did not succeed in the past, and is not likely to do so now. In fact, it may only serve to create a more aggressive and extremist response from conservative forces. This may prove to be a hurdle for even the moderate rationalists in moving their societies towards a healthier balance in the same way as happened in the past. The hopeful sign, however, is that, as will be discussed in Chapter 9, the ongoing spread of democracy will tend to serve as a positive force in favour of moderation because of the necessity of rallying the support of all groups.

Notes

1. The two *aḥādīth* are: "The quest for knowledge is the duty (*farīḍah*) of every Muslim", and "the superiority of a learned man (*'ālim*) over a mystic (*'ābid*) is like that of the full moon over all other stars". Both are reported by Ibn Mājah, the first from Anas ibn Mālik and the second from Abū al-Dardā', Volume 1, p. 81, numbers 224 and 223, *al-Muqaddimah, Bāb*: 17 – *faḍl al-'ulamā' wa al-ḥathth 'alā ṭalab al-'ilm*. For other *aḥādīth* on the subject of learning and teaching, see pp. 80-98. See also al-Qurṭubī (d. 463/1070), *Jāmi' Bayān al-'ilm wa Faḍluhū*, Volume 1, pp. 3-63, and al-Ghazālī (d. 505/1111), *Iḥyā'*, Volume 1, pp. 4-82.
2. Abū Zahrah, *Uṣūl al-Fiqh*, 1957, p. 350.
3. Berkey, 1992, p. 3.
4. Nicholson, 1956, p. 419.
5. *Bayt al-Ḥikmah* was established by al-Ma'mūn (198-218/813-833) in Baghdād and *Dār al-Ḥikmah* was established by the Saljūqid Sulṭān 'Aḍud al-Dawlah (367-372/977-983) in Baghdād. Several of the principal Spanish towns possessed what might be called universities in the present-day world. Chief among these were those in Cordova, Seville, Malaga and Granada. Such institutions were also established in other cities in the then Muslim world.
6. See Tibawi 1954; Makdisi, 1981; Berkey, 1992 and Zurayk, 1992.
7. See Sarton, 1927-48, Volume 1 and Book 1 of Volume 2 and Sezgin, 1983.
8. Faroghi, 1994, p. 542.
9. See for example, Makdisi, 1981, pp. 35-74 and Hodgson, 1977, Volume 2, p. 124.
10. Inalcik, 1970, p. 307.
11. Inalcik, 1994, p. 79; Hodgson, 1977; Cizakca, 2000; Behrens-Abouseif, et. al., 2002; Kahf, 2004 and Ahmed, 2004.

12. Hofmann, 1996, p. 85.
13. The Prophet (pbuh) said: "Any Muslim who plants a tree or cultivates a field, enabling birds, animals and human beings to eat from it, performs an act of virtue." (Al-Bukhārī, *Kitāb al-Ḥarth wa al-Zirā'ah, Bāb Faḍl al-Zirā'ah wa al-Ḥarth.*) According to this *ḥadīth,* any human act which fulfils the needs of not only human beings but also birds and animals is an act of virtue and is qualified to earn a reward in the Hereafter.
14. See McGowan, 1994, p. 712 and Cizakca, 2000.
15. See, "The Knowledge Factory: A Survey of Universities", *The Economist,* 4 October 1997, p. 4.
16. The word *i'tazala* means to withdraw, detach or isolate, and the term *Mu'tazilah* is used to signify the movement whose followers had withdrawn themselves from the extremist views of the Khārijites and the Murji'ites about a sinful Muslim and chose to follow the midway path. (See Abū Zahrah, *Ta'rīkh al-Madhāhib al-Islāmiyyah,* Volume 1, pp. 156-7; Valiuddin, 1963, pp. 199-200.) The movement started under the leadership of Wāṣil ibn 'Aṭā' (d. 131/748) and later on included in its fold a number of other stalwarts like Abū al-Hudhayl (d. 226/841), Ja'far ibn al-Bishr (d. 226/841), al-Naẓẓām (d. 231/845), al-Jāḥiẓ (d. 255/869), al-Jubbā'ī (d. 295/908) and 'Abd al-Jabbār (d. 415l/1024). Although the movement's influence spanned a period of almost five centuries, its classical period lasted for nearly two centuries from approximately the last quarter of the third/ninth century to the middle of the fifth/eleventh century. For some details on their views, see al-Shahrastānī (d. 548/1153), 1961, Volume 1, pp. 43-91 and al-Baghdādī (d. 429/1037), pp. 78-150. See also Valiuddin, 1963, pp. 204-18; Gimaret, 1993, pp. 783-93 and Gardet, 1971, pp. 1141-50.
17. Al-Fārābī defined *'Ilm al-Kalām* in his *Iḥṣā' al-'Ulūm* as "a science which enables a person to ensure the victory of beliefs and practices laid down by the *Shāri'* or God, the Provider of the Sharī'ah, and to logically refute all opinions contradicting them". Al-Ījī defined it in his *Kitāb al-Mawāqif fī 'Ilm al-Kalām* as "the science which is concerned with firmly establishing beliefs by supplying proofs and removing doubts", (both definitions are adapted with minor modifications in the translation from Gardet, 1971, p. 1141). In between the two, al-Ghazālī specified the purpose of *'Ilm al-Kalām* to be "to protect the Islamic faith and to defend it against the scepticism of heretics" (al-Ghazālī, *al-Munqidh,* p. 14).
18. Gardet, 1971, p. 1142.
19. Abū Zahrah, *Ta'rīkh,* Volume 1, pp. 162-3 and al-Ghazālī, *Tahāfut al-Falāsifah,* 1993, p. 26.
20. The first Muslim philosopher is generally acknowledged to have been al-Kindī, (d. 252/866), followed by a number of other illustrious names like Abū Bakr al-Rāzī, (d. 313/925), al-Fārābī (d. 339/950), Ibn Sīnā (d. 428/1037), Ibn Bājah (d. 533/1139), Ibn Ṭufayl (d. 581/1185) and Ibn Rushd (d. 595/1198).
21. For differences of opinion among the rationalists, see al-Shahrastānī, 1961, Volume 1, pp. 40-113 and 198-207.

22. The other three axioms were:
    - Reward and punishment (*al-wa'd wa al-wa'īd*), are both necessary?
    - A sinner is neither a believer (*mu'min*) nor an unbeliever (*kāfir*). He rather occupies an intermediate rank between the two (*al-manzilah bayna al-manzilatayn*). He is a malefactor (*fāsiq*).
    - It is the obligation of a Muslim to command the good and to forbid the evil (*al-amr bi'l-ma'rūf wa al-nahy 'an al-munkar*). (See al-Shahrastānī, 1961, Volume 1, pp. 43-6.)
23. Even the Prophet (pbuh), acknowledged this in a well-known and oft-repeated prayer, saying: "I cannot praise You fully: You are as You have described Yourself". (*Ṣaḥīḥ* of *Muslim* [1955], Vol. 1, p. 352:222, *Kitāb al-Ṣalāh*, also *Muwaṭṭa'*, Mālik, Abū Dāwūd, Tirmidhī, Nasā'ī and Ibn Mājah.)
24. For some details about the extreme rationalists and their views see Badawi, 1980, also Badawi, 1963, pp. 439-40.
25. See John Hicks, 1967, p. 190. See also Julian Huxley, 1957 and Ronald Hepburn, 1958.
26. Kraus, 1971, p. 905.
27. Cited from al-Kindī's book, *The Governors and Judges of Egypt* (ed. R. Guest, London-Leiden, 1912), by Hinds, 1993, p. 4.
28. Abū Zahrah, *Ta'rīkh*…, Volume 1, p. 178.
29. Cited from al-Kindī, op. cit., by Hinds, 1993, p. 4.
30. Abū Zahrah, op. cit., p. 183.
31. Hinds, 1993, p. 4, cited on the authority of al-Ṭabarī and al-Ya'qūbī.
32. See al-Mas'ūdī (d. 346/957) *Murūj al-Dhahab*, 1988, Volume 4, p. 52 and Abū Zahrah, *Ta'rīkh*, Volume 2, pp. 297-302. See also W. M. Patten, *Aḥmad ibn Ḥanbal and the Miḥnah*, Leiden, 1897, cited by Arberry, 1957, p. 19 and Hinds, 1993, p. 3.
33. Cited from al-Kindī, op. cit., by Hinds, 1993, p. 4.
34. See Hinds, 1993, p. 6.
35. Abū Zahrah, *Ta'rīkh* ..., Volume 1, p. 212.
36. Abū Ḥāmid al-Ghazālī, *Tahāfut*, 1993. The word *tahāfut* has been translated into English in different ways, including breakdown, disintegration, absurdity, bankruptcy, inconsistency and incoherence. Incoherence may perhaps reflect the meaning more closely (Van Den Bergh, 1987, p. xiii; also Watt, 1963, p. 59). Other books by al-Ghazālī which are of relevance to the subject include *Al-Munqidh min al-Ḍalāl* and *Iḥyā' 'Ulūm al-Dīn*.
37. Al-Ghazālī, *Tahāfut*, 1993, p. 28.
38. Hourani, 1961, p. 5.
39. Al-Ghazālī, *Al-Munqidh*, p. 31.
40. Arnaldez, 1971, p. 774.
41. The 'creation of the Qur'ān' is not included among these 20 theories, because this notion was put to rest in 234/849, during the reign of the Caliph al-Mutawakkil (232-47/847-61), long before al-Ghazālī (d. 505/1111).
42. Al-Ghazālī, *Tahāfut*, 1993, p. 31.
43. Ibid., p. 33.

44. Al-Ghazālī, *al-Munqidh*, p. 25.
45. Al-Ghazālī, *Iḥyā'*, Volume 1, p. 83.
46. Al-Ghazālī, *Tahāfut*, 1993, p. 169.
47. Ibid.
48. An English translation by Van Den Bergh was published in 1954. See also Hourani, 1961, for a translation of selections from Ibn Rushd's *Kitāb Faṣl al-Maqāl* and *Kitāb al-Kashf 'an Manāhij al-Adillah.*
49. Ibn Rushd, *Tahāfut al-Tahāfut*, 1992, p. 584.
50. Ibid., p. 527.
51. Ibid., p. 583.
52. Ibid., p. 527.
53. Ibid., pp. 585-6. It may be useful for the reader to read the entire Fourth Discussion on pp. 580-6; it indicates that Ibn Rushd's views were perfectly in tune with orthodoxy and that his defence of philosophers (not heretics) was not unfounded.
54. Ibid., p. 527.
55. Ibid.
56. Ibid., p. 519.
57. Ibid., p. 522. It may be useful to read the whole section on efficient causes, pp. 519-27.
58. "Thomas Aquinas quotes Averroes no less than five hundred and three times", (Urvoy, 1991, p. 127).
59. Van Den Bergh, in the Introduction to his translation of Ibn Rushd's *Tahāfut al-Tahāfut*, 1954, p. xii; Gardet, 1971, p. 1149.
60. De Boer, 1970, p. 200.
61. This book has been translated into English in two volumes by Imran Nyazee (1994).
62. See Dutton, 1994, p. 193.
63. See Watt, 1963, p. 13.
64. Ibn Taymiyyah, *Majmū' al-Fatāwā*, Volume 9, 1961-3, p. 186.
65. Ibid., p. 288.
66. Ibid.
67. *Muqaddimah*, pp. 514-19. (Rosenthal's translation, Volume 3, pp. 246-258.) Ibn Khaldūn includes metaphysics (*ilāhiyyāt*), magic and talismans, alchemy, philosophy, and astrology among the discredited sciences (pp. 495-531). However, Ibn Rushd had also earlier criticized in his *Tahāfut al-Tahāfut* many of these sciences in a manner not significantly different from that of Ibn Khaldūn. (See Ibn Rushd, *Tahāfut al-Tahāfut*, 1992, p. 51.)
68. *Muqaddimah*, pp. 514-19 (R: ibid.); See also De Boer, 1970, p. 202.
69. Al-Maqrīzī, *Khiṭaṭ*, Volume 2, p. 344.
70. See Reinhart, 1995, p. 183.
71. Al-Ghazālī, *Tahāfut*, 1993, pp. 219-20 and Abū Zahrah, *Ta'rīkh*, Volume 1, pp. 147-90.
72. See E. A. Burtt, 1955, p. 237.
73. Voltaire, *Selected Works*, p. 62, cited by Will Durant, *The Story of Philosophy*, 1970, p. 237.

74. Durant, *The History*, 1954, Volume 5, p. 571.
75. Hourani, 1961, p. 29.
76. Hinds, 1993, p. 6.
77. Zafar Ishaq Ansari, 1992, p. 157.
78. According to Prof. Robert Whaples, from whose comments on this manuscript I have benefited considerably, "the Church could not have the power to do this all by itself. It was given much/most of this power by the state – especially where the Inquisition was strongest, e.g. Iberia". This shows that if the state joins the repression of free debate on different issues by either the conservatives or the rationalists, the results can be even worse.
79. Ibn Taymiyyah, *Majmūʿ al-Fatāwā*, Volume 30, p. 80.
80. Ibid., Volume 35, p. 360.
81. Ibid., Volume 30, p. 79.
82. See Muṣṭafā al-Zarqā, 1967, Volume 1, pp. 147 and 171.
83. Ibn Taymiyyah, *Majmūʿ al-Fatāwā*, Volume 11, p. 490.
84. Ibid., Volume 1, p. 490.
85. Muṣṭafā al-Zarqā, *Al-ʿAql wa'l-Fiqh*, 1996, p. 14.
86. See Abū Zahrah, Volume 1, p. 190.
87. For the use of force by the Ashʿarites, see al-Maqrīzī, *al-Khiṭaṭ*, Volume 2, p. 358.
88. See Wael B. Hallaq, 1984, pp. 3-41. See also Zebīrī, 1993, p. 136.
89. Lewis acknowledges that "Muslim law has not been static, it has undergone a long, complex development. A careful scrutiny of juristic texts can produce valuable information on the changing conditions, pressures and influences to which the jurists were subject". (Bernard Lewis, 'Sources for the Economic History of the Middle East', in Cook, 1970, p. 91.)
90. Iqbal, *Reconstruction*, 1954, p. 151.
91. Ibn Khaldūn, *Muqaddimah*, p. 434.
92. Although this opposition to the translation of the Qur'ān may now appear to be irrational, it would not have appeared so at that time. As Arberry (1964) rightly put in the Introduction to his translation, "Since the Koran is to the faithful the very Word of God, from earliest times orthodox opinion has rigidly maintained that it is untranslatable, a miracle of speech which it would be blasphemous to attempt to imitate" (p. ix).
93. Gibb, 1947, p. 122.
94. Richard Antoun gave a valuable insight into the crucial role of the *ʿulamā'* by warning against "too firm faith in the power of the state and the influence of political elites" (Antoun, 1989, p. 244). This may perhaps be because of "the rapport which persists between the *ʿulamā'* and the majority of the Muslim population" (Leonard Binder, 1964, p. 24).
95. Dale Eickermann observes that "One pervasive element in Islam as a religious tradition is respect for those aspects of belief and ritual which are considered to be fixed and enduring" (Eickerman, 1989, p. 305).
96. From Abū Hurayrah; reported by al-Suyūṭī, Volume 1, p. 79, on the authority of al-Bukhārī and al-Nasā'ī.

6

SOCIAL DECLINE

Decline in some crucially important social areas

Cracks in solidarity between the government and the people

Historical experience indicates that it is difficult to sustain the progress of a society if there is a crack in solidarity between the government and the people. Such a crack tends to generate conflict and lack of cooperation and vitiates the climate for development. Since Islam continues to rule the hearts of people in the Muslim world and since the pious and competent among the *'ulamā'* have been commonly regarded as the traditional guardians and interpreters of Islam, a climate of trust between them and the government has proved to be indispensable for the popularity, efficient functioning, and stability of the government. Such solidarity is also indispensable to enable *Fiqh* to develop in step with the changing needs of society. The rapport between the *'ulamā'* and the government, however, has fluctuated considerably over the centuries. While there have been periods when cordial relations prevailed between the two, there has, unfortunately, been a long-run tendency towards decline.

During the reign of the Caliph Hārūn al-Rashīd (d. 193/809), competent and pious *'ulamā'* like Abū Yūsuf (d. 182/798) and al-Shaybānī (d. 189/804), both prominent students of Abū Ḥanīfah, were respected by the caliph and their advice was sought and generally implemented.[1] Hārūn al-Rashīd was, however, not an ideal ruler and behaved in a despotic manner when faced with an opinion that conflicted with his vested interest. This is evident from an incident narrated by al-Shaybānī, one of the most prominent contributors to the development of Ḥanafī *Fiqh*. Once when al-Shaybānī was a judge in al-Raqqah (Syria), Hārūn al-Rashīd asked him if he could withdraw a contractual assurance of protection given to Yaḥyā ibn 'Abdullāh al-Ḥasan. When al-Shaybānī replied that he could not do so within the purview of the Sharī'ah, al-Rashīd became so furious that he threw an inkpot at him, thereby injuring him and soiling his clothes with blood and ink. Another jurist, Abū al-Bakhtarī, who was also present, succumbed to the wishes of al-Rashīd and allowed him to do what he desired. Al-Shaybānī was, thereafter, prohibited from giving legal verdicts. However, al-Rashīd made up with him later on, promoted him and even eulogized him upon his death.[2]

Even though Hārūn al-Rashīd was not ideal when evaluated against Islamic criteria, he was better than many others after him who would perhaps have had al-Shaybānī executed for expressing an opinion that was against their interests even though in conformity with the Sharī'ah. Accordingly, a relationship of trust prevailed between the government and the *'ulamā'*. This, in turn, promoted cordial relations between the government and the people. Involvement of the *'ulamā'* in the affairs of the government had the effect of making them aware of the practical realities of life. *Fiqh*, therefore, stayed abreast of changing circumstances and developed in all its various ramifications, including moral, social, economic, political and international. This helped create a better environment for implementation of the Sharī'ah, maintaining law and order, and the realization of justice and development. A great boost was thereby provided to all nation-building activities and, in turn, political authority was also strengthened.

The solidarity between the *'ulamā'* and the government suffered a severe setback during the reign of Hārūn al-Rashīd's son, al-Ma'mūn (198-218/813-33) and his two successors, al-Mu'taṣim (218-27/833-42) and al-Wāthiq (227-32/842-47), even though they did a great deal to support science and intellectual debate. The reason being their effort to use coercive state power to impose *Mu'tazilism* as an official doctrine, in spite of the *'ulamā's* declaration that some of its elements were against the teachings of the Sharī'ah. This alienated the *'ulamā'* as well as the people against the government and led to a weakening of the latter.

If al-Ma'mūn and his successors had been accountable before the people, they may have sought ways of bridging the rift. Instead, they sought to counter the public's displeasure by hiring foreign guards, officers, and soldiers from Central Asia for their protection, thus setting a tradition which proved ultimately to be a destabilizing factor. The rulers became more and more aloof and withdrawn from the people in sharp contrast with what prevailed during the *Khilāfah al-Rāshidah*. This seclusion intensified during the Ottoman period after the sixteenth century, further weakening the solidarity between the government and the people and depriving the ruler of first-hand knowledge of what was going on in the country.[3]

Al-Mutawakkil (232-47/847-61), al-Wāthiq's successor, realized the dangers of this conflict and seclusion and tried to remedy the situation by rallying the support of the *'ulamā'* and the civilian population. He renounced *Mu'tazilism* and considerably reduced its strength. No ruler subsequently attempted to reinstate it. However, al-Mutawakkil was himself murdered by the foreign guards. This led initially to a period of anarchy, in the course of which caliphs were made and unmade by the foreign guards: of the four caliphs who succeeded him, three were assassinated.[4] Political authority thus continued to weaken until the ultimate downfall of the 'Abbāsids.

The stagnation of Fiqh

The question that pops up again and again is why did *Fiqh* become stagnant in later centuries when it had earlier shown rigorous dynamism? One has to look at the impact of historical factors on the various players in the field to be able to find clues to a reasonably satisfying answer. The conflict that had been simmering between the *'ulamā'* and the rulers after the introduction of political illegitimacy and the violation of a number of principles of the Sharī'ah by the rulers was, as discussed in Chapter 5, further aggravated by the persecution of the *'ulamā'* by al-Ma'mūn and his successors. This reduced the possibility of a friendly and constructive dialogue between the two. The position improved considerably at different times when conscientious rulers came to the helm and tried to placate the *'ulamā'*. However, non-implementation of the Sharī'ah in the highly crucial political field always remained a bone of contention and led increasingly to a number of ills, including inequity in the tax system, the corruption and luxury of the rulers, the development of a culture of sycophancy at the royal courts, and the exploitation of Islam for serving the rulers' own vested interest.

Pious and well-respected *'ulamā'* and Sufis, who resented all these evils, became more and more disenchanted with political authority and began avoiding the echelons of power. Service of the state became demeaning for the *'ulamā'* and anyone from among them who received salary or benefit from the state began to be considered as an accomplice in the rulers' wrongdoing. This had a far-reaching impact on Muslim society. Those *'ulamā'* who accepted government service and frequented the royal courts, forfeited their moral authority and began to be considered as power seekers and this-worldly. They were referred to as *'ulamā' al-sū'* (scholars of vice) or *'ulamā' al-dunyā* (world-seeking scholars) in comparison with those who avoided the royal courts and were called *'ulamā' al-khayr* (scholars of virtue) or *'ulamā' al-Ākhirah* (scholars seeking the Next world).[5] Al-'Attābī (d. 220/835) gives another plausible reason for the avoidance of royal courts by pious and outspoken *'ulamā'*. He argues that "the rulers may grant their courtiers an enormous amount for nothing, but may also have them put to death for nothing, and you may not wish to be in the place of any one of these two".[6] In addition, pious *'ulamā'*, in step with al-Ghazālī, considered all or most of the wealth of the corrupt sultans to be ill-gotten.[7] There was, therefore, a danger that their association with such sultans may beguile them away from the right path into not only different types of temptation and corruption but also to benefiting from a part of this ill-gotten wealth.[8] It was, therefore, morally safer that "you do not see them and they do not see you".[9] All these reasons – fear of being counted among the *'ulamā' al-sū'*, fear of being beguiled away from the right path, and fear of being executed – together reinforced the tendency of pious *'ulamā'* to stay away from the royal courts. This deprived rulers of the sincere advice which *'ulamā'* of the calibre of Abū Yūsuf were previously able to give to the likes of Hārūn al-Rashīd. Such a categorization, unfortunately, still continues to a certain extent in the Muslim world. Even now, *'ulamā'* who try to get close to government even with the objective of reforming it are generally looked upon with suspicion, particularly among Sufi circles.

This led to a paradox in Muslim societies. On the one hand, there was a desire for the realization of justice and general well-being in keeping with the demands of the Sharī'ah, and an emphasis on the need for the state to play an important role in this and for the *'ulamā'* to guide and help the state in fulfilling this role. On the other hand, the *'ulamā'* who were associated with the state were considered to be self-seekers and this-worldly. It was perhaps not appreciated how difficult it is to find *khalīfahs* of the calibre of Abū Bakr, 'Umar, 'Uthmān and 'Alī, who were not only pious and competent but also self-denying. So there may be no escape for the *'ulamā'* from learning to live with imperfect rulers and to squeeze out of them as much good as is possible. According to a genuine (*ṣaḥīḥ*) *ḥadīth*, faith (*al-Dīn*) stands for sincerity towards everyone, including rulers.[10] Sincerity towards rulers is generally understood to imply giving them candid advice and helping them in doing what is good and preventing them from, or at least warning them against, committing injustice. Sincere advice rendered to rulers by highly respected *ʿulamāʾ* would have carried a great deal of weight and, even if it was not implemented fully, it may at least have helped in reducing injustice to a certain extent and led gradually to an improvement in the condition of the people. The all or nothing approach was perhaps not the most practical. Seen in this light, the right attitude would have been that which the Qurʾān emphasizes: "Cooperate with each other in virtue and godliness but do not cooperate in evil and transgression" (5:2).

Avoidance of the echelons of power by pious and competent *ʿulamāʾ* has harmed Islam in a number of ways. First, it deprived the Muslim world of political reform. If righteous and prominent *ʿulamāʾ* and Sufis had struggled for political reform and the rights of the people instead of secluding themselves away, they may have been able, gradually over the centuries, to influence and effect the creation of democratic institutions. This might have helped impose checks and controls on rulers' powers, and reduced inequities, the misuse of state resources, and the appointment of incompetent people to senior positions. If ordinary people struggle for their rights, it is easier for despots to crush them. However, if well-respected *ʿulamāʾ*, with a substantial following among the masses, struggle for people's rights, rulers may not find it so easy to suppress and eliminate them. The struggle of the *ʿulamāʾ* against al-Maʾmūn and his followers did lead to sacrifices, but it ultimately succeeded. A number of rulers in the latter ʿAbbāsid period and other dynasties were perhaps not as powerful as al-Maʾmūn and a struggle of the kind continued against al-Maʾmūn and his successors could have gradually persuaded or coerced them to introduce political reforms.

Secondly, the conflict with *Mu'tazilism* aroused suspicion among the *'ulamā'* about *falsafah* (philosophy). Unfortunately, as discussed in Chapter 6, the teaching of *falsafah* was bracketed in those days with a number of physical sciences like physics and chemistry. Accordingly, all of these were unwittingly associated with *falsafah* and were, hence, suspect. The syllabi of *madrasahs*, therefore, primarily came to be confined to religious sciences. Grounding in various social and physical sciences and the tools of analysis which earlier jurists like Abū Yūsuf, al-Ghazālī and Ibn Rushd were able to receive, and without which they could not have played their roles effectively, did not become available to later generations of *'ulamā'*. They were, therefore, not trained to exercise the kind of independent judgement that earlier jurists did. In this way, they became incapable of creativity.

Thirdly, the seclusion of the *'ulamā'* from the echelons of power confined them primarily to the mosques and the *madrasahs*. This cut them off from the practical realities of life except during brief periods of reform in almost every dynasty, and, thereby, reduced the range of opportunities available to them to respond to the socio-economic and political challenges of their times and make the Sharī'ah a dynamic reality in the lives of Muslims. They were, thus, left with very little room for rational analysis and fresh contributions through *ijtihād*. Sciences develop in response to need, irrespective of whether they are religious or mundane. *Fiqh* is not an exception. It nearly became stagnant. Hence, the *'ulamā'* became engrossed in marginal aspects of the Islamic way of life.

What was written in the past became the beau ideal and led to undue emphasis on the unquestioned acceptance of previous verdicts in spite of changing needs and challenges. The *'ulamā'* continued to interpret the texts in the same way as was done by their teachers. Even the brightest of them, spent their time writing commentaries upon commentaries and, thus, perpetuating the rule of ancient textbooks written in entirely different circumstances. Students had no option but to memorize the old texts. Prestige lay in the number of books they had committed to memory rather than in their ability to analyze issues scientifically and to give realistic solutions to different problems.

The stagnation of *Fiqh* prevented it from developing as a system in which all of its parts could be interrelated through a focus on the realization of the overall *maqāṣid al-Sharīʿah* in different fields of human life.[11] Verdicts began to be given with increasingly greater reliance on legal stratagems (*ḥiyal*) in the interpretation of religious texts without giving due consideration to the *maqāṣid*.[12] This sapped the earlier dynamism of Islam. Its ideals of promoting a political, legal, and socio-economic system that would help realize a just socio-economic order were gradually relegated to the background. Even the crucial ingredients of Islamic teachings oriented towards the inculcation of noble character traits (*khuluq ḥasan*) like justice, honesty, integrity, conscientiousness, cooperation, hard work, punctuality, tolerance and dedication to duty began to receive less and less importance in clear violation of the Prophet's saying whereby: "The most perfect of Muslims is he who is best in character."[13] The *fiqh* that remained was ritualistic and not relevant to the needs of a dynamic civilization that Islam had established in earlier centuries. The skeleton remained but the spirit was weak.

The teaching of sciences, arts and languages was not revived in the Muslim world until the establishment of secular colleges and universities by Western powers after their occupation of most Muslim lands. This, unfortunately, led to the creation of a dual system of education, one concerned with the teaching of old religious texts and the other with modern sciences. Merging of the two systems in step with the earlier tradition was indispensable, but could not be undertaken by the Muslims for a number of reasons, not least because the *ʿulamāʾ* were not mentally prepared to accept the teaching of what they considered to be mundane sciences in religious schools. Furthermore, the teaching of religious sciences in colleges and universities and the injection of a spiritual dimension in modern 'secular' sciences required the preparation of textbooks that would rationally combine Revelation with reason. This was a difficult task that could not be accomplished in a short time, particularly because scholars who were well-versed in both were rare. This failure has hurt the Muslim world in a number of ways. First, it has further weakened social solidarity by creating two separate groups of scholars who are unable to communicate with each other. Secondly, since university graduates are able to get higher positions in the public as well as private sectors, and graduates of religious institutions generally achieve jobs that command less pay and lower social status, religious education has become materially unattractive. Parents, particularly of the social and political elite, do not generally send their children to religious institutions even if they are of a religious persuasion. This holding of senior positions in government by university graduates who are not well-versed in religious sciences makes the reinstatement of the Sharīʿah in the echelons of power even more difficult.

What the Muslim world needs is a fusion of the religious and secular education systems with maximum attention being given to the *maqāṣid* and *khuluq ḥasan*. Within the Islamic paradigm, there is no such thing as secular education. All sciences that help bring well-being or *falāḥ* to mankind are religious. Fortunately, as a result of the struggle of scholars like Jamāl al-Dīn al-Afghānī (d. 1315/1897) and Muḥammad ʿAbduh (d. 1323/1905) in the Arab world, and of Sir Sayyid Aḥmad Khān (d. 1316/1898) and Muhammad Iqbal (d. 1357/1938) in the Indo-Pakistan subcontinent, this needed fusion has gradually been taking place. The syllabi of *madrasahs* are, however, not changing as fast as they should. They have become locked-in through the operation of path dependence and self-reinforcing mechanisms and it is not easy to dislodge them. However, what is indirectly helping in the fusion is that the *madrasah* graduates are themselves seeking admission in modern educational institutions to learn English and modern sciences, and university graduates are learning religious sciences. Moreover, Muslim students receiving higher degrees in Islamic religious sciences from Western universities, are not only able to obtain better pay and higher status but are also able to analyze issues more scientifically. This fusion is gradually helping to accelerate the development of *Fiqh* and bring it closer to the echelons of power.

The role of Sufism

Another consequence of the corruption and worldliness of the royal courts was the refuge a number of pious and consciencious *ʿulamāʾ* sought in Sufism or asceticism. In spite of much opposition to Sufism from the *ʿulamāʾ* because of a number of concepts which were clearly in conflict with basic Islamic teachings,[14] the Sufis gradually began to attract more and more people and to dominate the religious environment of many Muslim countries. This was the result of their piety, simple lives, honest livelihood, easy accessibility and the helpful attitude of many (though not all) of them. They also played an important role in the spread of Islam in a substantial part of the world. The *really* pious among them act like religious psychiatrists; people go to them with difficulties and do succeed in finding spiritual solace and mental satisfaction.

In spite of the efforts by a number of scholars like al-Ghazālī (d. 505/1111) and Shaykh Aḥmad Sirhindī (d. 1034/1624) to cleanse Sufism of its objectionable elements, it has not become sufficiently reformed and has, therefore, hurt Islam in two very important ways. Firstly, the Sharīʿah that the Prophet (pbuh) preached, stood for the establishment of a just socio-economic order through the promotion of individual as well as social righteousness and the creation of institutions that were necessary for this purpose. It required Muslims to boldly face the different challenges in political, social and economic life, and not to run away from them. However, the Sufis did not pay much attention to social righteousness in its broader sense of struggling for the realization of justice and human rights. They rather promoted resignation to the prevailing political, social and economic fate.

Secondly, the Sharīʿah that the Prophet preached stood for the realization of a balance between material and spiritual pursuits. Sufism destroyed this balance by emphasizing individual piety in its extreme form. It eulogized poverty and asceticism and promoted ecstatic obliteration of the individual self. It stood for full-time devotion to prayer and lack of interest in worldly matters. By removing some of the most upright, competent and well-respected *'ulamā'*, who could have helped change the course of history, from the practical realities of life and from active political struggle for the establishment of a just socio-economic order, it unwittingly became one of the factors that helped perpetuate the prevailing unjust power structures.

Nevertheless, the Sufis can still play an important role in the moral regeneration of the Muslim world if they return to their original mission of spiritual purification, take part in the peaceful and non-violent struggle for the restoration of justice and people's rights, and rid themselves of the un-Islamic concepts that crept into its practice later on. The charisma that some of them still have as well as their simple lives and upright characters can be of great service in the moral, economic, and political reform of the Muslim world. However, if the Sufis continue to be glued steadfastly to their own ways and express disdain for those who get involved in the socio-political struggle, they may only serve to slow down the ongoing reform movement and also, in the process, marginalize themselves even more than what they are already.

Deterioration in the position of women

With the weakening of central government, the spread of political insecurity, and the decline in rationalism, the position of women also suffered in Muslim society. Essentially, the important role that woman had played earlier in nearly all aspects of life began to decline.

The Qur'ān prescribed for them rights equal to those of men (2:228). It also required men to treat them gently and fairly (4:19) and to fulfil their obligations towards them graciously (2:237), so as to be able to realize the ultimate goal of peace of mind as well as mutual love and affection (30:21).

The Prophet (pbuh) further reinforced these and other verses of the Qur'ān by characterizing women as sisters of men.[15] In the sermon that he delivered during his farewell pilgrimage, he exhorted men to fear God in their treatment of women because they (men) had accepted them (women) as "a trust from God".[16] On another occasion he warned them against usurping the rights of women by taking advantage of their weakness.[17] These, as well as a number of other *aḥādīth,* have been interpreted as a testimony for their equal (and not inferior) status and the playing of a complementary role to men in the betterment of society. 'Umar, the second Caliph, felt prompted, therefore, to say: "During the pre-Islamic period (*al-Jāhiliyyah*), we did not consider women to be anything. However, after the coming of Islam, when God Himself expressed His concern for them, we realized that they also had rights over us."[18]

During the days of the Prophet himself (pbuh), women played an important role, by participating in a number of religious, social, educational, economic and political activities. They "were accorded property rights not equalled in the West until modern times".[19] They even helped in the war effort.[20] As a result of their participation in various activities, everyone knew about the Prophet's wives, daughters and aunts as well as other prominent ladies of the time. This would not have happened if they had remained confined to their homes and did not come into contact with men.

Some women used to cover their faces before the Prophet's days, while others did not. In keeping with his humane attitude of not using coercion, the Prophet did not force them to uncover their faces. However, he did require them to leave their faces uncovered during prayers, '*Umrah* and *Ḥajj*. Some of his Companions wished to prevent women from going to the mosques, but he clearly and forcefully forbade them from doing so.[21] Accordingly, the verdict of a number of respected Islamic scholars of the past as well as the present is that, while women are required to be dressed modestly in keeping with the teachings of the Sharīʿah, they are not expected to cover their faces or to be confined to their homes.[22]

Women are well-represented in the books of history, *Tafsīr*, *Ḥadīth* and *Fiqh*. In the biographical literature devoted to the Companions, over 1,200 female Companions are included, roughly about 10 to 15 percent of the total entries.[23] During the Umayyad and the early ʿAbbāsid periods as well, women enjoyed more or less the same liberty as they did during the Prophet's time. A number of them, including Hārūn al-Rashīd's mother, wife and daughter, played an important role in their society. After reading the histories of thousands of women in 40 bibliographical collections dating from the ninth century, Ruth Roded, lecturer at the Hebrew University of Jerusalem, did not find any evidence to support the view that Muslim women were "marginal, secluded and restricted". She, therefore, concluded that "the role of women in traditional Islamic society has often been portrayed in extremely negative terms that are not justified by historic reality".[24]

Even down to the Ottoman period, women owned property, which her husband could not touch during her life-time. Women established *waqf* (charitable endowments) to support education and other benevolent causes. This demonstrates their ownership of property.[25] While studying *waqf* endowments in Ottoman Aleppo, Roded was "astounded to discover 41 percent of the endowments were founded by women and that women's endowments differed little from those of men".[26] Women also acted as farmers, merchants, artisans and landlords.[27] Courts were active in safeguarding women's rights, and particularly inheritance rights, in conformity with the Sharīʿah.[28] No stigma seems to have been attached to a woman's attending court in person, and quite a few women took care of their affairs without the mediation of a male representative. Schatzmiller, writing on labour in the medieval Islamic world, states that "stagnation, aversion to manual labour, and the limited participation of women in economic activities and in the labour force can no longer be upheld".[29]

The picture that emerges from all this differs considerably from what now prevails in most Muslim countries. Women are illiterate, secluded, and generally deprived of the rights that Islam has given them. They have little role to play in their societies. In some Muslim societies they are even deprived of the right to inherit property. Except for the *Ḥaram* in Makkah and the Prophet's Mosque in Madīnah, it is rare to see women in the mosques except during the month of Ramaḍān and that too in some countries. One may, therefore, wonder about what historical factors brought about the change. No sociological explanation seems to have been offered so far. It may be worth exploring whether one important cause was insecurity of life and property that resulted from the political upheavals and the weak law and order situation prevailing over a number of centuries starting from the later part of the ʿAbbāsid dynasty down through the Buwayhid (334-447/945-1055) and the Saljūqid (447-590/1055-1194) dynasties. The barbarian Mongol (656-756/1258-1355) and Tīmūrid (736-807/1336-1405) occupations may have further accentuated the seclusion to save Muslim women from being subject to molestation.[30] In periods of turmoil, disorder and anarchy (*fasād* or *fitnah*), *fiqh* allows the imposition of restrictions as precautionary measures (*sadd al-dharīʿah*) to prevent harm – restrictions that are not allowed by the Sharīʿah under normal circumstances.[31] Since the turmoil prevailed for centuries, the restrictions which may have been accepted for a temporary period became locked-in through path dependence and became a permanent characteristic of Muslim society. Furthermore, prevailing local customs and traditions helped provide the needed self-reinforcing mechanisms. People continued in their own ways, and many of the practices which Islam came to abolish or reform were not only left undisturbed but even became associated with Islam, there being no satisfactory arrangement for the education of the masses in the values of Islam.

In some Muslim countries the seclusion has become so strict that men and women live in two entirely separate worlds with little interaction between them except in the family. This has not only prevented men and women from playing their mutually supporting roles in society, but has also deprived women of education and economic independence. While in rural areas, women are at least able to work in the field, in urban areas they are unable to play any significant role except that of attending to household responsibilities. Women's ignorance, confinement to the house, and total dependence on their husbands for the fulfillment of practically all needs, prevents them from asserting themselves and obtaining the rights that Islam has given them. A number of *'ulamā'* have now come to their defence and tried to show the true Islamic position on the subject.[32] Any society where nearly half of the population becomes marginalized and is unable to play its potential role in keeping with the talents that God has granted to it, is bound to have stunted growth.

Notes

1. See Zaman, 1997.
2. This incident is cited in detail by the editor, 'Abd al-Fattāḥ Abū Ghuddah, from al-Saymarī's *Akhbār Abī Ḥanīfah wa Aṣḥābihī*, in his Introduction to Al-Shaybānī's, *Kitāb al-Kasb*, pp. 54-56. This incident was brought to my notice by Dr. Anas Zarqā.
3. Faroghi, 1994, p. 616.
4. See Lewis, 1960, p. 18.
5. See al-Ghazālī (d. 505/1111), *Iḥyā'*, Volume 1, pp. 58-82. See also al-Ṭurṭūshī (d. 520/1126), *Sirāj al-Mulūk*, 1994, Volume 2, chapter on "Warning against the company of the Sulṭān", pp. 480-4.
6. Cited by al-Ṭurṭūshī (d. 520/1126), 1994, p. 481.
7. al-Ghazālī, *Iḥyā'*, Volume 2, p. 139.
8. Ibid., p. 143.
9. Ibid., p. 142.

10. The full text of the *ḥadīth* is: "The Prophet (pbuh) said three times that faith stands for sincerity (*Inna al-Dīna al-Naṣīḥah*). When asked: 'For whom, Oh Prophet of God?' He replied 'For God, His Book, His Prophet, the Muslim leaders, and the common people'." (Narrated from Tamīm al-Dārī by Bayhaqī in his *Shu'ab al-Īmān*, Volume 6, pp. 25-26, No. 7400, on the authority of Muslim, Aḥmad, Abū Dāwūd and Nasā'ī.) For the implications of sincerity, see al-Mundhirī, Volume 2, p. 576, footnote 2.
11. Cf. Fazlur Raḥman, 1965, pp. 184-85 and Abū Sulaymān, 1993, p. 93.
12. See Ibn Taymiyyah, *Bayān al-Dalīl* 1425 H (= 2004 AC), p. 137.
13. Narrated from Abū Hurayrah by al-Bayhaqī in his *Shu'ab al-Īmān*, 1990, Volume 6, p. 230, No. 7976.
14. Some of these are: asceticism and rejection of the world; greater emphasis on *ṭarīqah* (Sufi practices) and *kashf* (Sufi intuition) than on the Sharī'ah and *Waḥy* (Revelation); veneration of saints when Islam does not recognize saintship; the Sufi acting as an intermediary (*wasīlah*) between man and God instead of the direct link that Islam has established, and dead 'saints' having a say in the affairs of the world as well as the ability to respond to the supplications of their followers.
15. Cited from 'Ā'ishah by al-Suyūṭī in his *al-Jāmi' al-Ṣaghīr* on the authority of Aḥmad, Abū Dāwūd and al-Tirmidhī, Volume 1, p. 102.
16. Cited from Jābir ibn 'Abdullāh by Muslim in his *Ṣaḥīḥ*, *Kitāb al-Manāsik, Bāb ḥajjat al-Nabiyy*, Volume 2, p. 889:147; Abū Dāwūd, *Kitāb al-Manāsik, Bāb ṣifāt ḥajj al-Nabiyy*; also Ibn Mājah and *Musnad* of *Aḥmad.*
17. The actual wordings of the *ḥadīth* are: "I forbid usurpation of the right of two weak people – the orphan and the woman" (narrated from Abū Hurayrah by al-Ḥākim in his *Mustadrak*, Volume 1, p. 63). This *ḥadīth* is *ṣaḥīḥ*, on the criteria of Muslim.
18. Narrated from 'Umar by al-Bukhārī in his *Ṣaḥīḥ, Kitāb al-Libās, Bāb mā kāna al-Nabiyyu yatajawwazu min al-libās wa'l-busṭ*, Volume 4, p. 281:735.
19. Lewis, 1995, p. 72.
20. See Abū Shuqqah, 1990, Volume 3, pp. 132-233; see also Ruth Roded, 1994, p. 35.
21. The *ḥadīth* is: "Do not prevent women (*imā' Allāh*) from the mosques (*masājid Allāh*)." Narrated from Ibn 'Umar, by Muslim in his *Ṣaḥīḥ*, Volume 1, p. 327: 136, *Kitāb al-Ṣalāt, Bāb Khurūj al-nisā' ilā al-masājid.*
22. Abū Shuqqah, Volume 2, 1990, pp. 15 and 83-137.
23. Roded, 1994, p. 19.
24. Ibid., pp. viii and ix.
25. Ibid., p. 123.
26. Ibid., p. vii.
27. Faroghi, 1994, pp. 599 and 605.
28. Schatzmiller, 1994, p. 362.
29. Ibid., p. 399.
30. For Tīmūr's savagery, see Hodgson, 1977, Volume 2, p. 433.
31. Cf. Abū Shuqqah, 1990, Volume 3, pp. 183 and 199.
32. Of particular significance is the work in six volumes by the late Shaykh Abū Shuqqah (1990), a prominent leader of the Muslim Brotherhood in Egypt.

7

SOME LESSONS (*ʿIBAR*) FROM MUSLIM HISTORY

Muslim history clearly demonstrates that all the different constituents of a civilization, including the people, their worldview, beliefs and values, the government, the economy, and justice and development, play a complementary and interdependent role in that civilization's rise or fall. One of these constituents may act as the trigger mechanism and the rest may be affected over time through the process of circular causation. It also shows that human beings themselves have a crucial role to play in this process because they are not just the end, but also the means of development. Since they are the end, their well-being needs to be ensured. If this is not done, they will not be motivated to work hard and innovate. However, since they are also the means, they may not be able to render their best for the overall development of their society and mankind unless some requisites are ensured. These include:

a. The proper moral upbringing and education of the people, and in particular the new generation, along with training in skills in demand;

b. Justice, law and order, and security of life, property, and honour for every individual;
c. Suitable employment and self-employment opportunities to enable people to utilize their talents fruitfully for raising their own well-being as well as that of their society, and
d. A proper environment that is conducive to the promotion of not only hard, efficient and creative work but also of mutual trust, cooperation and social solidarity.

It may not be possible to satisfy all these requisites without a proper worldview that provides values or rules of behaviour that clearly define the rights and responsibilities of all members of society. These values may, in turn, be meaningless unless they are enforced impartially for the benefit of all by an efficient, honest and strong government accountable before the people. While the moral uplift of all individuals is indispensable for human well-being, development of society's wealth is also important not only for improving the material well-being of the people to motivate them to do their best but also for providing resources to the government to fulfil its responsibilities effectively. Wealth and development acquire even greater importance with the passage of time as the number of people increases and the challenges faced by them as well as the government become more and more difficult, indeed complex. While a society may be able to advance in the short-run in spite of the weakness of any one of the variables included in Ibn Khaldūn's model, it may not be able to sustain the advance in the long-run. The weakness of one may become reflected over time in the weakness of all others.

The Muslims were able to strengthen all variables to a substantial extent, though not as much as desired, and thereby realized the rapid overall development and advance of their society. However, later on political authority started to neglect its responsibilities. It failed to implement some important aspects of the Sharīʿah and to ensure justice, security of life, property and honour, and to provide the educational, health and infrastructure facilities needed by the people to realize their full potential. Consequently, development suffered a setback as did the wealth at society's disposal and the government's military and political strength.

The first lesson

The question is: why did rulers start to neglect their responsibilities? The answer is provided by the first lesson of Muslim history that accountability before the people is indispensable for motivating rulers to perform their tasks effectively for the well-being of the people. For this purpose Islam instituted the system of *khilāfah* with *shūrā*. If these two institutions had been allowed to operate in earnest for a sufficiently long period of time, the embryonic framework that developed during the *Khilāfah al-Rāshidah* for both these and for the effective functioning of the government may have gradually evolved, with some frustrations and setbacks from time to time, into a more sophisticated constitutional and legal framework, which took place in the West. The environment for such evolution was perhaps not favourable in those days for a faith that was rapidly expanding over a vast geographical area in different communities with divergent cultural and political backgrounds. It thus became possible for Mu'āwiyah, who became *Khalīfah* in 41/661, 30 years after the Prophet's death, to nip the system in the bud by bequeathing the *khilāfah* to his son 20 years later through hereditary succession. There were revolts against this but these did not succeed because of the impossibility of successfully organizing widespread public agitation against this move, especially given the slow means of transportation and communication of those days.

The system of *khilāfah* and *shūrā* could not, therefore, become institutionalized, and instead of the transfer of power taking place in an orderly manner by virtue of ability and character through the consensus of the community, as envisaged by the Sharīʿah, it took place by hereditary means or force. This increasingly led to wars of succession, fragmentation and disunity, and to the absence of accountability and the neglect of responsibilities on the part of the government. The result has been the creation of the most damaging fault line in Muslim history. Kramer has hence rightly pointed out that "the causes of the decline were to be sought mainly within the body politic".[1]

Political authority did not, however, deteriorate into despotism immediately after the abolition of *khilāfah*. This was not possible in a society where the spirit of Islamic values had been infused by the Prophet (pbuh) himself. The Sharīʿah continued to be a source of inspiration for the people, and of at least some moral constraint on the government, which could not avoid wearing the cloak of the Sharīʿah, even if it did not care to implement its teachings fully. Moreover, there arose in almost all dynasties some conscientious and competent rulers who tried to set things right, at least partially. Such bouncing back was, however, due to the rulers' own initiative rather than to an institutional imperative built into the political system in keeping with what the system of *khilāfah* with *shūrā* had envisaged.

The second lesson

This leads to the second lesson of Muslim history, which is that the lack of political accountability gradually gives rise to a number of ills that hurt both justice and development. One of the first ill effects of this was the loss of freedom of expression whereby it was no longer possible for people to criticize rulers and to discuss government policies openly. This led to the creation of fertile ground for inequality before the law, in clear violation of the Sharīʿah, and the formation of a privileged class which could not be subjected fully to the discipline of the Sharīʿah.[2] A major mechanism for self-correction in the political system was, thus, nearly lost. Possibilities for reform hence receded more and more into the background. Corruption, inefficiency, and inequities accentuated and public resources were increasingly used for the luxury of the royal court and the pursuit of expensive military campaigns aimed at territorial expansion, particularly during the Ottoman period. Low priority was given to nation-building activities like education, health, research, and infrastructure construction, thereby sowing the seeds of ultimate Muslim backwardness, particularly in civilian and military technology.

Slow development was not conducive to an adequate rise in government revenues. Since expenditures, nevertheless, kept on rising, fiscal imbalances were accentuated. To cover these, there was increasing recourse to exploitative tax-farming, taxation beyond the ability of the people to bear, currency debasing, the sale of public offices, which led to the appointment of incompetent people to senior positions, and excessive borrowing. Socio-economic justice, the *raison d'être* of Islam and an indispensable requisite for development, suffered a severe setback. Agriculture stagnated, and peasants, artisans and traders became impoverished. The solidarity between the people and the rulers weakened. The quality of the people declined, their vitality and motivation suffered, and the economy could not keep pace with the growing needs of the people as well as the government. As a result, the Muslim world lagged behind in all-round development, and was thereby unable to face the economic and military challenges from a rapidly rising Western civilization.

The third lesson

The third lesson of Muslim history is that it is not possible for political authority to impose its own worldview on people. Such efforts rupture the solidarity between people and rulers, accentuate social turmoil, and vitiate the atmosphere for development. The effort of al-Ma'mūn to impose the *Mu'tazilī* worldview on people by the use of brute force alienated pious and well-respected *'ulamā'* who had already become disgruntled with the rulers after the introduction of political illegitimacy, increases in the luxury of the royal court and socio-economic inequities. Since these pious *'ulamā'* enjoyed the peoples' confidence, rulers' lack of solidarity with the *'ulamā'* was itself reflected in a decline in the rulers' rapport with the people. Tensions and conflict gradually became more aggravated, leading eventually to the 'Abbāsids' downfall.

The experience of al-Ma'mūn is corroborated by that of Soviet Russia, Eastern Europe, China, Turkey, Algeria and Tunisia. All show that discontent and unrest initiated by efforts to forcefully impose a worldview unacceptable to the people continues to simmer, leading to the breakdown of solidarity between the government and the people, and the accentuation of conflict and tension.

Repression has never succeeded and never will. The use of repressive methods by the Church was responsible, to a considerable extent, for the success of the Enlightenment in its anti-religious form. If the Church had adopted a more rational approach, religion may not have suffered as much of a set-back in the West as it actually did. If the *Mu'tazilites* had not used force, rationalism may not have suffered as much of a set-back in the Muslim world as it did. The free interaction of rationalist and conservative views might perhaps have ultimately led to a relatively more balanced equilibrium. The use of repression to enforce unacceptable views on people led to an extreme reaction against the rationalists and generated tensions in the Muslim world which ultimately meant a lack of emphasis on the teaching of science subjects in religious schools. Furthermore, since the government did not spare resources for the teaching of science, the development of science and technology suffered, making the Muslim world unable to successfully face the challenges it encountered. Such tension and suspicion also deprived students of religious schools of the tools of analysis that they needed for the development of *Fiqh* and other religious sciences.

The fourth lesson

Al-Ma'mūn's experience also teaches the fourth lesson of Muslim history, whereby once the people are alienated, the government loses its grass roots support and needs to rely on the help of external guards to stay in power. This, however, proves ultimately to be self-defeating. It makes rulers complacent, further reduces their contact and dialogue with people, leaves conflicts unresolved, increases tensions, lowers development and leads to the domination of the country by outsiders. If, instead, the government were to resort to a strategy of dialogue, sharing power, conflict resolution, and solving the people's problems, it would prolong its power base without reliance on external forces, and also save the country from ruin.

The fifth lesson

The fifth lesson of Islamic history is that Islam is not the cause of Muslim decline. Islam has, in fact, itself been, and continues to be, a victim of lack of political accountability, corruption and repression. The desire of political authority to exploit Islam for solving its own vested interests by trying to extract verdicts that were not in harmony with the Sharī'ah was one of the important factors that led to the closure of the *ijtihād* gate and the stagnation of *Fiqh*, making it unable to face newer challenges. It also led pious and competent *'ulamā'* and Sufis to avoid the royal courts so as to safeguard themselves from corruption and human rights violations, but in turn also isolated them from the practical realities of life. They, therefore, became less effective in fulfilling their natural role of contributing to the reform of the people and government, ensuring sanctity of human rights, and promoting the development of *Fiqh* so that it could successfully respond to the changing realities of life.[3]

The soft landing

The cycle of circular causation, however, took several centuries to complete. This is because some of the functions of the body politic were taken over by other social and political institutions and, thereby, helped soften the decline. The most important of these offsetting institutions was Islam itself, which, in spite of losing its dynamism, has continued to inspire the people as well as some sectors of the government in different dynasties. This has helped maintain at least some semblance of justice, reduced the misery of the poorer elements of the population, and also ensured family and social solidarity to a substantial extent. If it had not been for Islam, Muslim decline may have been more precipitous.

The people themselves, specially the conscientious among the well-to-do and the pious among the *'ulamā',* tried to offset the shortcomings of rulers. Many of the services that the government was expected to provide, were only enabled by private philanthropy, particularly through the institution of *waqf,* to build schools, hospitals, and markets and to ensure a number of other public goods and services. In addition to *waqf, zakāh* and *ṣadaqāt* were also used for the well-being of the poor and the vulnerable. This was primarily due to the great emphasis on charity, brotherhood and care of the distressed in Islamic values. If such philanthropy had not been available during periods of disorder, chaos and economic breakdown, the condition of the poor and those uprooted by civil shift would perhaps have been extremely miserable.

The *'ulamā'* continued to use mosques and *madrasahs* as centres of religious education. However, mosques, *madrasahs* and Friday sermons were not enough to fulfil the gigantic task of educating and reforming the people, who were expanding at an exponential rate with an enormously large mass of humanity entering into the fold of Islam. Such converts needed a more systematic and widespread system of education for orientation into the Islamic worldview and values, without which their moral transformation was impossible. Since this was not arranged, the people continued in their own ways, and many of the practices which Islam came to abolish or reform, not only continued undisturbed, but even became associated with Islam. The *'ulamā'* could not possibly have mustered the resources required for this task, particularly when economies were also slackening.

Notes

1. Kramer, "Othmanli", 1995, p. 197.
2. Dr. Anas Zarqa rightly pointed out in his valuable comments on this manuscript that this has been equally true of most human societies until recently.
3. Prof. Robert Whaples rightly pointed out in his valuable comments on this manuscript that the lessons of Muslim history could as likely be called lessons of human history, since these same forces and vicious cycles have been played out in virtually every society.

8

FAILURE TO LEARN THE LESSONS

Six hundred years have passed since Ibn Khaldūn wrote the *Muqaddimah.* One would have expected that the analysis made by a man of his moral and mental calibre would receive serious attention from rulers. This might have prompted them to implement in the body politic the reforms enunciated by Islam so as to ensure political accountability, justice and development, and, thereby, help reverse the cycle of circular causation in a positive direction. However, this did not happen. The overall Muslim decline has persisted even though it has not been a straight line phenomenon and some Muslim countries have done better than others. The primary reason for this overall decline is that the Muslim world has failed to learn the lessons of history indicated in the previous chapter. Lack of political accountability which triggered the decline, has continued until today. The Muslim world has not been able until now to establish a procedure for the orderly transfer of the reins of power to the most upright and competent in the eyes of the people as desired by the Qur'ān (49:13), the efficient and equitable use of public resources in accordance with the Sharī'ah, and the free and fearless criticism of government policies.

The present position

The absence of Democracy

Only 13, or a little less than 23 percent, of the 57 member countries of the Organization of the Islamic Conference (OIC) have democracy, while 44, or 77 percent, do not. Of these 44 countries, 31 have pseudo-democracy, 5 have absolute monarchy, 3 have dictatorship, and 5 are in transition.[1] However, even those Muslim countries that do enjoy democracy, have it only in a formal sense: they hold elections and the democratic structures provide an alternance of power. Powerful vested interests, nevertheless, succeed in getting elected and re-elected. The poor and disadvantaged are in most cases not free to vote as they wish and are poorly represented in the echelons of power.[2] Democracy has, thus, not been able to take hold in a real sense. While effective democratic processes have gone a long way in ensuring good governance and the effective use of public resources for development in the Western world, the Muslim world has lagged behind because of the near absence of accountability of the rulers and of good governance, which democracy tends to bring.[3]

The impact of this on the socio-economy

The absence of democracy has led to a number of evils through the operation of circular causation. One of these is lack of freedom of the press. Only 4 Muslim countries[4] are free, 14 are partly free and 39 are not free.[5] The inability to criticize the government in the news media or other forums like the parliament (*shūrā*) or through peaceful demonstrations contributes to poor governance, lack of transparency and unhealthy policies. It also promotes corruption and misuse of public resources for the private benefit of the rich and the powerful. Even if the press is free in some countries, public criticism does not have any impact if the ruler is able to use different machinations to prolong his stay in power. Empirical studies have led to a consensus in economic literature that corruption and poor governance have substantial adverse effects on development.[6]

The "Corruption Perception Index" prepared by the Berlin-based Transparency International includes 159 countries and ranges from 10 (least corrupt) to zero (most corrupt).[7] A score of 5 on this index indicates a borderline country. Only 6 Muslim countries are above this borderline with scores ranging from 5.1 to 6.3. 42 countries fall below this borderline. No data are available for the rest. The likelihood, however, is that most of these other countries for which no data are available may also lie below the borderline. It is disheartening to note that six of the ten most corrupt countries are Muslim and that all of the three most corrupt countries are also Muslim. This is so in spite of the fact that the Qur'ān emphatically prohibits wrongful acquisition of wealth and the taking of bribes (2:188 and 4:29).

Corruption, combined with lack of freedom of expression, tends to corrupt the courts as well, in which case, there is little likelihood that the power elite will be punished. When the wrongdoers are not punished, the vice tends to spread until it becomes locked-in through the operation of path dependence and self-reinforcing mechanisms. It then becomes difficult to root out the evil. If only the poor are punished, then there is a rise in discontent and a decline in solidarity between the government and the people. This contributes to social and political instability, which is among the major factors that hurt economic development.

As a result of corruption, a substantial part of the scarce public resources of these countries is diverted to the building of palaces and the financing of luxury and conspicuous consumption of the power elite, making governments unable to spend adequately on education, health, infrastructure construction and the provision of public services needed for accelerated development. Corruption also raises the transactions costs of the private sector and, thereby, adversely affects the rate of return. Savings, therefore, go abroad and domestic investment tends to decline. This is bound to affect growth as confirmed by the inferior performance of most Muslim countries. Even though the total population of the 57 Muslim countries is 1,415 million and constitutes around 22 percent of the world's population of 6,438 million,[8] their total real GDP at constant 2000 dollars is only 1,891 billion. This represents only 5.2 percent of the world real GDP of $36,411 billion.[9] Their PPP adjusted per capita GDP is $3,381, which is 40 percent of the PPP adjusted GDP of $8,477 for the world, and 12 percent of the PPP adjusted GDP of $29,144 for high income countries. Only four Muslim countries, all of whom happen to be oil-producing, are able to get into the high income category (HIC) and only six into the upper middle income (UMC) category. 18 fall into the low middle income category (LMC) and 29 fall into the low income category (LIC).[10]

Education, which received high priority in the early history of Islam and which was one of the causes of its rise, has not received the emphasis it needs in government budgets. Accordingly, the average adult illiteracy rate in these countries was 30 percent in 2004.[11] This means that around 425 million people are illiterate and unable to contribute their full potential to development. All these countries together have only 600 universities whereas the US alone has 1,975, or more than three times as many, when its population is a little over one-fifth.[12] Democracy, education and development reinforced each other in the Western world. Education promoted development and development led to a rise in the demand for education, which it was possible to satisfy because of state support for it as a result of the rise in revenues. Education and development together helped reinforce democracy.

The Human Development Index

No wonder only 7 Muslim countries score high on the UNDP Human Development Index (HDI), while 28 and 18 receive medium and low scores respectively.[13] However, the problem with the HDI is that it incorporates only three variables: life expectancy at birth, literacy, and GDP per capita adjusted for purchasing power parity. It, thus, reflects the restricted framework of Development Economics before it recognized the crucial role played in development by social, cultural and political institutions, which Ibn Khaldūn emphasized in his model and which Development Economics has now belatedly come to recognize.

It is, therefore, necessary to prepare a more comprehensive index. This would lead to the inclusion of a number of other variables, including justice, family integrity, social harmony, mental peace, reward for merit and hard work, and minimization of crime, tension and anomie. Also important are democracy, freedom of expression, the equitable distribution of income and wealth, and an honest and effective judiciary. Data may not be available on all these. It is, nevertheless, important to construct as comprehensive an index as possible and to strive for the collection of data not as yet available.

It may not be surprising if Muslim countries, which do not score high on the existing HDI, may perhaps turn out to be even more so on the scale of a more comprehensive index. This is because, after centuries of operation of Ibn Khaldūn's model, political illegitimacy is no longer the only problem faced by Muslim societies. All the socio-economic and political institutions of these countries have gradually become vitiated through the operation of circular causation so that it is now difficult to distinguish the cause from the effect. There is, therefore, need for comprehensive reform. Paying attention to only economic or even political variables to reverse the cycle of decline may not be enough.

Notes

1. Based on data for the year 2002 given in "The Index of Electionworld. org". Democracy is defined by the Index of Electionworld as a country in which democratic structures provide an alternance of power. Pseudo-democracy is

defined as a country having democratic structures but without a real chance of alternance of power.

2. See Besley and Burgess, 2003, p.17.
3. There is a great deal of literature available now on the positive effect of democracy on good governance and of good governance on development (see, for example, Mulligan et al., 2004; Kaufmann and Kraay, 2002; Hall and Jones, 1999, and Kaufmann et al., 1999). A few authors have, however, argued that democracy hinders economic growth, particularly in less developed countries, because democratic governments are unable to vigorously implement policies that are necessary for accelerated development (Sirowy and Inkles, 1990; Johnson, 1964 and MacIntyre, 1996). This line of thinking gained prominence during the heyday of the Soviet Union and of China's great leap forward but seems to have fewer followers now.
4. Wherever the term 'Muslim countries' is used in this chapter, it refers to the 57 members of the Organization of the Islamic Conference (OIC), which is like a United Nations of Muslim countries.
5. Based on data given in "Freedom of the Press 2004", www.freedomhouse.org. The definition of 'free', 'partly free' and 'not free' by Freedomhouse is based on each country's prevailing legal (0-30 points), political (0-40 points) and economic (0-30 points) environment affecting the press. The higher the restrictions, the higher the number of points the country receives. A country's final score is based on the total of these three criteria. A score of 0 to 30 places the country in the free press group; 31 to 60 in the partly free group, and 61 to 100 in the not free group.
6. Kaufmann et al., 1999; Knack and Keefer, 1995; Mauro, 1995, 2004, p. 1.
7. The data are for the year 2005. Corruption is defined by Transparency International "as the abuse of public office for private gain". The index tries to measure the degree to which corruption is perceived to exist among a country's public officials and politicians.
8. This data are for the year 2005 given in Islamic Development Bank (IDB), 2007, Table 1.1, p. 9. There are Muslims in non-Muslim countries and non-Muslims in Muslim countries. This figure does not, therefore, indicate the total number of Muslims all over the world. The total number of Muslims is estimated to be somewhere between 1.5 and 1.8 billion.
9. Islamic Development Bank (IDB), 2007, Table 2.5b, p. 43.
10. World Bank, 2004, p. 251.
11. Islamic Development Bank, 2007, Table 1.5, p. 15.
12. Based on data given in www.universitiesworldwide; Islamic Development Bank, 2007 and IMF, April 2007.
13. Based on the data for the year 2004 given in Islamic Development Bank, 2007, Table 1.8b, p. 20. No data are given for four countries. Data for Guyana, which is a member of OIC but not of IDB, is for 2002 and obtained from UNDP, 2003, pp. 237-240.

9

THE NEED FOR REFORM

Where to start?

The call for comprehensive reform in Muslim countries to reverse the cycle of circular causation, brought into operation by the end of political accountability and the intensification of authoritarian rule, automatically raises the crucial question of where to start? The best place to start would be where the Prophet himself (pbuh) started – the reform of human beings. They play the role of a locomotive in the rise or fall of any civilization. However, even though they need to receive the topmost priority, this does not necessarily mean that other socio-economic and political factors that have been vitiated over the centuries through the process of circular causation do not need to be given simultaneous attention.

Moral reform

The crux of the problem, however, is how to reform individuals in such a way that they are transformed into better human beings and become a source of blessing not only for their own society but also for mankind as a whole, in keeping with the Prophet's mission specified in the Qur'ān (21:107). For this purpose it is necessary to change their character, ability, motivation and mental outlook by giving maximum attention to their moral upbringing and education. This is what all the Messengers of God, including Abraham, Moses, Jesus and Muḥammad, peace be upon them all, tried to do.[1]

Such an emphasis on moral upbringing may appear to be odd and uncalled for in the present-day secularist and liberal environment. The undeniable fact, however, is that it is the religious worldview which carries the potential to help strengthen all the qualities of character that are needed for sustained development and realization of the Islamic vision of justice, brotherhood and the well-being of all. It may not be possible to ensure the well-being of all if everyone is committed to serving just their own self-interest and is not willing to make the kind of sacrifices that the well-being of all demands.[2] It is the religious worldview, with accountability in the Hereafter and the sanctity of moral values, that can help motivate individuals to make the needed sacrifice. The religious worldview does this by giving the serving of self-interest a long-run perspective – in this world as well as the Hereafter. The more individuals sacrifice their self-interest to fulfill their moral, socio-economic and political obligations in this world, which is after all transient, the more their self-interest is served in the Hereafter, which is eternal. Raising peoples' moral consciousness is, therefore, unavoidable. In this respect, the Qur'ān clearly emphasizes the role of belief, moral reform and justice in the rise and fall of societies. (See for example, 57:25; 20:111; 87:14; 91:10 and 103:1-3.)

History is replete with examples of where a society has reached its climax as a result of moral reform. Intellectual and economic advance have then generally followed. Kroeber too rightly pointed out: "I cannot think of a single people which first evolved a high science, philosophy, or art, and thereafter a religious pattern."[3] Schweitzer has also emphasized that "if ethical foundation is lacking, then civilization collapses even when in other directions creative and intellectual forces of the strongest nature are at work".[4] Therefore, according to him, "moral control over men's dispositions is much more important than control over nature".[5] Toynbee has also argued that "the command over non-human nature, which science has in its gift, is of almost infinitely less importance to Man than his relations with himself, with his fellow men, and with God".[6] More recently, Nigel Lawson, British Chancellor of the Exchequer, 1983-1989, stressed that "no political or economic order can long survive except on a moral base".[7] Friedman, a Harvard professor, has also argued in his recent book that moral growth and economic growth go hand in hand, reinforcing each other.[8] Even empirical evidence has established the positive impact of religiosity on a wide variety of outcomes.[9] This is a clear vindication of the religious worldview, which Ibn Khaldūn and even a number of Western scholars represent, but which the Enlightenment movement tried to undermine with only transient success. It is gratifying that the reinstatement of the religious worldview is gaining momentum day by day.

Justice, development and the alleviation of poverty

It may, however, be difficult to raise the moral calibre of the people unless justice is also ensured. Al-Māwardī (d. 450/1058) rightly observed that "there is nothing that destroys the world and the conscience of the people faster than injustice".[10] Justice, in spite of being a distinguishing characteristic of Islamic teachings, is conspicuously missing from Muslim countries and constitutes a source of many internal and external problems. One of the first reflections of any programme to ensure justice has to be the removal of poverty, which leads to incapacity, helplessness and crime, and can even, according to the Prophet (pbuh), drive a person close to disbelief.[11] It may not, however, be possible to remove poverty without effectively using all the available resources to accelerate the pace of rural as well as urban development and promote employment and self-employment opportunities.

Proliferating education and microfinance

The overly ideological effort to impose neo-liberalism and market fundamentalism on developing countries in the guise of a Washington Consensus is generally considered to have failed.[12] Recent literature on development indicates that there is no unique universal set of rules that can be followed by developing countries to accelerate development.[13] Muslim countries can choose the strategy that suits them most in accordance with their goals and circumstances.[14] However, while every effort needs to be made to accelerate development, the focus should simultaneously be on ensuring justice. This will remain a false hope if poverty is not alleviated and the prevailing flagrant inequalities of income and wealth are not reduced. Two of the most important hurdles on the path to realizing this goal are the exorbitant cost of education and microfinance. It is, therefore, important to make high quality education accessible to the poor, preferably free of charge and, if this is not feasible, at affordable prices, so as to raise their moral and intellectual quality and to teach them the skills in demand. It is also equally important to make microfinance available to them at an affordable cost so as to enable them to establish their own micro-enterprises.

Since the decline in education, research and technology has been one of the most important causes of Muslim decline, it is imperative to remove the existing gap in these areas between the Muslim and developed countries by providing high quality education and research facilities through the proliferation of properly equipped schools, colleges and universities all over the country. In this process special care needs to be taken to ensure that education is accessible to all sectors of the society and not just to the rich. It is, however, unfortunate that privatization of education has made education so expensive that it is now beyond the reach of the poor. If this condition is not corrected, it is primarily the rich who will be able to acquire higher education. This will raise inequalities of income and wealth instead of reducing them and, thereby, aggravate the prevailing tensions and unrest in Muslim societies. It is, therefore, imperative to considerably reduce the cost of education for the poor. This may not be possible without substantially raising government subsidies for education and streamlining the collection and distribution of zakāh, *waqf* and other charitable private contributions. If the human factor is the most important for development, there is no reason why a greater proportion of government resources should not be allocated for the spread of education, which seems to have been one of the greatest victims of the lack of political accountability in the Muslim world.

Another important and unavoidable requirement for alleviating poverty is to make microfinance available to the poor to enable them to realize their dream of establishing their own micro-enterprises. It seems that interest-based microfinance has not proved an effective way of helping them in this task. A timely study (2007) edited by Dr. Qazi Kholiquzzaman Ahmad, President of the Bangladesh Economic Association, about the working of major microfinance institutions in Bangladesh has revealed that in a majority of cases the desired improvements have not been realized in the lives of borrowers. The effective rate of interest turns out to be as high as 30 to 45 percent and causes serious hardship to the borrowers in servicing the debt. They are often constrained to not only sacrifice essential consumption but also borrow from money-lenders. This engulfs them unwittingly into an unending debt cycle which will not only perpetuate poverty but also ultimately lead to a rise in unrest and social tension.[15] It is, therefore, important that, while the innovative group-based mechanism for lending adopted by the Grameen Bank and other institutions in Bangladesh is retained, microfinance is provided to the very poor on a humane interest-free basis. This will necessitate the integration of microfinance with zakāh and *waqf* institutions. For those who can afford them, profit-and-loss sharing and sales and lease-based modes of Islamic finance need to be popularized. Microfinance may not, however, be sufficient by itself. It is also necessary to expand vocational training along with infrastructure and marketing facilities to support micro-enterprises.[16]

Even though the alleviation of poverty may, by itself, be a great achievement, it will not be sufficient to realize the Islamic goal of human brotherhood. It is also necessary to bring about an equitable distribution of income and wealth and to ensure social equality, dignity and respect for every individual in Muslim societies. Therefore, justice, moral as well as socio-economic uplift, and brotherhood are all interrelated, for it may not be possible to bring about a sustained improvement in one without an improvement in the other areas.

The reform of all institutions

Such an overall improvement in the human condition may be difficult to realize without reforming all the institutions that affect human behaviour. The most important of these institutions is the family. It is the first and the most important institution in the life of a child for moral upbringing as well as education.[17] The father and the mother are the child's mentors from the very beginning and unless they themselves are educated and their character reflects Islamic values, they may not be able to play their roles satisfactorily. The love and affection of both parents, and particularly of the mother, are crucial for bringing up a new generation which is morally upright, mentally alert, socially responsible, cooperative and caring. If the family fails to play this role, no one else can take its place. This is why Islam, like most other religions, has stressed family integrity and a climate of love and affection between parents (Qur'ān, 30:21).

The role of the family needs to be reinforced by educational institutions to provide high quality education in all fields of learning, and particularly in science and technology, to enable Muslim societies to compete successfully in the international arena and to attain a reasonably high rate of economic growth. However, while educational institutions played a crucial role in the earlier centuries of Muslim history, as a result of both private philanthropy and unflinching government support, they are now unable to play that role. One of the reasons for this is that government support for education and research has substantially declined as a result of political illegitimacy, lack of adequate appreciation of education's crucial role in development and excessive spending on unproductive showpieces and defence. The neglect of moral as well as material education has had its impact on the family as well. As a result, it is unable to play its upbringing role effectively as a result of the lack of education of both parents, and particularly mothers.

Other institutions that have an important role to play in upbringing and education, but which have also become ineffective, need to be strengthened as well. Among these are the mosques which have a crucial role to play in Muslim societies but which they are now unable to do. This is because the imāms (prayer leaders), who are supposed to act as models and play a dynamic role in the moral education and character uplift of their congregations, are not only ill-equipped in terms of education to play this role but are also isolated from their congregations. They arrive just before the start of the prayer (*iqāmah*) and leave shortly after the end (*salām*). They do not generally interact with the congregation and, even if they did, they would not be able to enhance its moral awareness because in many cases, their own vision of Islam is also extremely limited. Indeed it is often confined merely to the performance of prayers and the observance of certain rules of outward appearance. The imāms' weak economic condition along with their low social status also stand in the way of their being able to play an effective role in social change. The prevailing condition cannot, however, be improved without streamlining *madrasah* education to teach the students the skills in demand along with a revised syllabus in religious education to enable them to analyze issues scientifically, to avoid extremism and stereotypes, and to appreciate more clearly the importance of justice and good character (*khuluq ḥasan*) in the Islamic value system.

While schools, colleges and institutions of higher learning need to complement the role of the family, the mosque and the *madrasah* in moral upbringing, their primary role needs to be to provide high quality education, particularly in science and technology, and the needed skills to enable students to have better prospects in the employment market whereby they can help accelerate their country's development. The quality of education at all these institutions needs to be greatly improved by a change in their syllabi and the allocation of a substantial part of government resources. Investment in education to raise its quality will be more productive in the long run than that on most other heads of spending, including military hardware. Kennedy, a Yale University professor, has rightly reached the conclusion that nations which stretch themselves militarily beyond what their economies will sustain are looking for a fall.[18]

Political reform

Reform and the socio-economic uplift of human beings would, however, be relatively less difficult if the political system were also supportive. Political reform, along with freedom of expression, an honest judiciary, and accountability of the power elite would help at least reduce, if not eliminate, the now prevalent corruption and mismanagement. This would, in turn, enable the efficient use of public resources for education, health, and rural as well as urban development, leading thereby to socio-economic uplift. It would also help introduce land reforms, thereby not only enabling the peasants to get a just share of their existing output but also providing them with the resources they need to acquire training, along with better seeds, tools and fertilizers, to raise their future output. The Muslim world would then be able to generate the kind of agricultural surplus needed for investment in technological, industrial and infrastructure development – the surplus that the Muslim world was able to generate in the earlier centuries and which Japan, South Korea and Taiwan were able to generate in recent history. Incidentally, the land reforms introduced into these latter countries by occupation authorities helped destroy the power base of feudal lords.[19]

How to bring about political reform

The crucial question, however, is how to bring about political reform in countries where political illegitimacy is well-entrenched, and where governments use all forms of repression to curb any struggle for political reform. Armed struggle has, nevertheless, to be ruled out. It has, rarely succeeded in Muslim countries in the past, and is even less likely to succeed now when governments have more sophisticated means of suppressing it and of torturing and impoverishing those involved. Any effort to overthrow prevailing governments by resort to force and violence could lead to enormous losses in terms of both life and property. It may also destabilize the societies, accentuate inequities, slow down development and reform, and exacerbate existing problems. The suffering of the poor and the underprivileged could also be unbearably high. According to the Prophet (pbuh), it is not becoming of a Muslim to put himself into a tribulation which he does not have the strength to bear.[20]

The best strategy for political reform is, therefore, peaceful and non-violent struggle, even though this may appear to be time-consuming. The Qur'ān has clearly expressed its preference in favour of dialogue for resolving conflict by emphasizing: "Call towards the way of your Lord with wisdom, friendly admonition, and convincing argument" (16:125). The Prophet (pbuh) also emphasized peaceful struggle by saying: "Whoever is deprived of gentleness is deprived of goodness", and "God is gentle and likes gentleness; He rewards for gentleness what He does not reward for harshness or anything else".[21] The teachings of the Qur'ān, the Prophet's (pbuh) example, and the lessons of history are all clearly against any resort to force or violence in the revival of Islam. It is difficult to understand how it is possible for a person to call himself a Muslim and yet kill and maim innocent people in clear violation of Islamic teachings. This cannot be considered a "blessing", which the Qur'ān wants the Muslims to be.

Can peaceful struggle be successful?

This brings to mind a number of questions. One of these is: is there any hope for success through peaceful struggle? Thankfully, a number of factors inspire one's confidence in the future. The international environment is now unfriendly towards illegitimate governments and these have been gradually falling.[22] The international environment is also against corruption and money laundering, making it difficult to hide ill-gained wealth. Moreover, domestic pressures for the introduction of democracy are also gaining momentum in practically all Muslim countries. The spread of education and the gradual improvement in the economic condition of the poor will also help weaken existing power structures that thrive on the illiteracy and poverty of the masses.

The establishment of democratic governments, even if feudal lords initially dominate them, should weaken the power structures over time because of the voting power of the electorate. The pressures on elected governments to fulfill their promises, may also help reduce corruption and military spending,[23] divert more resources to education, health and development, and also make possible the introduction of land reforms. The resulting improvement in the socio-economic condition of the rural poor, which is already taking place to some extent as a result of the remittances of expatriate labour, will then give rise to a broader and healthier middle class willing and able to fight for its rights democratically.

Globalization is also acting as a check on despotic governments. The absence of freedom of expression domestically has become substantially offset by criticism in the international news media. The spread of news through radio and satellite television, fax machines, and the worldwide Web has frustrated the efforts of repressive governments to censor external criticism and to prevent its circulation among people inside the repressed country. Therefore, even if governments are not accountable domestically, they have become accountable internationally for their corruption and human rights violations. Though this is not sufficient, it will exercise a healthy influence on the future course of events.

Difficulties that lie ahead

Making democracy successful in these countries may not, however, be an easy task. This is because of the die-hard autocratic attitude of the present ruling elites, who will perhaps continue to use all means at their disposal to win elections. Their attitudes may not change easily and they may try to use a number of contrivances to avoid true accountability. There may not, therefore, be a significant difference between the behaviour of dictators and elected rulers in the initial phase. The real difference will, however, come gradually with the success of the struggle to see democracy buttressed by the international monitoring of elections and a free press as well as a number of badly needed legal, political and judicial reforms. One of the most important of these reforms will have to be a restructuring of the election process, to remove, or at least minimize, the influence of money, power, and manipulation in the choice of political leadership. Excessive campaign spending works in favour of the wealthy and the powerful and against worthy middle class candidates. It also invites corruption by the post-election effort of successful candidates to recover the amount spent or to provide benefits to financiers. Such reform may, however, meet with great resistance and take time to be put in place successfully. Incompetent and corrupt political authority accentuates injustice, impoverishes the people, and retards development.

Historically inherited land holding and land tenure systems are also a great hindrance to democracy by being among the primary causes of inequities and underdevelopment and of several economic, social and political problems. Exploitation of the peasants renders them incapable of even feeding themselves and their families, leave alone the generation of a surplus needed for investment in improved seeds, fertilizers and tools, and the establishment of micro industries in rural as well as urban areas to increase output and income. Such exploitation tends to weaken their moral fibre and induces them to lie and cheat. It hurts their pride and their incentive to work. Their low productivity and output further reduces their ability to save and invest. It also deprives them of the education and training they need to raise their productivity and economic condition. Peasants, who constitute a preponderant majority of the population, are unable to vote freely to choose political representatives of their own choice. Feudal lords are also able to influence the armed forces and the government bureaucracy as well as the judiciary and the police through their sons and relatives, who occupy important positions in these institutions, and the use of their power and resources to suppress all opposition. The entire government machinery, thus, becomes their handmaid serving their vested interest. The deprivation of the peasantry does not lead to higher savings on the part of feudal lords, who either fritter away their income on luxury and conspicuous consumption or invest it abroad. This forces the country to resort to large doses of external borrowing which has raised the debt-servicing burden and reduced resources available for development.

Can the Western world help?

The Western world can certainly play a catalytic role in the restoration of democracy and the promotion of socio-economic uplift in Muslim countries. This is also in its own long-run interest. Greater political accountability would lead to the more effective use of all available resources for better education and increased opportunities for employment and self-employment. This, in turn, would help promote socio-economic uplift, remove the difficulties and inequities that people face, and mitigate the turmoil and unrest in the Muslim world.[24] It would also widen the market for mutual exports. More trade would lead to greater interdependence and better understanding and frustrate the efforts of all those who have a vested interest in promoting conflict.

The West cannot, however, help restore democracy or reduce militancy by the use of force. Force has never worked and will never work. The use of force by the United States and its allies in Afghanistan and Iraq and by Israel in Palestine and Lebanon with the help of the United States has led to the unwarranted killing of more than 100,000 innocent people and the destruction of precious infrastructure, industries, farms, schools and hospitals.[25] Instead of removing poverty and enhancing socio-economic uplift and justice, which are the need of the hour in these countries, these attacks have done the reverse. This will only serve to intensify the dislike for the West, accentuate militancy, and lead to a clash of civilizations. This will be bad for all, but in particular for the Muslim world because it will slow down not only its development but also the pace of badly needed socio-economic and political reform.

The West needs to realize that the Muslim world, with a population estimated to be between 1.3 to 1.8 billion, is not a homogeneous whole. While fundamental beliefs are common among all Muslims, there is a great deal of diversity of languages, cultures and behavioural patterns. In spite of this diversity, the mainstream Muslim population has always been, and continues to be, moderate, peace loving, cooperative and easy to get along with.[26] Lewis has frankly admitted this by stating: "There is something in the religious culture of Islam which inspired in even the humblest peasant or peddler a dignity and a courtesy toward others never excelled and rarely equalled in other civilizations."[27]

There are, of course, extremists and militants in Muslim society just as they are in every other society around the world. It is not right to exaggerate the existence of extremists in Muslim society because they constitute a very small proportion of the total and the militants among the extremists constitute an even smaller proportion. Muslims in general abhor what the militants are doing because of its being in clear violation of Islamic teachings. The Qur'ān equates the killing of even one innocent person with the killing of the whole of mankind (5:32). It also condemns *fasād* (2:11, 27; 7:56, 85; 13:25 and 26:152) which refers to all varieties of crime, including the unwarranted destruction of life and property, non-fulfilment of socio-economic and political obligations, and everything that creates disorder, fear, insecurity and misery.[28] Therefore, to equate Islam or Muslims with 'terrorism' or 'fascism' is highly unjust, offensive and infuriating. It is only going to increase ill will and accentuate tension.

The West also needs to bear in mind that all people around the world love their own religion, values and culture, and will not accept any monolithic concept of globalization, irrespective of whether they are in China, Japan, India or the Muslim world. The Muslim world is, thus, not unique in this respect. Any effort to impose on them an unacceptable alien culture is bound to meet with resistance. It also needs to be borne in mind that modernization or globalization are not necessarily equivalent to 'Westernization'. There is no doubt that the adoption of modern technology is indispensable for development. Technology is, however, the cumulative result of contributions made by several civilizations, including the Chinese, Indian, Byzantine, Sassannian and Islamic. If technology is not Western, then what else is implied by Westernization? Is it values? Yet every country has the right to stick to its own values. This should be welcomed because it adds diversity and richness to the social and cultural panorama of the world. This does not, of course, mean that what is good in other cultures should not be willingly adopted. However, history bears witness to the fact that Muslims have always done this.

There is no doubt that Muslims, like all other people, have their own weaknesses. These have nothing to do with Islam and must be removed. This can, however, be done only gradually through proper upbringing, education, socio-economic uplift and political reform. Bringing about social change is one of the most difficult and time-consuming tasks and most of the literature on social change suggests that change can only be brought about gradually. This demands a great deal of patience. Governments as well as educational institutions and social reform movements need to coordinate their efforts if they wish to succeed.

The West also needs to realize that there is already a great deal of misunderstanding about it in the Muslim world because of the crusades and the vicious attacks on Islam and the Prophet (pbuh).[29] It was to be expected that these attacks, which occurred over the last several centuries, would decline in the age of globalization. This has, unfortunately, not happened. The attacks have not only increased but have rather become more vicious. This has intensified tension and exacerbated the prevailing misunderstanding. What the West needs to do is to change its strategy by adopting three badly needed measures. One of these is to refrain from attacks on Islam by emphasizing the common beliefs and values of Christianity and Islam. The second is to provide the assistance that the Muslim countries badly need to expedite socio-economic uplift. The third is to promote political reform.

Fortunately, this is already happening to a certain extent. There are a number of scholars who have been emphasizing the common beliefs and values of both Christianity and Islam. According to Richard Bulliet, these two faiths are siblings without essential differences so much so that there is a strong case for an "Islamo-Christian civilization".[30] According to Lewis there is even a significant majority of Muslims "with whom we share certain basic cultural and moral, social and political, beliefs and aspirations".[31] He even goes on to say: "Islam has brought comfort and peace of mind to countless millions of men and women. It has given dignity and meaning to drab and impoverished lives. It has taught people of different races to live in brotherhood and people of different creeds to live side by side in reasonable tolerance. It inspired a great civilization in which others besides Muslims lived creative and useful lives and which, by its achievement, enriched the whole world."[32] If there is such a great deal that is common between the two faiths and such a great deal that they can offer to each other, then why not emphasize the need for peaceful coexistence instead of a clash of civilizations.

Humanitarian help has also been forthcoming and this is helping the cause of socio-economic uplift. Moreover, a large number of Muslims are studying and working in Western countries. The remittances of expatriate workers has helped promote socio-economic uplift. This can be further reinforced by increased help in the elimination of poverty and unemployment. If the US had diverted the billions of dollars it spent on the destruction of Afghanistan and Iraq to the development of these countries it would have achieved what it aspired for. The West can also help in political reform by monitoring elections and promoting legal and institutional reform.

Such help will create a better climate not only for accelerated reform and development but also for mutual cooperation and peaceful coexistence.

Can Islam play a catalytic role once again?

A crucial question which arises here is whether the revival of Islam that is now taking place in the Muslim world can be of any help in reforming and developing Muslim societies. Can it help them realize justice and the needed socio-economic and political reform as it did in the classical period? Can it also help them face the challenges that they are confronted with in the modern world? The general consensus in the Muslim world seems to be in favour of a positive answer. This was also acknowledged by Ramsey Clark, US Attorney General in the Lyndon Johnson Administration, when he stated that Islam: "is probably the most compelling spiritual and moral force on earth today".[33]

This may perhaps be because Islam is the only living reality in the Muslim world that has the charisma to attract the masses, unite them in spite of their great diversity, and motivate them to act righteously in spite of centuries of degeneration. It has its own programme for comprehensive moral, social, economic and political reform which is more suitable for these countries than any programme that may be imported from abroad. Its strong emphasis on moral values and character building, socio-economic justice, accountability of the political authority and rule of law, combined with its strategy of using education and dialogue for bringing about change, should prove to be a great blessing for the Muslim world. It encourages simple living, which helps reduce conspicuous consumption and thereby weakens one of the major causes of corruption and low savings and investment. It can also help inculcate in people a number of other desirable qualities like honesty and integrity, punctuality, conscientiousness, diligence, frugality, self-reliance, tolerance, fulfillment of contracts and all socio-economic obligations, and concern for the rights and well-being of others – qualities which are necessary to promote development as well as justice. It places a strong emphasis on family and social solidarity, which are essential for even the survival of a society, leave alone its development. It is also flexible enough to enable adjustment to changing circumstances.

Since Islamic revival has become a deeply-rooted phenomenon in the Muslim world, any effort to undo Islam and transplant secularism in its place would necessitate the use of force. This would have tragic results in the Muslim world as it did in the past when al-Ma'mūn and two of his successors tried to force upon people certain elements of *Mu'tazilism* which were considered by the *'ulamā'* to be against the Sharī'ah. This use of force created, as we saw in Chapter 5, a chain reaction which has plagued Muslim societies to the present day. In the same way, the use of force would accentuate social conflict and instigate violence even in modern times. Once this takes place, it may be difficult to bring under control. What is even worse is that the place of Islam may be taken by the prevailing materialist and hedonist philosophy, which would promote conspicuous consumption, sexual promiscuity, and self-gratification. This would further weaken the moral fibre, encourage living beyond means, exacerbate corruption, reduce savings and investment, worsen imbalances, aggravate inequities, and weaken family and social solidarity. The consequences of this for development and socio-economic uplift should not be difficult for anyone to figure out.[34]

The first ruthless effort in modern times to undo Islam by a Muslim government in a predominantly Muslim country took place in Turkey. This led, as indicated earlier, to an excessive role in the government for the military which exercized real authority in spite of an outward façade of democracy. It arbitrarily removed duly elected governments four times over the last 40 years, in 1960, 1971, 1981 and 1997. In spite of the ruthless use of force by the army to undo

Islam, it did not succeed and Islam is now enjoying a revival even in Turkey: "If ever there was a Kemalist wish for Islam to wither away, it has not done so and is unlikely to do so in the future when human rights are expected to flourish rather than diminish."[35]

The lack of accountability and the misuse of public resources, both of which were the cause of Turkey's underdevelopment, continued uninterruptedly. Turkey, a developing country, has maintained the biggest army of any NATO power except the US, leading to a very high rate of growth of 7.0 percent in defence spending over the five years from 2002 to 2006 as compared with 2.5 and 2.9 percent for the UK and the US over the same period. As a percent of GDP (3.4 percent), its defence spending is also higher than that of any other NATO country except the US (3.8 percent).[36] The country has, thus, experienced excessively large budgetary deficits, more than what prevailed in the past during the days of the corrupt sultans. These were financed by borrowing as well as monetary expansion. The deficits were, however, not utilized productively as a result of corruption, excessive military spending, and mismanagement. The budget's largest item was interest payments, which soaked up 79 percent of the central government's tax revenue in 2001.[37] As is to be expected, budgetary deficits were reflected in one of the highest rates of inflation around the world – 32.1 percent per annum during 1961-2000, as compared with 6.2 percent in the OECD, 8.2 percent in East Asia and 26.0 percent in Latin America.[38] There was, thus, a steep decline in the rate of exchange, which depreciated from 3 and 9 liras per US Dollar in 1950 and 1960 to 2,234,642 in December 2002.[39] So in what way was government by the 'secularist' generals different from that by the corrupt sultans? The military's effort to get rid of Islam in the name of secularism, in effect, brought about nothing but greater political corruption, inflation and social conflict. A *New York Times* editorial rightly stated: "The secular parties favoured by the military have failed to establish deep popular roots. They are increasingly perceived as aloof from the problems of ordinary Turks and consumed by personal vendettas and corruption."[40]

Secularism has led some other Muslim countries to even worse conditions. While in Turkey, the basic democratic and judicial framework remained in place, in some other countries the rulers have been more ruthless and unscrupulous than any that one can imagine. There is hardly any freedom of expression and there are greater inequities and human rights violations. Some of these countries had great potential for development, but have declined precipitously and the condition of the people has worsened to a distressing extent.

Reform in the understanding of Islam

The fact that Islam has not been a cause of Muslim decline does not necessarily mean that there is no need for reform in the present-day understanding of Islam. The Islamic emphasis on justice, the brotherhood of mankind, and tolerance seems to have become substantially diluted in certain sectors of Muslim societies as is its emphasis on character building. This may perhaps be due largely to historical factors arising from centuries of political illegitimacy, lack of educational facilities, socio-economic decline, and inequities, followed by long foreign occupation. It may not even be possible to correct the situation without creating a proper understanding of Islam. This would demand a substantial change in the curricula of all educational institutions and, in particular those of the *madrasahs*. The revised curricula should place greater emphasis on the *maqāṣid* (objectives of) *al-Sharī'ah* and *khuluq ḥasan* (nobleness of character).

Even though the *maqāṣid* constitute the ethos of Islamic teachings, they have been pushed into the background over the last few centuries. They need, therefore, to be brought back into the forefront to set the stage for a better understanding of the Qur'ān and the Sunnah. This will help release *Fiqh* (Islamic jurisprudence) from the shackles of blind following (*taqlīd*) of past verdicts given in entirely different circumstances, and enable it to regain the dynamism that it reflected in the earlier centuries of Islam. Without this it may not be able to successfully meet the challenges that the Muslim world faces in modern times when circumstances are entirely different from those confronting classical jurists. This will also help restore the real lustre of Islamic teachings by helping reduce the prevailing differences of opinion as well as the conflicts, fanaticism, intolerance and undue emphasis on appearances which have arisen largely as a result of neglect of the *maqāṣid* in the interpretation of texts. Imām al-Ḥaramayn, Abū'l-Ma'ālī al-Juwaynī (d. 478/1085) rightly emphasized: "Whoever does not comprehend the role of the *maqāṣid* in the do's and dont's of the Sharī'ah lacks insight into its implementation."[41]

The decline in the emphasis on *maqāṣid* has led to an increasing use of *ḥiyal* (legal stratagems) in the interpretation of texts in spite of opposition from a number of prominent *'ulamā'*.[42] While the use of *ḥiyal* is allowed to reduce hardship in strained circumstances in keeping with the objectives of the Sharī'ah, excessive resort to them tends to have the unintended effect of frustrating the realization of the *maqāṣid.* Shaykh Muḥammad al-Ṭāhir ibn 'Āshūr, a prominent jurist, deplores this fact, saying: "Most of the issues in *uṣūl al-fiqh* (principles of Islamic jurisprudence) have become confined to the derivation of verdicts from the words of the Law-Giver rather than being used to serve the purpose or objectives of the Sharī'ah."[43] The unhealthy result of this excessive reliance on *ḥiyal* is that "many of the religious sciences (*al-'Ulūm al-Dīniyyah*), including *uṣūl al-fiqh*, have lost the true spirit from which they benefited in the earlier periods. The revival of this spirit is the most crucial imperative for the renaissance of religious knowledge".[44]

This emphasis on the *maqāṣid* needs to be accompanied by greater significance given to character building, in keeping with the Prophet's (pbuh) saying that "the most perfect of Muslims is he who is best in character".[45] This should help inculcate in Muslims the good traits of character that are emphasized by Islam but which have generally become weakened in present-day Muslim societies. It is also necessary to bring into focus once again a number of the Prophet's (pbuh) sayings, two of which are: "Mankind is the family of God and the most beloved of them before Him is one who is most beneficial to His family", and "Do not say like a characterless person (*imma'ah*) that 'if people are good to us we will be good to them and if they are bad to us we will be bad to them'; instead, get yourself accustomed to being good to them when they are good to you but not to ill-treat them when they are bad to you."[46] This will help change the attitude towards non-Muslims, who are also the *khalīfahs* of God just like Muslims and need to be treated fairly and well (Qur'ān, 60:8). It will also set the stage for greater tolerance and cordial relations with them. The reform of Muslim character in the light of these and other teachings of the Qur'ān and the *Sunnah* will enable Muslims to once again fulfill the Prophet's mission of being a "blessing for mankind".

This reform in the understanding of Islam can take place through a friendly dialogue between the moderate rationalists and moderate conservatives, both of whom recognize the role of Revelation as well as reason in human life. However, if governments try to impose secularism by the use of force, the consequence cannot but be a stiffening of attitudes. This will hurt the progress of the dialogue and slow down the needed reform. The role of governments should only be to create a conciliatory environment for the dialogue. This will help create a rapport between the government and the *'ulamā'* as well as the people. The result may also be a decline in resistance to change. This may not only make it easier to introduce changes in *fiqhī* verdicts, but also help create a more conducive atmosphere for development.

The role of Islamic movements

Islamic movements would be more successful if they tried to endear themselves not only to the people in their own societies but also to the world at large by being a blessing and not a menace. This they can do only by being worthy representatives of Islam, setting a good moral example, adopting a moderate posture free from fanaticism and intolerance, and avoiding internal as well as external conflict and confrontation as much as possible. They need to bear in mind that Islamization and the development of their societies after centuries of decline is a difficult task. It can only come gradually through a great deal of hard work coupled with wisdom and patience. Since the human and material resources at their disposal are extremely limited, they cannot afford to overstretch themselves.[47] It is necessary for them to establish priorities if they wish to succeed in Islamizing and developing their societies and realizing the *maqāṣid.*

Their first and foremost priority needs be to educate people about the high moral standards that Islam expects from its followers. This is the stepping-stone for the Islamization of their societies. Without this, the light that they wish to project to their societies will not have the lustre that is needed. The Islamic state they wish to establish is not possible without the minimum level of moral uplift that Islam envisages. This brings into focus the question of when will they be able to bring about moral uplift to such a vast population? This may not be immediately necessary. If they can succeed in changing the character of a sufficient minority, the rest will tend to follow. The Qur'ān states: "How often has a small group overcome, by the will of God, a large one", (2:249). Toynbee has also asserted that: "All growth originates with creative individuals or small minorities of individuals, and their task is … the conversion of the society to this new way of life."[48] Once the creative minority has shown its worth, the rest of the people will find it worthwhile to follow them. The immediate task of the

Islamic movements is, therefore, to establish their worthiness, and to gain respect and regard for themselves among not only their own masses but also around the world.

Their second, but equally important priority, should be socio-economic uplift by removing illiteracy and poverty, making high quality education available to the poor, increasing the availability of microfinance as well as employment and self-employment opportunities, and helping solve as much as possible the problems of all people irrespective of whether they are Muslims or not. They cannot accomplish all this on their own. They can, however, put pressure on the government and try to mobilize private sector resources as best they can for this purpose. This will help everyone realize that the revival of Islam will bring an improvement in the lives of all and be a source of blessing for them. It will, thus, help promote the peaceful coexistence of all people in society. It is only social service-oriented programmes of this type, and not just slogans, that help minimize crime and conflict and instill in the minds of people the central message of Islam about human brotherhood, justice and the well-being of all.

Their third priority should be to struggle for political reform, freedom of expression, and human rights. For this purpose, it is not necessary to take part in elections directly. They may do so if they wish. However, they need to bear in mind that this will unnecessarily bring them into conflict and confrontation with the government as well as other parties and make them ineffective in realizing their objectives. Since it may be a long time before they can themselves come into power in many countries, it may be better for them to be on friendly terms with all parties and seek their help in achieving whatever political and judicial reforms and socio-economic uplift that they can without themselves being in power. Without creating such a friendly atmosphere, they may not be able to get the cooperation for reform that they need, and will continue to need, even when they themselves come into power. Corrupt civilian and military bureaucracies and powerful rural and urban vested interests will not enable them to succeed without the help of all well-meaning groups. By the use of wisdom and a friendly attitude, they may be able to attain a great deal even from their die-hard opponents as the Prophet (pbuh) said: "God will help this religion even by an unrighteous person (*al-rajul al-fājir*)."[49]

The fourth priority should be to try to create a better understanding among different groups of Muslims and also to build consensus about various educational, social, economic and political reforms through dialogue by following the Qur'ānic advice of first calling towards commonly agreed principles (Qur'ān, 3:64). This necessitates the establishment of a think tank with qualified and well-meaning representatives from different socio-economic, political and religious groupings. A programme prepared by such a group would enable them to mobilize the support of a larger mass of people.

Their fifth, but not the least important, priority should be to build cordial relations with other countries and societies. They need to realize that non-Muslims represent close to four-fifths of the world's population and, just like Muslims, do not constitute a homogenous whole. While some of them are definitely anti-Islam, not all of them are necessarily so. It is our own behaviour towards them which determines their attitude towards us. The more we resort to confrontation and militancy, the more hostile they will become towards us. Therefore, even if there have been unjust attacks on Islam and Muslims by the West, the Qur'ānic advice to them is: "Good and evil are not equal. Respond to evil with what is best. This will help turn your enemy into your intimate friend" (41:34). The Qur'ān also says: "You will certainly be tested [with losses] in your possessions and lives and hear much that will hurt you from those who received the Book before you and from those who associate partners unto God. But if you have patience and abstain from doing what is wrong, then that is a more dignified behaviour" (3:186). Murad Hofmann has rightly emphasized that:

"I know of nothing better to propose than to urge the Muslim world to become 'fundamentalist' in the original sense of the word – to go back to the real foundations of our Islamic creed, and to analyze the factors which were instrumental for the Madīna, Andalus and 'Abbāsid experiments."[50]

Prospects for the future

Prospects for the future seem to be bright because the reversal of the tide desired by Ibn Khaldūn 600 years ago seems to be taking place now. This is clear from a number of crucial indicators, one of which is a decline in political illegitimacy. The authoritarian role of the generals in Turkish politics has now become weakened as a result of the country's commitment to join the European Union and the electoral victory of the Islamically-oriented Justice and Development Party which has, according to the *Economist*, "enacted a swathe of reforms", brought about a "silent revolution" in Turkey's politics and economics, and has, thus, been able to increase its support base.[51] It has provided a relatively clean and effective government which, along with its fiscal prudence, has generated primary (pre-interest) budget surplus. This has not only helped shrink the debt burden but also brought down steeply the rate of inflation to single digit levels for the first time in 30 years. This has enabled Turkey to issue a new lira, dropping six zeros from the old one. Turkey's GDP grew at the healthy average rate of more than 8 percent per annum over the years 2004 and 2005. All this has encouraged the IMF to say that "the fortunes of the Turkish economy have been transformed".[52]

Dictators in a number of countries have seen their downfall and more are expected to see the same fate. Moreover, nearly all Muslim countries have become independent from foreign domination and are now free to adopt policies that are in their own interests. There is also an acute awareness among the public that they need good governance to alleviate a number of difficulties. This has made them realize the need for political accountability. It is hoped that the future will see rapid progress towards real democracy in all Muslim countries irrespective of whether they have dictatorship or pseudo-democracy.

Political illegitimacy is, thus, losing ground in the Muslim world. Even the major industrial countries, with whose moral and material support it has thrived, seem to have now realized that the spread of democracy is also in their own long-run interest. The writing on the horizon clearly indicates a movement in the direction of democracy, along with land reforms, a free press, a strong and independent judiciary, and the growth of effective and impartial institutions for detecting and punishing corruption and inefficiency.

The spread of democracy should be helpful in a number of ways. First, it should help promote moderation in the political stand of secular as well as religious parties. They will have to appeal to all sectors of the population if they do not wish to be disappointed at the polls. Since the masses have a strong sentimental attachment to Islam, efforts by the secularists to create a dichotomy between the sacred and the secular, of the kind that took place in the West, will be frustrated. Extreme orthodoxy may also likewise fail because it does not fit into the pluralist framework of modern democratic societies. Secondly, it should help realize the Islamic imperative of socio-economic justice and the well-being of all as a result of the political pressure on all parties to remove poverty and misery and to include a range of socio-economic, judicial, and political reforms in their manifestos. Thirdly, it should enable women to assert their rights more successfully. This will enable them to obtain better education, which will, in turn, help them provide a proper upbringing for their children and thereby, remove one of the major causes of Muslim decline and contribute richly to the development of their societies. Fourthly, it should lead to not only greater integrity in the use of government resources, but also the establishment of priorities and the employment of more realistic strategies. This will ultimately promote the use of public resources for the development and well-being of the people through the elimination of illiteracy, the provision of better quality education, the improvement of health facilities, the construction of infrastructure beyond showpiece highways and buildings, and the accelerated but balanced and just development of these countries.

Consequently, corrupt secularist bureaucracies as well as extreme orthodoxies should lose ground. The former, because of their association with an ideology not acceptable to the people, in addition to their corruption, inertia, and loyalty to internal or external vested interests; and the latter because of their lack of a proper understanding of Islam as well as the complexities of modern economies, their suspicion of everything foreign, and their refusal to borrow from successful strategies employed elsewhere. This should lead to the development of a strategy that is tailored to the promotion of development with justice.

Democracy will, thus, force secular as well as religious parties to moderate their views to make themselves acceptable to broader sectors of the population, thus increasing tolerance and reducing extremist views. Moreover, the ongoing revival of Islam should make it possible to have material advance accompanied by moral uplift, justice and social harmony which are important for providing the needed moral and ethical capital for sustained development. This will become further buttressed if the *'ulamā'* as well as the political elite realize the role of *maqāṣid* in the interpretation of texts. The continually rising number of books and papers on the *maqāṣid* indicates that this has started taking place. Once this gains momentum, it will help bring about the needed change in the understanding of Islam. The real character of a Muslim has also started receiving greater focus in the writings and sermons of a number of scholars.

In other words, a number of indicators point toward the reversal of Ibn Khaldūn's cycle of circular causation from the negative to the positive direction. It is appropriate, therefore, to end this chapter with the following verse of the Qur'ān:

> *So lose not heart,*
> *Nor fall into despair,*
> *For you are bound to rise,*
> *If you are true in faith* (3:139).

Notes

1. The Qur'ān does not make any mention of the Messengers sent by God to people other than those in the Middle East. Their names were not familiar to the people there and the Qur'ān is not intended to be an encyclopaedia. It, however, states clearly that: "And indeed We have sent Our Messengers to every community in every period" (16:36). "And We sent Messengers before you; some of them We have mentioned to you, while some others We have not mentioned" (40:78). According to a weak *ḥadīth* of the Prophet (pbuh), there has been a total of around 124,000 Messengers who were sent to different countries around the world at different times in history (cited by Mawdūdī, 1962, in his commentary of verse 51 of *Sūrah* 19, Volume 3, p. 72).
2. The emphasis in economics on the serving of self-interest could not become a practical reality in the West. Rather, it served primarily as an analytical tool. Christian values continued to influence the general behaviour of people even though their influence seems to have gradually declined.
3. Alfred Kroeber, 1994, pp. 803-4.
4. Schweitzer, 1949, p. xii; see also Toynbee, Somervell's abridgement, Volume 2, p. 364.
5. Schweitzer, ibid., pp. 22-23, 38, 39, 91.
6. Toynbee, abridgement by Somervell, 1957, Volume 2, p. 99. In fact Toynbee goes to the extent of saying that "a crushing victory of science over religion would be disastrous for both parties; for reason as well as religion is one of the essential faculties of human nature," ibid., p. 99.
7. Lawson, 1995, p. 35.
8. Friedman, 2005.
9. Gruber, 2005, p. 1. See also Ellison, 1991; Barrow and McCleary, 2003 and Iannaccone, 1998.
10. Al-Māwardī, *Adab*, 1955, p. 125.
11. Cited by al-Suyūṭī in his *al-Jāmiʿ al-Ṣaghīr* from Anas ibn Mālik on the authority of Abū Nuʿaym's *al-Ḥilyah,* under the word *kāda,* p. 89.

12. Rodrik, 2006, p. 974.
13. World Bank, 2005, p. xiii.
14. See Chapra, 1993 and 2000.
15. Ahmad, 2007, see the whole book, which is short, but in particular pp. xvii-xix and 32.
16. For some details, see Chapra, 2007, pp. 336-338.
17. For a valuable discussion about the need for moral upbringing and the crucial role of the family in this, see Abū Sulaymān, 1991 and 2005.
18. Kennedy, 1987, see, in particular, pp. 536-40. See also Toynbee, Somervell's abridgement, Volume 2, p. 370.
19. See Chapra, 1993, pp. 175-77.
20. The full text of the *ḥadīth* is: "It is not rightful for a Muslim to degrade himself". When asked about how he could degrade himself, the Prophet (pbuh) replied: "He undertakes to burden himself with a tribulation which he cannot bear." (Narrated from al-Ḥudhayfah by al-Tirmidhī as *ḥadīth Ṣaḥīḥ* in his *Jāmi*ʿ: *Kitāb al-Fitan*.)
21. Reported from Jābir ibn ʿAbdullāh and ʿĀ'ishah respectively, by Muslim in his *Ṣaḥīḥ*, Volume 4, p. 2004:2592 and 2593, *Kitāb al-Birr wa al-Ṣilah wa al-Adab: Bāb Faḍl al-Rifq*.
22. In 1974, only 39 countries worldwide – one in every four – were democratic. Today 115 countries – a little more than two in three – use open elections to choose their national leadership. (The figure for 1974 is from World Bank, *World Development Report*, 1997, p. 111, while the latest data are as of 14 January 2004 from Electionworld.org.)
23. Global military spending had fallen significantly from $1.2 trillion in 1985 to $809 billion in 1998. However, it rose to $950 billion in 2003. This is unfortunate but is supposed to be primarily due to the US attack on Iraq and the huge budgetary deficits this caused. (World Military Spending, 16 June 2004. (www.globalissues.org/geopolitics/armstrade/spending.asp#world military spending.)
24. Education will help reduce turmoil only if it inculcates in students the noble characteristics of character and provides them with those skills in demand to enable them to earn an income which is adequate to fulfill their needs. (See Krueger and Maleckova, 2003.)
25. The number of people killed by the US and its allies is far more than that by the Mongols, who are considered to have been extremely ruthless. The figure of those killed by the Mongols when they sacked Baghdād and the surrounding areas in 656/1258 ranges from 200,000-800,000. (See Morgan, 1993, p. 231.)
26. See also Esposito, 1992.
27. Lewis, 1990, Part II, p. 8.
28. See the Qur'ānic verses under the root *fasada* in the index of the Qur'ān by Muḥammad Fu'ād ʿAbd al-Bāqī. See also Abū Sulaymān, 1993, pp. 139-141.
29. For a very good analysis of tensions between Islam and the West, see Esposito, 1992, particularly Chapter 2.

30. See Bulliet, 2004.
31. Lewis, September 1990, Part I, p. 2.
32. Ibid.
33. Clark, 1997.
34. See also Richards, 2003 and Etzioni, 2004.
35. Mehmet, 1990, p. 125. Even in pre-revolution Iran, efforts by the shah to Westernize the country and traditional values created a great deal of resentment against him and served as one of the major causes of the revolution. (Algar, 1972; Graham, 1979 and Arani, 1980.)
36. See the Defence Expenditures of NRC Countries (1985-2006), Tables 2, 3 and 6 (www.nato.int/docu/pr/2006/p06-159e.htm).
37. IMF Occasional Paper No. 242, 2005, Table 5.1, p. 34.
38. Ibid., Table 2.3, p. 7.
39. IMF, *International Financial Statistics*, CD-ROM, and Yearbook 2004, p. 4.
40. Reproduced by the *International Herald Tribune*, 26 March 1996, p. 6, from the editorial entitled 'Civilian Rule for Turkey' in the *New York Times*.
41. Al-Juwaynī, *al-Ghiyāthī*, 1400, Volume 1, p. 295.
42. See Ibn Taymiyyah, *Bayān al-Dalīl*, (1425/2004), p. 137.
43. Muḥammad al-Ṭāhir ibn 'Āshūr, *Maqāṣid al-Sharī'ah al-Islāmiyyah*, 2nd ed., 2001, p. 166.
44. Abū al-Faḍl, 'Abd al-Salām (1425/2004), pp. 576-7.
45. Narrated from Abū Hurayrah by al-Bayhaqī in his *Shu'ab al-Īmān*, 1990, Volume 6, p. 230, No. 7976.
46. The first *ḥadīth* is narrated from Anas ibn Mālik by al-Bayhaqī in his *Shu'ab al-Īmān*, 1990, Volume 6, p. 43, No. 7446. The second is narrated from Ḥudhayfah by al-Mundhirī (Volume 3, p. 341:23) on the authority of al-Tirmidhī.
47. According to Muḥsin 'Abd al-Ḥamīd, Islamic movements try to accomplish several times more than what their resources permit. This is one of the reasons for their failures and reversals (*tarāju'*) and for putting themselves into the jaws of their enemies ('Abd al-Ḥamīd, 1996, pp. 198-9).
48. Toynbee, abridgement by Somervell, 1957, Volume 2, p. 364.
49. Reported from 'Amr ibn al-Nu'mān as *ṣaḥīḥ ḥadīth* by al-Suyūṭī in his *Al-Jāmi' al-Ṣaghīr* (Volume 1, p. 72 under the word *inna*) on the authority of Ṭabarānī's *al-Kabīr*.
50. Hofmann, 1996, p. 86; see also al-'Alwānī, (1412/1991), p. 61.
51. See *The Economist*, 18 September 2004 and 22 January 2005, pp. 13 and 32 respectively.
52. For a more detailed picture of the transformation that has taken place in the Turkish economy, see IMF Occasional Paper No. 242, 2005.

REFERENCES

'Abd al-Bāqī, Muḥammad Fu'ād (1986), *al-Mu'jam al-Mufahras li Alfāẓ al-Qur'ān al-Karīm* (Istanbul: Dār al-Da'wah).

'Abd al-Ḥamīd, Muḥsin (1996), *Tajdīd al-Fikr al-Islāmī* (Herndon, VA: IIIT).

'Abdullāh, 'Alī Aḥmad, (n.d.) *Al-Shakhṣiyyah al-I'tibāriyyah fī al-Fiqh al-Islāmī* (Legal Personality in Islamic Jurisprudence). (Khartoum, Sudan: Al-Dār al-Sūdāniyyah li al-Kutub).

Abū al-Faḍl, 'Abd al-Salām (2004), *Al-Tajdīd wa'l-Mujaddidūn fī Uṣūl al-Fiqh* (Cairo: Al-Maktabah al-Islāmiyyah).

Abū Dāwūd al-Sījīstānī, Imām (d. 275/888) *Sunan Abū Dāwūd* (Cairo: 'Īsā al-Bābī al-Ḥalabī).

Abū El-Fadl, Khaled (1992), 'Tax Farming in Islamic Law (*Qabālah and Ḍamān of Kharāj*): A Search for a Concept', *Islamic Studies* (Islamabad), Spring, pp. 5-32.

Abū Fāris, M. 'Abd al-Qādir (1988), *Ḥukm al-Shūrā fī al-Islām wa Natījatuhā* (Jordan: Dār al-Furqān).

Abū Shuqqah, 'Abd al-Ḥalīm M. (1990), *Taḥrīr al-Mar'ah fī 'Aṣr al-Risālah* (Kuwait: Dār al-Qalam), 6 volumes.

Abū Sulaymān, 'AbdulḤamīd (1991), *Azmat al-'Aql al-Muslim* (Virginia, USA: International Institute of Islamic Thought).

Abū Sulaymān, 'AbdulḤamīd (1993), *Crisis in the Muslim Mind,* Yusuf Talal Delorenzo (tr.), (Virgina, USA: IIIT).

Abū Sulaymān, 'AbdulḤamīd (2005), *Azmat al-Irāḍah wa'l-Wujdān al-Muslim: al-Bu'd al-Ghā'ib fī Mashrū' Iṣlāḥ al-Ummah* (Damascus: Dār al-Fikr).

Abū 'Ubayd Qāsim ibn Sallām (d. 224/839), (1968), *Kitāb al-Amwāl,* M. Khalīl al-Ḥarrās (ed.), (Cairo: Maktabah al-Kulliyyah al-Azhariyyah).

Abū Yūsuf, Ya'qūb ibn Ibrāhīm (d. 182/798), *Kitāb al-Kharāj* (Cairo: al-Maṭba'ah al-Salafiyyah, 2nd ed., 1352 AH). This book has been translated into English by Ben Shemesh (q.v.), Volume 3, 1969.

Abū Zahrah, Muḥammad (1957), *Uṣūl al-Fiqh* (Cairo: Dār al-Fikr al-'Arabī).

Abū Zahrah, Muḥammad (n.d.), *Tārīkh al-Madhāhib al-Islāmiyyah* (Dār al-Fikr al-'Arabī)

Aghnides, Nicholas P. (1916), *Mohammedan Theories of Finance with an Introduction to Mohammedan Law and a Bibliography* (New York: Columbia University).

Ahmad, Mumtaz, (ed.) (1986), *State Politics and Islam* (Washington: American Trust Publications).

Ahmad, Qazi Kholiquzzaman (ed.) (2007), *Socio-Economic and Indebtedness-Related Impact of Micro-Credit in Bangladesh* (Dhaka: Bangladesh Unnayan Parishad).

Ahmed, Habib, (2004), *Role of Zakāh and Awqāf in Poverty Alleviation.* Occasional Paper No. 8, Islamic Research and Training Institute/Islamic Development Bank, Jeddah.

Algar, Hamid (1972), 'The Oppositional Role of the *'Ulamā'* in Twentieth-Century Iran' in Keddie (ed.), *Scholars, Saints, and Sufis* (Berkeley: University of California Press), pp. 23-55.

Allouche, Adel, (1994), *Mamluk Economics: A Study and Translation of Al-Maqrīzī's Ighāthah* (Salt Lake City: University of Utah Press).

'Alwānī, Ṭahā Jābir al- (1412/1991), *Iṣlāḥ al-Fikr al-Islāmī Bayna al-Qudrāt wa'l-'Aqabāt* (Herndon, Washington, DC: International Institute of Islamic Thought).

Ansari, Zafar Ishaq (1992), 'The Contribution of the Qur'ān and the Prophet to the Development of Islamic Fiqh', *Journal of Islamic Studies,* July.

Arani, S. (1980), 'Iran: From the Shah's Dictatorship to Khomeini's Demagogic Theocracy', *Dissent,* Winter, pp. 9-26.

Arberry, A. J. (1957), *Revelation and Reason in Islam* (London: George Allen and Unwin).

Arberry, A. J. (1964), *The Koran Interpreted* (London: Oxford University Press).

Arnaldez, R. (1971) '*Falsafa*', *The Encyclopaedia of Islam* (Leiden: Brill, new ed.), Volume 2, pp. 769-775.

Arrow, Kenneth J. (1973), 'Social Responsibility and Economic Efficiency', *Public Policy.* Volume 21, pp. 303-17.

Arrow, Kenneth J. (2000), 'Observations on Social Capital', in Dasgupta and Serageldin, pp. 3-5.

Arsalan, Amir Shakib (1962), *Our Decline and its Causes,* tr., M. A. Shakoor (Lahore: S. M. Ashraf, 1962).

Asad, Muhammad (1982), *The Principles of State and Government in Islam* (Gibraltar: Dār al-Andalus, 1982).

'Āshūr, Muḥammad al-Ṭāhir ibn, (d. 1393/1973) (1421/2001), *Maqāṣid al-Sharī'ah al-Islāmiyyah,* ed. Muḥammad al-Ṭāhir al-Miysāwī (Jordan: Dār al-Nafā'is, 2nd. ed.).

Australian Bureau of Agricultural and Research Economics (1988), *Japanese Agricultural Policies.* Policy Monograph No. 3. Canberra, Australia.

Badawi, Abdurrahman (1963), 'Muḥammad ibn Zakariyyā al-Rāzī', in M. M. Sharif, Volume 1, pp. 434-49.

Badawi, Abdurrahman (1980), *Min Tārīkh al-Ilḥād fi'l-Islām* (Beirut: Al-Mu'assasah al-'Arabiyyah li al-Dirāsāt wa al-Nashr, 2nd. ed.).

Baeck, Louis, (1994) *The Mediterranean Tradition in Economic Thought* (London: Routledge).

Baghdādī, 'Abd al-Qāhir ibn Ṭāhir al- (d. 429/1037), *Al-Farq Bayn al-Firaq* (Beirut: Dār al-Kutub al-'Ilmiyyah, n.d.).

Bairoch, Paul, (1982), 'International Industrialization Levels from 1750 to 1980', *The Journal of European Economic History* (Rome, Italy), pp. 269-333.

Barrow, Robert, and Rachel McCleary (2003), 'Religion and Economic Growth', Harvard University, April 8.

Bayhaqī, Imām Abū Bakr al- (d. 458/1065), *Shu'ab al-Īmān*, Muḥammad Sa'īd Bisyūnī Zaghlūl (ed.), (Beirut: Dār al-Kutub al-'Ilmiyyah, 1990).

Behrens-Abouseif, Doris (2002), '*Waqf*, *Encyclopaedia of Islam*, Volume 11, pp. 59-109 (Leiden: Brill).

Ben Shemesh, A. (1965), *Taxation in Islam,* translation of *Kitāb al-Kharāj* by Qudāmah ibn Ja'far (d. 337/948) as Volume 1, Yaḥyā ibn Ādam (d. 203/818) as Volume 2 (1967), and Abū Yūsuf (d. 182/798) as Volume 3 (1969) (Leiden: E. J. Brill; and London: Luzac).

Berkey, Jonathan (1992) *The Transmission of Knowledge in Medieval Cairo: A Social History of Islamic Education* (Princeton, NJ: Princeton University Press).

Besley, Timothy and Robin Burgess (2003), 'Halving Global Poverty', *Journal of Economic Perspectives,* 17:3, Summer, pp. 3-22.

Besley, Timothy (2005), 'Political Selection', *Journal of Economic Perspectives,* 19:3, Summer, pp. 43-60.

Binder, Leonard (1964), *Ideological Revolution in the Middle East* (New York), (Leiden: Brill).

Bjorkman, W. (1991), '*Maks*', in *Encyclopaedia of Islam*, Volume 6, pp. 194-95, (Leiden: Brill).

Bosworth, C. E. (1995), 'Saljūḳids', in *The Encyclopaedia of Islam*, Volume 8, pp. 936-73 (Leiden: Brill).

Boulakia, Jean David C. (1971), 'Ibn Khaldun: A Fourteenth Century Economist', *Journal of Political Economy,* September/October, pp. 1105-1118.

Bowles, Samuel, and Herbert Gintis (2002), 'Social Capital and Community Governance', *The Economic Journal,* November, F419-F436.

Brandel, Fernand and Frank Spooner (1967), 'Prices in Europe from 1450 to 1750', in E. E. Rich and C. H. Wilson (eds.), *The Cambridge Economic*

History of Europe, (Cambridge: Cambridge University Press), Volume 4, pp. 374-486.

Brenner, Robert (1987), 'Feudalism', *The New Palgrave Dictionary of Economics*. Macmillan, London, Volume 2, pp. 309-16.

Bukhārī, Imām Abū 'Abdullāh Muḥammad ibn Ismā'īl al- (d. 256/869) (1407/1987), *Ṣaḥīḥ al-Bukhārī*, ed., al-Shaykh Qāsim al-Shammā'ī al-Rifā'ī (Beirut: Dār al-Qalam).

Bulliet, Richard W. (2004), *The Case for Islamo-Christian Civilization* (New York: Columbia University Press).

Burtt, Edwin A. (1955), *The Metaphysical Foundations of Modern Science* (Garden City, New York: Doubleday).

Cahen, Claude (1970), 'Economy, Society, Institutions', in Holt, Lambton and Lewis (eds.), Volume 2, pp. 511-38.

Cahen, Claude (1986), 'Buwayhids or Buhids', in *The Encyclopaedia of Islam*, Volume 1, pp. 1350-7, (Leiden: Brill).

Cahen, Claude (1990), '*Kharāj* in the Central and Western Islamic Lands', in *The Encyclopaedia of Islam*, Volume 4, pp. 1030-4, (Leiden: Brill).

Chapra, M. Umer (1979), *The Islamic Welfare State and its Role in the Economy*, (The Islamic Foundation, Leicester, UK).

Chapra, M. Umer (1985), *Towards a Just Monetary System*, (The Islamic Foundation, Leicester, UK).

Chapra, M. Umer (1992), *Islam and the Economic Challenge*, (The Islamic Foundation, Leicester, UK.)

Chapra, M. Umer (1993), *Islam and Economic Development* (Islamabad: The International Institute of Islamic Thought)

Chapra, M. Umer (2000), *The Future of Economics: An Islamic Perspective*, (The Islamic Foundation, Leicester, UK).

Chapra, M. Umer (2007), 'Challenges Facing the Islamic Financial Industry', in M. Kabir Hassan and Mervyn Lewis, *Handbook of Islamic Banking*, pp. 325-357 (Northampton, MA, USA: Edward Elgar).

Checkland, S. G. (1987), 'Industrial Revolution', *The New Palgrave Dictionary of Economics,* Macmillan, London, Volume 2, pp. 811-15.

Cizakca, Murat (1996), *The Comparative Evolution of Business Partnerships* (Leiden: E. J. Brill).

Cizakca, Murat (2000), *A History of Philanthropic Foundations: The Islamic World from the Seventh Century to the Present* (Istanbul: Bogazici University Press).

Clark, Ramsey (1997), Interview with *Impact International,* London: UK, December 10.

Cook, M. A., ed. (1970), *Studies in the Economic History of the Middle East from the Rise of Islam to the Present Day* (London: Oxford University Press).

Dasgupta, Partha, and Ismail Serageldin (2000), *Social Capital: A Multifaceted Perspective* (Washington, D.C., The World Bank).

De Boer, T. J. (1970), *The History of Philosophy in Islam,* tr. Edward R. Jones (London: Luzac).

Desai, M. (1971), 'Demand for Cotton Textiles in Nineteenth Century India', *The Indian Economic and Social History Review*, December, pp. 337-361.

Desfosses, Helen, and Jacques Levesque, eds. (1975), *Socialism in the Third World* (Praeger, New York).

Dobb, M. (1946), *Studies in the Development of Capitalism* (Routledge and Kegan Paul, London).

Durant, Will (1954), *The History of Civilization* (New York: Simon & Schuster).

Durant, Will (1970), *The Story of Philosophy* (New York: Washington Square Press).

Dutton, Yasin (1994), 'The Introduction to Ibn Rushd's *Bidāyat al-Mujtahid*', *Islamic Law and Society*, August.

Economist, The (1977), 'The Knowledge Factory: A Survey of Universities', 4 October.

Economist, The (2004), 'Why Europe Must Say Yes to Turkey', 18 September, p. 13.

Economist, The (2005), 'Turkey's Booming Economy: Babacan's Miracle', 22 January, p. 32.

Ehrenkreutz, A. S., Halil Inalcik and J. Burton-Page (1991), '*Dār al-Ḍarb*', in *The Encyclopaedia of Islam,* Volume 2, pp. 117-21 (Leiden: Brill).

Eickermann, Dale (1989), *The Middle East: An Anthropological Approach* (Englewood Cliffs, N.J.).

Ellison, Christopher (1991), 'Religious Involvement and Subjective Well-being', *Journal of Health and Social Behaviour,* 31:1, pp. 80-99.

Esposito, John L. (1992), *The Islamic Threat: Myth or Reality?* (Oxford: Oxford University Press).

Essid, M. Yassine (1995), *A Critique of the Origins of Islamic Economic Thought* (Leiden: Brill).

Etzioni, Amitai (1988), *The Moral Dimension: Towards a New Economics.* The Free Press, New York.

Etzioni, Amitai (2004), 'Religious Civil Society is Antidote to Anarchy in Iraq and Afghanistan' *The Christian Science Monitor,* 1 April (www.csmonitor.com/2004/0401/p09s01-coop.html).

Faroghi, Suraiya (1994), 'Crisis and Change', in Inalcik (ed.), 1994, pp. 411-636.

Friedman, Benjamin (2005), *Moral Consequences of Economic Growth* (New York: Knopf).

Fukuyama, Francis (1995), *Trust, Social Virtues and the Creation of Prosperity,* (New York: Free Press).

Gardet, L. (1971), '*Ilm al-Kalām*', *The Encyclopaedia of Islam* (Leiden: Brill, new ed.), Volume 3, pp. 1141-50.

Ghazālī, Abū Ḥāmid al- (1953), *al-Munqidh min al-Ḍalāl,* along with three other books by al-Ghazālī, *Kīmyā' al-Sa'ādah, al-Qawā'id al-'Asharah,* and *al-Adab fī al-Dīn,* Muḥammad Jābir (ed.), (Beirut: Maktabah al-Thaqāfah, n.d.). *Al-Munqidh* has been translated into English by W. Montgomery Watt under the title: *The Faith and Practice of al-Ghazālī* (London: George Allen and Unwin).

Ghazālī, Abū Ḥāmid al- (1993), *Tahāfut al-Falāsifah*, Jirār Jihāmī (ed.), (Beirut: Dār al-Fikr al-Lubnānī). An English translation by Sahib Aḥmad Kamali was published in 1963 by the Pakistan Philosophical Conference, Lahore.

Ghazālī, Abū Ḥāmid al- (d. 505/1111), *Shifā' al-Ghalīl*, ed. Muḥammad al-Kubaysī, (Baghdād: Maṭba'ah al-Irshād, n.d.).

Ghazālī, Abū Ḥāmid, al- (d. 505/1111) (1947), *Iḥyā' 'Ulūm al-Dīn* (Cairo: Maktabah wa Maṭba'ah al-Mashhad al-Ḥusaynī, n.d.), 5 volumes.

Gibb, H. A. R. (1947), *Modern Trends in Islam* (Chicago: University of Chicago Press).

Gibb, H. A. R. (1962), *Studies on the Civilization of Islam* (London: Routledge and Kegan Paul).

Gibbon, Edward (1960), *The History of the Decline and Fall of the Roman Empire* (J. B. Bury's ed., in 7 Vols., abridged in 1 Volume by D. M. Low).

Gimaret, D. (1993), '*Mu'tazila*', in *The Encyclopaedia of Islam* (Leiden: Brill, new ed.), Volume 7, pp. 783-93.

Gintis, Herbert (2002), 'Social Capital and Community Governance', in *The Economic Journal,* November, F419-F436.

Graham, R. (1979), *Iran: The Illusion of Power* (New York: St. Martin's Press).

Gruber, Jonathan (2005), 'Religious Market Structure, Religious Participation, and Outcomes: Is Religion Good for You?', NBER Working Paper 11377, May.

Ḥākim, Abū 'Abdullāh Muḥammad al- (d. 848/1444), *Al-Mustadrak* (Riyadh: Maktabah wa Maṭābi' al-Naṣr al-Ḥadīth, n.d.)

Hall and Jones (1999), 'Why Do Some Countries Produce So Much More Output per Worker Than Others?' *Quarterly Journal of Economics,* 114(1), pp. 83-116.

Hallaq, Wael B. (1984), "Was the Gate of *Ijtihād* Closed?" *Journal of Middle East Studies,* March, pp. 3-41.

Haque, Ziaul, (1977) *Landlord and Peasant in Early Islam* (Islamabad: Islamic Research Institute).

Hepburn, Ronald, (1958), *Christianity and Paradox* (London: C. A. Watts).

Hessen, Robert (1987), 'Corporation' *The New Palgrave Dictionary of Economics,* Macmillan, London, Volume 1, pp. 675-77.

Hicks, John (1967), 'Revelation', *The Encyclopaedia of Philosophy* (New York: Macmillan and the Free Press), Volume 7, pp. 189-91.

Hilton, R. H. (1969), *The Decline of Serfdom* (London: Macmillan).

Hinds, M. (1993), '*Miḥna*', in *The Encyclopaedia of Islam* (Leiden: Brill).

Hitti, Philip (1958), *History of the Arabs* (London: Macmillan).

Hodgson, Marshall G. S. (1977), *The Venture of Islam: Conscience and History in a World Civilization* (Chicago: University of Chicago Press).

Hofmann, Murad Wilfried (1996), 'Backwardness and the Rationality of the Muslim World', *Encounters* (UK), March, pp. 76–87.

Hollingsworth, J. Rogers, and Robert Boyer (1998), *Contemporary Capitalism: The Embeddedness of Institutions* (Cambridge: Cambridge University Press).

Holt, P. M., Ann Lambton and Bernard Lewis (eds.) (1970), *The Cambridge History of Islam* (Cambridge: The University Press).

Hourani, George F. (1961), *Averroes on the Harmony of Religion and Philosophy* (A translation, with introduction and notes, of Ibn Rushd's *Kitāb Faṣl al-Maqāl* with its appendix (*Ḍamīmah*) and an extract from *Kitāb al-Kashf 'an Manāhij al-Adillah* (London: Luzac).

Huxley, Julian (1957), *Religion Without Revelation* (London: Harper, 1st ed., 1947; 2nd ed., 1957).

Iannaccone, Laurence (1998), 'Introduction to the Economics of Religion', *Journal of Economic Literature,* September, pp. 1465-1496.

Ibn 'Ābidīn, Muḥammad Amīn (d. 1258/1842) (1386/1966), *Ḥāshiyat Radd al-Mukhtār* (Cairo: Muṣṭafā al-Bābī al-Ḥalabī).

Ibn al-Athīr (1980), 'Izz al-Dīn 'Alī (d. 630/1233), *Al-Kāmil fī al-Tārīkh* (Beirut: Dār al-Kitāb al-'Arabī).

Ibn Khaldūn, ʿAbd al-Raḥmān, (1370/1951) *Al-Taʿrīf bi Ibn Khaldūn wa Riḥlatuhū Gharban wa Sharqan,* Muḥammad Tāwīt al-Ṭanjī, (Cairo).

Ibn Khaldūn, ʿAbd al-Raḥmān, (1967), *Muqaddimah* (Cairo: Al-Maktabah al-Tijāriyyah al-Kubrā, n.d.). See also its translation under Rosenthal, and selections from it under Issawi (1950).

Ibn Khaldūn, ʿAbd al-Raḥmān, *Kitāb al-ʿIbar wa Dīwān al-Mubtada' wa'l-Khabar fī Ayyām al-ʿArab wa'l-ʿAjam wa al-Barbar wa man ʿĀsharahum min Dhawī al-Sulṭān al-Akbar,* (Beirut: Maktabah al-Madrasah wa Dār al-Kitāb al-Lubnānī), 1983-1986

Ibn Mājah, Imām (d. 273/886) (1952), *Sunan* (Cairo: ʿĪsā al-Bābī al-Ḥalabī).

Ibn Qudāmah, Abū Muḥammad ʿAbdullāh (d. 620/1223), *Al-Mughnī* (Cairo: Maṭbaʿah al-ʿĀṣimah, n.d.)

Ibn Rushd (d. 595/1198), *Bidāyat al-Mujtahid wa Nihāyat al-Muqtaṣid* (Cairo: Maṭābiʿ al-Bābī al-Ḥalabī, 3rd ed., 1960). Translated into English by Imran Ahsan Khan Nyazee under the title, *The Distinquished Jurists' Primer* (Reading, UK: Garnet, 1996).

Ibn Rushd (d. 595/1198), *Tahāfut al-Tahāfut,* ed., Maurice Bouyges (Beyrouth: Dār al-Mashriq, 3rd ed., 1992). An English translation in 2 volumes by Simon Van Den Bergh was published in 1954, reprinted in 1969, 1979 and 1987 by Luzac & Co., London. The second volume consists of only the translator's notes. References in the text pertain to the 1987 reprint.

Ibn Taymiyyah, Imām Aḥmad (d. 728/1328) (1381-83/1961-63), *Majmūʿ al-Fatāwā Shaykh al-Islām Aḥmad Ibn Taymiyyah,* ed., ʿAbd al-Raḥmān al-ʿĀṣimī, (Riyadh: Maṭābiʿ al-Riyāḍ, 1st ed.).

Ibn Taymiyyah, Imām Aḥmad (d. 728/1328) (1967), *Al-Ḥisbah fī al-Islām,* ed., ʿAbd al-ʿAzīz Rabāḥ (Damascus: Maktabah Dār al-Bayān). Translated by Muhtar Holland under the title *Public Duties in Islam: the Institution of the Ḥisba* (Leicester, UK: The Islamic Foundation, 1982).

Ibn Taymiyyah, Imām Aḥmad (1425/2004), *Bayān al-Dalīl ʿAlā Buṭlān al-Taḥlīl,* ed. Aḥmad ibn Muḥammad al-Khalīl (Dammam: Dār Ibn al-Jawzī).

Imām, Zakariyyah Bashir (1977), *Tarīq al-Taṭawwur al-Ijtimā'ī al-Islāmī.* (Jeddah: Dār al-Shurūq).

Inalcik, Halil (1970), 'The Heyday and Decline of the Ottoman Empire', in Holt, et al., Volume 1, pp. 324-31.

Inalcik, Halil (1970), 'The Rise of the Ottoman Empire', in Holt, et al., Volume 1, pp. 295-323.

Inalcik, Halil and Dovald Quataert (eds.) (1994), *An Economic and Social History of the Ottoman Empire, 1300-1914* (Cambridge, UK: Cambridge University Press).

International Monetary Fund (IMF) (2004), *International Financial Statistics*, CD-ROM and Yearbook.

International Monetary Fund (IMF) (2005), *Turkey at the Crossroad: From Crisis Resolution to EU Accession,* Occasional Paper No. 242 prepared by a team led by Reza Moghadam (Washington, DC: IMF).

International Monetary Fund (IMF) (2007), *International Financial Statistics*, April.

International Herald Tribune, (1996) 26 March.

International Monetary Fund, *International Financial Statistics* (Washington, DC: IMF), CD-ROM, Annual Yearbooks, and monthly.

Iqbal, Muhammad (1954), *Reconstruction of Religious Thought in Islam* (Lahore: Shaikh Muhammad Ashraf).

Islamic Development Bank (IDB) (2007), *Statistical Monograph* No. 27, May (Jeddah: Islamic Development Bank, Jeddah).

Issawi, Charles (1950), *An Arab Philosophy of History: Selections from the Prolegomena of Ibn Khaldūn of Tunis (1332-1406).* (London: John Murray).

Issawi, Charles (1966), *The Economic History of the Middle East, 1800-1914*, (Chicago: University of Chicago Press).

Issawi, Charles (1970), 'The Decline of Middle Eastern Trade, 1100-1850', in Richards, 1970.

Jāḥiẓ, 'Amr ibn Baḥr al- (d. 255/869) (1964-65), *Rasā'il*, ed. A. M. Hārūn (Cairo).

Jansen, Marius B. (1973-74), 'Japan, History of', *The New Encyclopaedia Britannica*, 15th ed., Volume 10.

Jaṣṣāṣ, Abū Bakr al- (1347 AH), *Aḥkām al-Qur'ān* (Cairo: Maṭba'ah al-Bahiyyah al-Miṣriyyah).

Johnson, John W. (1964), *The Military and Society in Latin America*. Stanford University Press, Stanford.

Juwaynī, Abū al-Ma'ālī al- (d. 478/1085) (1979), *Al-Ghiyāthī: Ghiyāth al-Umam fī Iltiyāth al-Ẓulam* (Helping Nations to Eliminate Injustice), Fu'ād 'Abd al-Mun'im and Muṣṭafā Ḥilmī (eds.) (Alexandria: Dār al-Da'wah).

Kahf, Monzer, 2004. '*Sharī'ah* and Historical Aspects of *Zakah* and *Awqaf*', background paper prepared for the Islamic Research and Training Institute/ Islamic Development Bank, Jeddah.

Kaufmann, Daniel, Aart Kraay, and Pablo Zoido-Lobaton (1999), 'Governance Matters', World Bank, Policy Research Working Paper No. 2196, Washington, DC (hhtp://www.worldbank.org/wbi/governance/pubs/growthgov/html).

Kaufmann, Daniel, and Aart Kraay (2002), 'Growth without Governance', World Bank Policy Research Paper No. 2928, Washington, DC (hhtp://www.worldbank.org/wbi/ governance/pubs/growthgov/html).

Kennedy, Paul (1987), *The Rise and Fall of the Great Powers: Economic Change and Military Conflict from* 1500-2000. (New York: Random House).

Khadduri, Majid (1984), *The Islamic Conception of Justice* (Baltimore: Johns Hopkins University Press).

Khafīf, 'Ali al- (1962), *Al-Shirkah fī al-Fiqh al-Islāmī*. (Corporations in Islamic Jurisprudence). Ma'had al-Dirāsāt al-'Arabiyyah al-'Aliyyah, Cairo.

Khallāl, Abū Bakr al- (d. 311/923) (1407 AH), *Al-Ḥathth 'alā al-Tijārah wa al-Ṣinā'ah wa al-'Amal* (Riyadh: Dār al-'Āṣimah).

Knack, Stephen and Philip Keefer (1995), 'Institutions and Economic Performance: Cross-Country Tests Using Alternative Institutional Measures', *Economics and Politics*, Vol. 7, No. 3, pp. 207-27

Kramer, J. H. (1952), '*Geography and Commerce*', in Thomas Arnold and Alfred Guillaume, *The Legacy of Islam* (London: Oxford University Press).

Kramer, J. H., 'Othmanli', *The Encyclopaedia of Islam*, Vol. 8, p. 1995 (Leiden: Brill).

Kraus, P., (1971), 'Ibn al-Rāwandī', *The Encyclopaedia of Islam* (Leiden: Brill, revised edition), Volume 3, pp. 905-6.

Kroeber, Alfred (1994), *Configurations of Culture Growth* (Berkeley: University of California Press).

Krueger, Alan, and Jitka Maleckova (2003), 'Education, Poverty and Terrorism: Is there a Causal Connection?' *Journal of Economic Perspectives*, 17:4, Fall, pp. 119-144.

Kuran, Timur (1997), 'Islam and Underdevelopment: An Old Puzzle Revisited', *Journal of Institutional and Theoretical Economics*, March.

Kuran, Timur (2004), 'Why the Middle East is Economically Underdeveloped: Historical Mechanisms of Institutional Stagnation', *The Journal of Economic Perspectives*, Summer, 18:3, pp. 71-90.

Lal, Deepak (1998), *Unintended Consequences: The Impact of Factor Endowments, Culture, and Politics on Long-Run Economic Performance* (Cambridge, MA: MIT Press).

Lambton, Ann K. S. (1970) 'Persia: The Breakdown of Society', in Holt, et al., 1970, Volume 1, pp. 430-67.

Lambton, Ann K. S. (1981), *State and Government in Medieval Islam* (Oxford: Oxford University Press).

Lambton, Ann K. S. (1990), '*Kharāj* in Persia' in *The Encyclopaedia of Islam*, Volume 4, pp. 1034-53 (Leiden: Brill).

Lawson, Nigel (1995), 'Some Reflections on Morality and Capitalism', in Samuel Brittan and Alan Hamlin, eds., *Market Capitalism and Moral Values: Proceedings of Section (Economics) of the British Association for the Advancement of Science*, Keele, 1993 (Aldershot, UK: Edward Elgar).

Lewis, Bernard, (1960), 'Abbāsids', in *The Encyclopaedia of Islam*, Volume 1, pp. 15-26, (Leiden: Brill).

Lewis, Bernard (1962), 'Ottoman Observers of Ottoman Decline', *Islamic Studies*, I, pp. 71-87.

Lewis, Bernard (1970), 'Sources for the Economic History of the Middle East', in Cook, pp. 78-92.

Lewis, Bernard (September 1990), 'The Roots of Muslim Rage' (The Atlantic online, digital edition, Parts I and II).

Lewis, Bernard, (1991), '*Duyūn-e-'Umumiyye*', in *The Encyclopedia of Islam*, Volume 2, p. 677 (Leiden: Brill).

Lewis, Bernard, (1995), *The Middle East: 2000 Years of History from the Rise of Christianity to the Present Day* (London: Weidenfeld & Nicolson).

Lewis, Bernard, (2007), '*The 2007 Irving Kristol Lecture by Bernard Lewis,*' posted on the internet 20 March 2007.

MacIntyre, Andrew (1996), 'Democracy and Markets in Southeast Asia', in *Constructing Democracy and Markets: East Asia and Latin America*, ed., International Forum for Democratic Studies and Pacific Council on International Policy, Pacific Council, Los Angeles, pp. 39-47.

Maddison, Angus (1995), *Monitoring the World Economy, 1820-1992* (Paris: OECD, Development Centre Studies).

Mahdi, Muhsin (1964), *Ibn Khaldun's Philosophy of History* (Chicago: University of Chicago Press).

Makdisi, G. (1981), *The Rise of Colleges: Institutions of Learning in Islam and the West* (Edinburgh: Edinburgh University Press).

Maqrīzī, Taqī al-Dīn Aḥmad ibn 'Alī al- (d. 845/1442) (n.d.), *Al-Khiṭaṭ al-Maqrīziyyah* (Beirut: Dār Ṣadr, n.d.).

Maqrīzī, Taqī al-Dīn Aḥmad ibn 'Alī al- (d. 845/1442) (1994), *Ighāthah al-Ummah bi Kashf al-Ghummah*, 'Abd al-Nāfi' Tulaymāt (ed.), (Ḥams: Dār ibn al-Wahīd, 1956). See its English translation by Adel Allouche, 1994.

Maqrīzī, Taqī al-Dīn Aḥmad ibn 'Alī al- (d. 845/1442) (1971), *Kitāb al-Sulūk li Ma'rifah Duwal al-Mulūk*, ed., Sa'īd 'Abd al-Fattāḥ 'Āshūr (Cairo: Dār al-Kutub wa al-Wathā'iq al-Qawmiyyah, Markaz Taḥqīq al-Turāth, Egyptian Arab Republic).

Masud, M. Khalid (1977), *Islamic Legal Philosophy: A Study of Abū Isḥāq al-Shāṭibī's Life and Thought* (Islamabad: Islamic Research Institute).

Mas'ūdī, Abū al-Ḥasan 'Alī (d. 346/957), *Murūj al-Dhahab wa Ma'ādin al-Jawhar*, M. Muḥyī al-Dīn 'Abd al-Hamīd (ed.), (Beirut: Al-Maktabah al-'Aṣriyyah).

Mauro, Paolo (1995), 'Corruption and Growth', *Quarterly Journal of Economics*, Vol. 110, No. 3, pp. 681-712.

Māwardī, Abū al-Ḥasan 'Alī al- (d. 450/1058) (1955), *Adab al-Dunyā wa al-Dīn*, Muṣṭafā al-Saqqā (ed.), (Cairo: Muṣṭafā al-Bābī al-Ḥalabī).

Māwardī, Abū al-Ḥasan 'Alī al- (d. 450/1058) (1960), *Al-Aḥkām al-Sulṭāniyyah wa al-Wilāyat al-Dīniyyah* (Cairo: Muṣṭafā al-Bābī al-Ḥalabī). The English translation of this book by Wafa Wahba was published in 1960 under the title, *The Ordinances of Government* (Reading: Garnet).

Mawdūdī, Sayyid Abul A'lā, (1962), *Tafhīm al-Qur'ān* (Lahore: Maktabah Ta'mīr-e-Insāniyat), 6 Volumes published between 1962-73. The 3rd Volume was published in 1962.

Mawdūdī, Sayyid Abul A'lā, (1966), *Khilāfat-o-Mulūkiyyat* (Lahore: Islamic Publications).

McGowan, Bruce (1994), 'The Age of the Ayans', in Inalcik (ed.), pp. 637-758.

Mehmet, Ozay (1995), *Islamic Identity and Development: Studies in the Islamic Periphery* (London: Routledge).

Meyer, M. S. (1989), 'Economic Thought in the Ottoman Empire in the 14th-Early 19th Centuries', *Archiv Orientali*, 4:57, pp. 305–18.

Miles, G. C. (1992), 'Dīnār' and 'Dirham', in *The Encyclopaedia of Islam,* Volume 2, pp. 297-99 and 319-20 (Leiden: Brill).

Ministry of *Awqāf* and Islamic Affairs, Kuwait (1983), *Al-Mawsū'ah al-Fiqhiyyah* (Kuwait: Wizārat al-Awqāf wa al-Shu'ūn al-Islāmiyyah, 2nd ed.), 43 volumes issued so far up to the letter *wāw*.

Mirakhor, Abbas (1987), 'The Muslim Scholars and the History of Economics: A Need for Consideration', *The American Journal of Islamic Social Sciences,* December, pp. 245-276.

Misri, Rafīq Yunus al- (1990), *Al-Islām wa al-Nuqūd* (Jeddah: King Abdul Aziz University).

Morgan, D. O. (1993), 'Mongols', in *The Encyclopaedia of Islam,* Volume 7, pp. 230-5 (Leiden: Brill).

Mulligan, Casey, Richard Gil and Xavier Sal-i-Martin (2004), 'Do Democracies Have Different Public Policies than Non-democracies?', *Journal of Economic Perspectives*, Winter, pp. 51-74.

Mundhiri, Ibn 'Umar al- (1986), *Al-Targhīb wa al-Tarhīb,* ed. Muṣṭafā M. 'Ammārah (Beirut: Dār al-Kutub al- 'Ilmiyyah).

Musallam, B. F. (1981), 'Birth Control and Middle Eastern History: Evidence and Hypotheses', in Udovitch, pp. 419-470.

Muslim, Imām Abū al-Ḥusayn Muslim ibn al-Ḥajjāj al-Naysābūrīy (d. 261/874) (1374/1955), *Ṣaḥiḥ*, ed., Muḥammad Fu'ād 'Abd al-Bāqī (Cairo: 'Īsā al-Bābī al-Ḥalabī).

Myrdal, Gunnar (1968), *Asian Drama* (New York, The Twentieth Century Fund).

Najjar, Zaghlul Raghib al- (1409/1989), *Qadiyyah al-Takhalluf al-'Ilmī wa al-Taqanī fī al-'Ālam al-Islāmī* (Qatar: Ri'āsah al-Maḥākim al-Shar'iyyah wa al-Shu'ūn al-Dīniyyah).

Nawas, John A. (1994), 'A Re-Examination of Three Current Explanations for al-Ma'mūn's Introduction of the *Mihna*', *International Journal of Middle East Studies* (Cambridge, UK), pp. 615-29.

Nicholson, R. A. (1956), *A Literary History of the Arabs* (London: Cambridge University Press, 1st ed., 1907).

Noland, Marcus, 'Religion, Culture, and Economic Performance', Unpublished paper (mnoland@ iie.com)

North, Douglass C. and Robert Paul Thomas (1973), *The Rise of the Western World: A New Economic History* (Cambridge: Cambridge University Press).

North, Douglass C. (1990), *Institutions, Institutional Change, and Economic Performance* (Cambridge: Cambridge University Press).

North, Douglass C. (1994), 'Economic Performance through Time', *The American Economic Review*, June, pp. 359-68.

Nyazee, Imran, Ahsan Khan (1994), *The Distinguished Jurist's Primer* (Reading, UK: Garnet).

Nyazee, Imran, Ahsan Khan (2000), *Theories of Islamic Law* (Islamabad: Islamic Research Institute).

Oesterle, Dale Arthur (1994), 'Limited Liability', *The New Palgrave Dictionary of Money and Finance*, Macmillan, London, Volume 2, pp. 590-91.

Oghli, Sahili Khalil (1989), *'Māliyat al-Dawlah al-'Uthmāniyyah'*, in *Mu'assasah Āl al-Bayt,* Volume 2, pp. 591-656.

Osman, Fathi (1986), 'The Contract for the Appointment of the Head of an Islamic State' in Mumtaz Aḥmad, 1986, pp. 51-85.

Otaibi, Moneer M. al- and Hakim M. Rashid, 'The Role of Schools in Islamic Society. Historical and Contemporary Perspectives', *The American Journal of Islamic Social Sciences* (*AJISS*), Winter 1997, pp. 1-18.

Ozmucur, Suleyman, and Sevket Pamuk (2002), 'Real Wages and Standards of Living in the Ottoman Empire, 1489-1914', *The Journal of Economic History,* Volume 62, No. 2, June.

Pamuk, Sevket, 'Money in the Ottoman Empire, (1326-1914)' (1994), in Inalcik (ed.), pp. 947-85.

Pamuk, Sevket (1987), *The Ottoman Empire and European Capitalism, 1820-1913: Trade, Investment and Production* (Cambridge: Cambridge University Press).

Pamuk, Sevket (2004), 'The Evolution of Financial Institutions in the Ottoman Empire, 1600-1914', *Financial History Review,* 11.1, pp. 7-12 (Cambridge University Press, 2000).

Patten, W. M. (1897), *Aḥmad ibn Ḥanbal and the Miḥnah* (Leiden: Brill).

Qala'ji, M. R. (1981), *Mawsū'ah Fiqh 'Umar ibn al-Khaṭṭāb* (Kuwait: Maktabah al-Falāḥ).

Qaradawi, Yusuf al- (1969), *Fiqh al-Zakāh* (Beirut: Dār al-Irshad).

Qaradawi, Yusuf al- (1991), *Awlawiyyāt al-Ḥarakah al-Islāmiyyah fī al-Marḥalah al-Qādimah* (Cairo: Maktabah Wahbah).

Quataert, Donald (1994), 'The Age of Reforms, 1812-1914', in Inalcik, pp. 861-943.

Qurashī, Yaḥyā ibn Ādam al- (d. 203/818), (1384 AH), *Kitāb al-Kharāj*, Aḥmad Muḥammad Shākir (ed.), (Cairo: Al-Maṭba'ah al-Salafiyyah, 2nd ed.). This book has been translated into English by Ben Shemesh (q.v.).

Qurṭubī, Abū 'Umar Ḥāfiẓ ibn 'Abd al-Barr al-Namīrī al- (d. 463/1070), *Jāmi' Bayān al-'ilm wa Faḍluhū* (Madīnah: al-Maktabah al-'Ilmiyyah, n.d.).

Qurṭubī, Abū 'Abdullāh Muḥammad al- (1957), *Al-Jāmi' li-Aḥkām al-Qur'ān*, ed. Aḥmad 'Abd al-'Alīm Bardūnī (Dār al-Kitāb al-'Arabī).

Quṭb, Sayyid (1986), *Fī Ẓilāl al-Qur'ān* (Jeddah: Dār al-Qalam).

Rabie, Hassanein (1970), 'The Size and Value of the Iqtā' in Egypt, 564-741/1169-1341', in Cook (1970), pp. 129-138.

Rabie, Hassanein (1972), *The Financial System of Egypt: 564-741/1169-1341* (London: Oxford University Press).

Rahman, Fazlur (1965), *Islamic Methodology in History* (Islamabad: Islamic Research Institute).

Raysūnī, Aḥmad al- (1992), *Naẓariyyat al-Maqāṣid 'Inda al-Imām al-Shāṭibī* (Riyadh: Al-Dār al-'Ālamiyyah li al-Kitāb al-Islāmī, 2nd ed.).

Rayyis, Muḥammad Diyā' al-Dīn al- (1961), *Al-Kharāj wa al-Nuẓum al-Māliyyah li al-Dawlah al-Islāmiyyah* (Cairo: al-Maktabah al-Angelo al-Misriyyah, 2nd ed.).

Reinhart, A. Kevin (1995), *Before Revelation: The Boundaries of Muslim Moral Thought* (Albany: State University of New York).

Rheinstein, Max, and Mary Glendon (1994), 'Inheritance and Succession' *The New Encyclopaedia Britannica*, 15th ed., pp. 638-47.

Richards, D. S. (ed.), (1970), *Islam and the Trade of Asia* (Philadelphia: University of Pennsylvania Press).

Richards, Alan (2003), 'Explaining the Appeal of Islamic Radicals' (Centre for Global Economic and Regional Studies), January, No. 1.

Roded, Ruth (1994), *Women in Islamic Biographical Collections from Ibn Sa'ad to Who's Who* (Boulder and London: Lynne Reinner Publishers).

Rodrik, Dani (2006), 'Goodbye Washington Consensus, Hello Washington Confusion? A Review of the World Bank's Economic Growth in the 1990s: Learning from a Decade of Reform', *Journal of Economic Literature,* December, pp. 973-987.

Rosenthal, Franz (1967), *Ibn Khaldūn: The Muqaddimah, An Introduction to History* (London: Routledge and Kegan Paul, 1st ed., 1958, 2nd ed.), 3 vols.

Rostow, W. W. (1978), *The World Economy: History and Prospects* (London: Macmillan).

Sachs, Jeffrey D. (1987), 'Trade and Exchange Rate Policies in Growth Oriented Adjustment', in Carlos Vittoria, Moris Goldstein and Mohsin Khan, *Growth-Oriented Adjustment Programmes: Proceedings of a Symposium Held in Washington, DC, February 25-27, 1986.* IMF/IBRD, Washington, DC.

Samarrā'ī, Nu'mān 'Abd al-Razzāq al- (1993), *Tāfsīr al-Ta'rīkh* (Riyadh: Maktabah al-Ma'ārif).

Sarton, George, *Introduction to the History of Science* (Washington, DC: Carnegie Institute, 3 volumes issued between 1927 and 1948, the 2nd and 3rd each in two parts).

Saunders, John J. (ed.), (1966), *The Muslim World on the Eve of Europe's Expansion* (Englewood Cliffs, NJ: Prentice Hall).

Schatzmiller, Maya (1994), *Labour in the Medieval Islamic World,* (Leiden: Brill).

Schweitzer, Alfred (1949), *The Philosophy of Civilization,* (New York: Macmillan).

Sezgin, Fu'ad (1983), *Ta'rīkh al-Turāth al-'Arabī* (History of Arab Legacy), Maḥmūd Fahmī Ḥijāzī (tr.), (Riyadh: Imām Muḥammad ibn Sa'ūd Islamic University. First Volume, followed by other volumes in later years.)

Sezgin, Fu'ād (2004), *Science and Technology in Islam* (Frankfurt: Institut für Geschihte der Arabisch-Islamischen Wissenschaften).

Shahrastānī, Abū al-Fatḥ Muḥammad ibn 'Abd al-Karīm, al- (d. 548/1153) (1961), *Al-Milal wa al-Niḥal,* ed. Muḥammad Sayyid Kaylānī (Cairo: Muṣṭafā al-Bābī al-Ḥalabī).

Sharif, M. M., ed. (1963), *A History of Muslim Philosophy* (Wiesbaden, Otto Harrasowitz), 2 volumes.

Shaybānī, Muḥammad ibn al-Ḥasan al- (d. 189/804), (1977), *Kitāb al-Kasb*, 'Abd al-Fattāḥ Abū Ghuddah (ed.), (Halab, Syria: Maktab al-Maṭbū'at al-Islāmiyyah).

Shihabi, Mustafa al-, et al. (1965), *'Filāḥa'*, in *The Encyclopaedia of Islam*, Volume 2, pp. 899-910 (Leiden: Brill).

Sirowy, Larry, and Alex Inkles (1990), 'The Effects of Democracy on Growth and Inequality: A Review', *Studies in Comparative International Development*, 25, pp. 125-126.

Solow, Robert M. (2000), 'Notes on Social Capital and Economic Performance', in Dasgupta and Serageldin, pp. 6-10.

Sorokin, Pitirim (1951), *Social Philosophies of an Age of Crisis,* (Boston: Beacon)

Spengler, Joseph (1964), 'Economic Thought in Islam: Ibn Khaldun', *Comparative Studies in Society and History.* April, pp. 268-306.

Spengler, Oswald (1947), *Decline of the West* (New York).

Spuler, Bertold and R. Ettinghausen (1986), 'Ilkhāns', in *The Encyclopaedia of Islam*, Volume 3, pp. 1120–7 (Leiden: Brill).

Suyūṭī, Jalāl al-Dīn, al- (d. 911/1505), *al-Jāmi' al-Ṣaghīr* (Cairo: 'Abd al-Ḥamīd Aḥmad Ḥanafī, n.d.) Volume 2, p. 96.

Ṭabarī, Abū Ja'far Muḥammad ibn Jarīr al- (d. 310/923) (1979), *Ta'rīkh al-Rusul wa al-Mulūk* (Beirut: Dār al-Fikr).

Talbi, M. (1986), *'Ibn Khaldūn'*, in *The Encyclopaedia of Islam* (Leiden: Brill), Volume 3, pp. 825-31.

Ṭanṭāwī, 'Alī al- and Nājī al-Ṭanṭāwī, (1959), *Akhbār 'Umar wa 'Abdullāh ibn 'Umar* (Damascus: Dār al-Fikr).

Tibawi, A. L. (1954), 'Muslim Education in the Golden Age of the Caliphate', *Islamic Culture* (Hyderabad), pp. 418-38.

Tirmidhī, Imām Muḥammad ibn 'Īsā al- (d. 279/892), *Jāmi' al-Tirmidhī* with commentary, *Tuḥfat al-Aḥwadhī* (Beirut: Dār al-Kitāb al-'Arabī, n.d.).

Toynbee, Arnold J. (1935), *A Study of History* (London: Oxford University Press, 2nd ed.).

Toynbee, Arnold J. (1957), *A Study of History,* abridgement by D. C. Somervell (London: Oxford University Press).

Toynbee, Arnold (uncle of the great historian Arnold J. Toynbee) (1961), *Industrial Revolution.* First published in 1884 as *Lectures on the Industrial Revolution in England.* (Boston: Beacon Press.)

Ṭurṭūshī, Abū Bakr Muḥammad al-Walīd al-Fahrī al- (d. 520/1126), (1994), *Sirāj al-Mulūk,* Muḥammad Fatḥī Abū Bakr (ed.), (Cairo: Al-Dār al-Miṣriyyah al-Lubnāniyyah), 2 volumes.

Udovitch, Abraham L. (1970), *Partnership and Profit in Medieval Islam* (Princeton, NJ: Princeton University Press).

Udovitch, Abraham L. (1981), *The Islamic Middle East 700-1900: Studies in Economic and Social History* (Princeton, NJ: The Darwin Press).

Urvoy, Dominique (1991), tr., Olivia Stewart, *Ibn Rushd* (London: Routledge).

Usmani, Muhammad Taqi (1998), *An Introduction to Islamic Finance* (Karachi: Idaratul Ma'arif).

Vaglieri, Laura (1970), 'The Patriarchal and Umayyad Caliphates', in Holt, Lambton and Lewis, 1970, Volume 1, pp. 57-103.

Valiuddin, Mir (1963), '*Mu'tazilism*', in M. M. Sharif, Volume 1, pp. 199-220.

Van Den Bergh, Simon, (1954), tr. *Averroes' Tahāfut al-Tahāfut* (The Incoherence of the Incoherence) (Cambridge, UK: The Gibb Memorial Trust, 1954; reprinted in 1969 and 1987 by Luzac and Co., London), 2 volumes.

Watson, Andrew M. (1981), 'A Medieval Green Revolution: New Crops and Farming Techniques in the Early Islamic World', in Udovitch, 1970, pp. 29-58.

Watson, Andrew M. (1983), *Agricultural Innovation in the Early Islamic World: The Diffusion of Crops and Farming Techniques: 700-1100* (Cambridge: Cambridge University Press).

Watt, W. Montgomery (1963), *Muslim Intellectual: A study of Al-Ghazali* (Edinburgh: University Press).

Watt, W. Montgomery (1970), 'Muḥammad', in Holt, Lambton and Lewis, Volume 1, pp. 30-56.

World Bank (1982, 1997), *World Development Report.*

World Bank (2005), *Economic Growth in the 1990s: Learning from a Decade of Reform* (Washington, DC: World Bank).

Zaheer, A., B. Mc Evily and V. Perrone (1998), 'Does Trust Matter: Exploring the Effects of Inter-organizational and Impersonal Trust on Performance', in *Organization Science*, pp. 141-159.

Zaman, M. Qasim (1997), *Religion and Politics Under the Early Abbasids* (Leiden: Brill).

Zarqā, Muṣṭafā Aḥmad al- (1967), *Al-Fiqh al-Islāmī fī Thawbihī al-Jadīd* (Damascus: Maṭābi' Alif Bā' al-Adīb).

Zarqā, Muṣṭafā Aḥmad al- (1996), *Al-'Aql wa'l-Fiqh fī Fahm al-Ḥadīth* (Damascus: Dār al-Qalam).

Zebiri, Kate (1993), *Mahmud Shaltut and Islamic Modernism* (New York: Oxford University Press, Inc.).

Zurayk, C. K. (1992), '*Jāmi'a*', in *The Encyclopaedia of Islam*, Volume 2, pp. 422-27 (Leiden: Brill).

INDEX

ʿAbbās, 59, 92
ʿAbbāsid caliphate, 10, 42
ʿAbbāsids, 54, 59, 60, 66, 72, 78, 92, 109, 117, 125, 135, 138, 145, 146, 154, 189
ʿAbd al-Raḥmān, 97
ʿAbduh, Muḥammad, 126, 141
ʿAbdullāh al-Ḥasan, 134
Abraham, 19, 165
Abū al-Bakhtarī, 134
Abū Bakr, 103, 107, 118, 129, 137
Abū Ḥanīfah, 120, 134
Abū ʿUbayd, 44, 76, 93
Abū Yūsuf, 44, 76, 93, 134, 137, 139
Abū Zahrah, 97, 128, 129, 130, 131, 132
ʿadl, 17, 105, 106
Afghanistan, 176, 179
Al-Afghānī, Jamāl al-Dīn, 126, 141
Africa, 11, 54, 91, 93
agriculture, 2, 37, 38, 41, 43, 44, 48, 73, 74, 76, 79, 84, 87, 97, 153
Ahmad, Qazi Kholiquzzaman, 168
Aḥmad ibn Abī Du'ād, 110
Akhīsārī, Muṣṭafā ʿAlī, 83, 94
Aleppo, 145
Algeria, 11, 12, 154
ʿAlī, 137
alleviation of poverty, 166, 169
America, 47, 48, 182
American Revolution, 47
Al-Amīn, 59
al-Amīrī, al-Kāmilī, 78
Anatolia, 69
Andalusia, 11
ʿaql, 114, 132
Arab provinces, 75
Arabia, 37, 63
Arabian bedouin, 10, 11, 34
Arnaldez, R., 130
ʿaṣabiyyah, 21, 22, 38
Al-Asadī, 78
Ashʿarites, 111, 113, 116, 118, 123, 132

Al-Ashʿarī, Abū al-Ḥasan, 111, 118
Al-ʿAttābī, 137
authoritrian rulers, 70
awqāf, 31, 51, 65
Al-Ayyūbī, Ṣalāḥ al-Dīn, 76

Baeck, Louis, 35, 43, 80, 94
Baghdād, 10, 40, 60, 73, 93, 109, 110, 128, 129, 193
Bangladesh, 168, 169
Al-Bāqillānī, 14
Barada, 40
Battle of Ḥarrah, 55
Bayt al-Ḥikmah, 97, 128
Bayt al-Māl, 49
Bedouin society, 11, 34, 42
Bible, 120
Bidāyat al-Mujtahid (of Ibn Rushd), 115
Bijāyah, 11
Al-Bishr, Jaʿfar ibn, 103, 129
Black Death, 10, 11
Bougie (Algeria), 11
budgetary deficit, 70, 82, 182, 193
Bulliet, Richard, 67, 179, 194
Burjī Mamlūks, 82
business enterprises, 51
Buwayhids, 59, 72, 73
Byzantine fiscal system, 40

Cairo, 12, 15
capital, 15, 20, 22, 25, 28, 29, 37, 38, 41, 47, 50, 51, 85, 191
Celali Rebellion, 69
Central Asia, 43, 54, 111, 135
China, 7, 41, 43, 154, 163, 177
Christians, 40, 42
Christian history, 119
Christian values, 29, 192
Christianity, 120, 179
Church, 50, 57, 119, 120, 121, 126, 132, 154
Circassian Mamlūks, 10
Clark, Ramsey, 180
classical Muslim scholars, 23, 54
consensus, 105, 110, 116, 120, 122, 152, 160, 167, 180, 188
conservatives, 101, 103, 105, 108, 111, 118, 121, 122, 123, 124, 125, 132, 185
consumer prices, 69, 92
corporation, 47, 48, 49, 50, 51, 53, 85
Corruption, 4, 13, 19, 36, 51, 52, 62, 64, 81, 82, 83, 89, 99, 119, 136, 137, 142, 155, 159, 160, 163, 171, 173, 174, 175, 180, 181, 182, 183, 190, 191
Corruption Perception Index, 160
crafts, 2, 25, 37, 41, 84, 92
Crimea, 91
Crusaders, 42
Crusades, 10, 178
currency, 33, 77, 78, 79, 80, 94, 153
Cyprus, 91

Danilevsky, 13
Dār al-Ḥikmah, 97, 128
dawlah, 12
democracy, 8, 29, 55, 56, 57, 61, 101, 128, 159, 161, 162, 163, 173, 174, 175, 176, 181, 190, 191
development, 3, 4, 5, 6, 7, 8, 9, 10, 12, 13, 15, 17, 18, 19, 20, 21, 22, 23, 24, 25, 26, 27, 28, 29, 31, 34, 35, 36, 37, 38, 40, 41, 43, 44, 46,

47, 48, 49, 50, 51, 52, 53, 54, 60, 61, 62, 67, 69, 71, 72, 74, 77, 79, 80, 81, 83, 85, 87, 89, 91, 98, 99, 101, 103, 108, 119, 122, 123, 124, 127, 132, 133, 134, 136, 142, 149, 150, 151, 152, 153, 154, 155, 156, 158, 159, 160, 161, 162, 163, 165, 166, 167, 168, 170, 171, 172, 174, 175, 176, 177, 178, 179, 180, 181, 183, 185, 186, 187, 190, 191
development economics, 28, 162
dīnārs, 77, 78
dirhams, 77, 78
Divine Laws, 22
division of labour, 21, 25
Durant, Will, 119, 131, 132
dynasties, 11, 13, 26, 40, 59, 60, 63, 75, 76, 78, 82, 97, 138, 146, 152, 156

East Asia, 48, 54, 182
East Asian tigers, 48
economic development, 6, 20, 46, 47, 83, 99, 160
economic forces, 20
economic growth, 20, 43, 163, 166, 170
economy, 2, 5, 21, 28, 29, 32, 38, 41, 47, 73, 85, 89, 91, 94, 149, 153, 159, 189, 194
education, 1, 6, 7, 15, 25, 28, 29, 30, 34, 38, 48, 51, 52, 53, 54, 71, 77, 82, 84, 85, 89, 92, 96, 97, 98, 99, 100, 101, 118, 123, 124, 126, 140, 141, 144, 145, 147, 149, 151, 153, 156, 157, 160, 161, 165, 167, 168, 169, 170, 171, 173, 174, 175, 176, 178, 180, 183, 187, 188, 190, 191, 193
Egypt, 11, 60, 93, 130, 148
England, 50, 51, 94, 95
Enlightenment movements, 108, 119, 166
entrepreneurial drive, 21
Euphrates, 40
Europe, 37, 42, 43, 47, 48, 71, 79, 81, 84, 91, 92, 97, 154

falāsifah, 102, 103, 111, 113, 129
family, 6, 10, 11, 15, 28, 36, 45, 48, 57, 61, 66, 72, 147, 156, 159, 162, 169, 170, 171, 181, 185, 193
Al-Fārābī, 129
Far East, 79
farmers, 26, 36, 39, 40, 49, 75, 79, 83, 85, 89, 93, 145
fasād, 146, 177, 193
Faṣl al-Maqāl (of Ibn Rushd), 115
Fāṭimids, 72, 74, 93
fay', 39, 72
feudal lords, 39, 49, 91, 172, 173, 175, 176
feudalism, 47, 51, 72
Fez, 11
Fihrist (of Ibn al-Nadīm), 73
finance, 37, 41, 50, 68, 71, 72, 80, 88, 89, 92, 98, 99, 169, 182
fiqh, 14, 31, 42, 91, 93, 97, 115, 119, 123, 124, 125, 126, 127, 128, 132, 133, 134, 136, 139, 140, 142, 145, 146, 155, 156, 184
fiscal imbalances, 2, 68, 70, 77, 153
fitnah, 146
France, 86, 87, 88, 89, 90
freedom of expression, 56, 60, 61, 109, 152, 160, 162, 171, 174, 183, 187

freedom of opinion, 122
freedom of thought, 7
French Revolution, 47
Friedman, Benjamin, 166, 192
fulūs, 77, 79
Fusṭāṭ, 110

GDP data, 89
Gardet, Louis, 103, 129, 131
Gaykhatu, 73
Germany, 86, 87, 88, 90
Al-Ghazālī, 14, 66, 93, 111, 112, 113, 114, 115, 118, 123, 128, 129, 130, 131, 137, 139, 142, 147
Ghazān Khān, 72, 73
Gibb, H.A.R., 44, 124, 132
Gibbon, Edward, 9
globalization, 174, 177, 178
God's Messengers, 19
governance, 8, 23, 48, 159, 160, 163, 190
Grameen Bank, 168
Greece, 86, 87, 88, 90
Greek philosophy, 103
Gresham's Law, 78

Habsburgs, 68, 70
ḥadīth, 15, 42, 58, 66, 76, 93, 97, 120, 128, 129, 138, 144, 145, 148, 192, 193, 194
Ḥakam II, 97
Hārūn al-Rashīd, 41, 42, 59, 78, 121, 134, 135, 137, 145
Ḥashawiyyah, 107, 118
Hebraic scriptures, 119
heretics, 107, 113, 115, 117, 122, 129, 131
historiography, 11
Hitti, Philip, 14, 35, 44, 92, 93
Hodgson, Marshall G.S., 35, 44, 46, 61, 64, 65, 67, 93, 94, 128, 148
Hofmann, Murad, 129, 188, 194
Hourani, G.F., 120, 130, 131, 132
Human Development Index, 161

Ibn ʿĀbidīn, 52, 65
Ibn ʿĀshūr, Shaykh Muḥammad al-Ṭāhir, 184
Ibn Baʾra, 78, 94
Ibn Khaldūn, 9, 10, 11, 12, 13, 14, 15, 16, 17, 18, 19, 20, 21, 22, 23, 24, 26, 27, 28, 29, 30, 31, 32, 33, 38, 41, 53, 54, 63, 64, 67, 76, 81, 82, 92, 94, 116, 117, 124, 131, 132, 150, 158, 162, 166, 189, 191
Ibn Khaldūn's model, 10, 12, 13, 14, 16, 20, 26, 28, 30, 31, 54, 64, 92, 150, 162
Ibn Khaldūn's theory of development and decline, 5, 9, 19, 27, 28
Ibn al-Nadīm, 73
Ibn al-Rāwandī, 103, 107, 108, 117, 118
Ibn Rushd, 103, 114, 115, 116, 118, 122, 129, 131, 139
Ibn Sīnā, 103, 129
Ibn Taymiyyah, 14, 116, 117, 121, 122, 124, 131, 132, 148, 194
Al-Ījī, 116, 129
ijmāʿ, 110, 116, 120
ijtihād, 123, 126, 139, 155
Ilkhānid, 60, 72, 73
Ilkhāns, 75
ʿilm al-kalām, 42, 103, 105, 111, 112, 113, 129

Inalcik, Halil, 14, 44, 65, 70, 71, 80, 90, 92, 93, 94, 95, 128
incentives, 22, 24
income, 1, 24, 25, 26, 34, 37, 49, 71, 79, 85, 100, 101, 161, 162, 167, 168, 169, 175, 176, 193
India, 54, 86, 87, 88, 90, 95, 98, 177, 178
Industrial Revolution, 51, 84, 99
industry, 25, 86, 87
injustice, 5, 20, 21, 23, 40, 62, 72, 89, 90, 93, 138, 166, 175
Inquisition, 109, 120, 122, 132
institutional economics, 22
Introduction to the History of Science (by George Sarton), 43
investment, 2, 5, 6, 24, 44, 161, 171, 172, 175, 180, 181
Iqbal, Muhammad, 123, 126, 141
*iqṭāʿ*s, 39
Iran, 54
Iraq, 194
irrigation, 40, 73
Islamic beliefs and practices, 104, 111, 112, 114
Islamic lands, 30, 54
Islamic learning, 126
Islamic movements, 186, 187, 194
Islamic sciences, 112
Islamic values, 101, 152, 156, 169
Islam's rationalist spirit, 98
Israel, 176
Italy, 86, 87, 88, 90

Jāhiliyyah, 58, 144
Japan, 43, 48, 84, 172, 177
Jesus, 19, 65
Jews, 42
Johnson, Lyndon, 180
judiciary, 8, 52, 162, 171, 175, 190
jurisprudence, 40, 49, 50, 122, 124, 127, 184
Al-Jurjānī, 116
justice, 1, 5, 6, 8, 9, 12, 15, 17, 18, 20, 21, 22, 23, 24, 27, 28, 29, 31, 36, 38, 40, 43, 45, 49, 53, 54, 57, 61, 62, 64, 72, 76, 83, 84, 89, 90, 91, 93, 105, 107, 134, 137, 138, 140, 142, 143, 149, 150, 152, 153, 156, 158, 162, 165, 166, 167, 169, 171, 175, 176, 180, 181, 183, 189, 190, 191
Al-Juwaynī, 14, 111, 184, 194

kalimāt ḥikamiyyah, 18
Al-Kāmil, 78
Karbalā', 55
Kennedy, Paul, 9, 44, 171, 193
Khabūr, 40
Khalīfah, Ḥājjī, 14, 69, 70, 71, 83
Khān, Sir Sayyid Aḥmad, 141
kharāj, 39, 40, 93
khilāfah, 33, 42, 54, 55, 56, 57, 58, 60, 61, 62, 63, 66, 67, 135, 151, 152
Khulafā' al-Rāshidūn, 39, 66
Al-Kindī, 103, 129, 130
Kitāb al-ʿIbar (of Ibn Khaldūn), 10, 12
Kitāb al-Manṭiq (of Ibn Taymiyyah), 116
Kochu Bey, 14, 83, 94
Kramer, J.H., 94, 152, 157
Kroeber, Alfred, 165, 192
Kuran, Timur, 14, 46, 47, 49, 50, 52, 53, 64, 65

labour, 20, 21, 25, 26, 40, 41, 47, 85, 149, 174
laissez faire, 23, 33
Lal, 50, 65
land grants, 39, 72, 93
Lawson, Nigel, 166, 192
Lebanon, 176
Lewis, Bernard, 14, 35, 43, 44, 66, 67, 70, 71, 89, 92, 94, 132, 147, 148, 177, 179, 193, 194
life expectancy, 162
literacy, 1, 54, 85, 97, 101, 161, 162, 173, 187, 191
Luṭfī Pāshā, 14, 69, 81, 83, 92, 94
Luther, Martin, 40, 44
luxuries, 26
luxury goods, 25

Madīnah, 55, 146, 189
madrasah, 32, 54, 99, 100, 139, 141, 156, 171, 183
Makkah, 55, 58, 146
Mālik, 15, 33, 60, 66, 120, 122, 128, 130, 192, 194
Mamlūks, 10, 54, 74, 76, 82, 93
Ma'mūn, 59, 109, 128, 135, 136, 138, 154, 155, 181
maqāṣid al-sharīʿah, 1, 7, 14, 96, 127, 140, 141, 183, 184, 186, 191
Al-Maqrīzī, 40, 44, 78, 93, 94, 116, 117, 131, 132
market, 24, 25, 32, 36, 37, 39, 41, 48, 60, 64, 75, 84, 85, 87, 156, 167, 169, 171, 176
Al-Māturīdī, Abū Manṣūr, 111
Al-Māwardī, 44, 76, 89, 93, 95, 166, 192
Mazdean 36, 103
medieval England, 50, 51, 75, 146
Mehmed II, 68, 76, 91
Mehmed III, 70
Mehmed IV, 91
merchandise exports, 88
merchant, 23, 36, 65, 145
microfinance, 167, 168, 169, 189
Middle East, 37, 97, 132, 192
Miḥnah, 109, 110, 120, 130
modern education, 124, 126, 141
Mongols, 10, 44, 60, 72, 73, 74, 79, 93, 124, 146, 193
Mongol invasions, 10
moral degeneration, 2, 53, 54
moral development, 6
moral law, 57
moral reform, 164, 165
moral values, 7, 12, 22, 23, 165, 180
Morocco, 11
Moses, 19, 165
Muʿāwiyah, 55, 65, 66, 151
muḍārabah, 49, 65
Muḥammad (the Prophet), 7, 8, 19, 34, 36, 49, 55, 58, 65, 96, 101, 127, 144, 145, 146, 152, 164, 165, 172, 173, 178, 185, 193
mulk, 17, 55, 62, 63
Muqaddimah (of Ibn Khaldūn), 10, 12, 13, 14, 15, 16, 17, 18, 30, 32, 33, 53, 66, 94, 117, 128, 131, 132, 158
muqāsamah, 39
Al-Murdār, Abū Mūsā, 103
Muslim backwardness, 153
Muslim civilization, 11, 13, 38, 45, 63
Muslim countries, 2, 3, 14, 24, 27, 46, 74, 80, 125, 126, 127, 142,

146, 147, 158, 159, 160, 161, 162, 163, 164, 166, 167, 172, 173, 174, 179, 183, 189
Muslim decline, 2, 3, 31, 45, 46, 53, 54, 155, 156, 158, 186, 183, 190
Muslim history, 55, 60, 62, 92, 149, 151, 152, 153, 155, 157, 170
Muslim law of succession and inheritance, 46, 47, 75, 145
Muslim malaise, 2
Muslim society, 1, 9, 10, 13, 22, 38, 55, 75, 108, 109, 110, 122, 123, 124, 136, 143, 146, 177
Muslim thinking, 23
Mutakallimūn, 103
Al-Muʿtaṣim, 38, 43, 109, 135
Al-Mutawakkil, 110, 130, 135
Muʿtazilah, 59, 129, 102, 103, 108, 109, 113, 121, 122, 123, 128, 154
Al-Muwaṭṭa' (of Imam Malik), 122, 130

Napoleonic Code, 47
NATO, 182
natural theology, 107
necessities, 26
neoclassical economics, 29
neo-liberalism, 167
Nile Valley, 40
Noland, Marcus, 46, 64
North, Douglas and Robert Thomas, 9, 28, 29, 33, 65
North Africa, 11, 91, 93

OECD, 182
OIC, 127, 159, 163
Ottomans, 40, 54, 60, 64, 70, 72, 74, 76, 86, 87, 91, 99

Palestine, 93, 176
parliament, 159
Pāshā, Sārī Mehmed, 14, 83
planning, 31
political accountability, 29, 52, 68, 84, 90, 99, 152, 155, 158, 164, 168, 176, 190
political authority, 12, 18, 22, 23, 26, 27, 33, 38, 61, 91, 100, 109, 135, 136, 150, 152, 153, 155, 175, 180
political illegitimacy, 51, 54, 55, 62, 64, 137, 154, 162, 170, 172, 183, 184, 190
political reform, 30, 55, 138, 143, 171, 172, 177, 178, 179, 180, 187, 188, 190
population, 1, 2, 25, 26, 31, 40, 41, 73, 89, 101, 102, 110, 129, 132, 133, 137, 147, 161, 175, 177, 186, 188, 190, 191
predestination, 107
prices, 26, 38, 69, 78, 88, 92, 167
primogeniture, 47, 48, 49, 51, 75
production, 26, 41, 61, 64, 74, 85, 86, 87, 95
property rights, 21, 28, 29, 50, 51, 52, 53, 83, 85, 91, 144
prophethood, 104, 106
prosperity, 25, 26, 41, 42, 75, 84, 91
public expenditure, 40
public resources, 27, 62, 68, 101, 153, 158, 159, 160, 171, 182, 191
public services, 99, 160

Qalʿat ibn Salamah, 12
Al-Qushayrī, 111

Rābiṭah (OIC), 127
Al-Raqqah, 134
rationalism, 113, 115, 118, 121, 125, 143, 154
rationalists, 99, 100, 101, 102, 105, 106, 107, 108, 111, 112, 113, 114, 116, 118, 120, 122, 123, 124, 125, 127, 128, 129, 130, 132, 154, 185
Al-Rāzī, Abū Bakr, 103, 107, 118, 129
Al-Rāzī, Fakhr al-Dīn, 14, 116
Reconquista, 11
Red Sea, 91
religious sciences, 103, 111, 139, 140, 141, 142, 155, 184
revelation, 35, 96, 104, 105, 106, 107, 108, 112, 114, 115, 118, 121, 124, 148, 185
Risālah fī Dhamm al-Maks (by al-Suyūṭī), 76
Roded, Ruth, 145, 148
Rosenthal, Franz, 15, 17, 32, 67, 131
rural population, 41
rural society, 38
Russia, 79, 86, 87, 88, 90, 91, 154

Sabians, 42
ṣadaqāt, 156
Safavids, 68, 91
Saljūqids, 40, 44, 59, 72, 73
Sarton, George, 43, 44, 93, 128
Sassanian and Byzantine Empires, 34, 37, 39, 59, 98, 102
savings, 5, 6, 24, 49, 85, 160, 176, 180, 181
Schatzmiller, Maya, 37, 43, 44, 64, 67, 146, 148
Schweitzer, Alfred, 9, 165, 192
secularism, 57, 61, 125, 127, 181, 182, 183, 185
Seville, 11, 128
al-Shāfiʿī, 120
Al-Shahrastānī, 116, 129, 130
Al-Shaybānī, 134, 147
shūrā, 55, 56, 60, 61, 65, 66, 127, 151, 152, 159
Siege of Vienna, 91
Sirhindī, Aḥmad, 142
social solidarity, 2, 5, 6, 12, 21, 22, 31, 36, 84, 91, 141, 150, 156, 181
socialism, 24
socio-economic policies, 29
Sorokin, Pitirim, 9, 10, 15, 16, 44
South Korea, 172
Soviet Union, 28, 163
Spain, 11, 54, 97
Spengler, Joseph, 32
Spengler, Oswald, 9, 13, 16
Sufis, 136, 137, 138, 142, 143, 155
Sufism, 142, 143
Suleyman the Magnificent, 69, 76, 82, 91
Sunnah, 4, 10, 49, 66, 104, 106, 107, 110, 111, 116, 120, 121, 122, 125, 126, 127, 184, 185
surplus, 24, 25, 71, 75, 172, 175, 189
sustainable development, 5, 8, 9, 20, 67
Al-Suyūṭī, Jalāl al-Dīn, 76
Syria, 60, 93, 134

Tabrīz, 60
tafsīr, 145
Tahāfut al-Falāsifah (by al-Ghazālī) 111, 129

Tahāfut al-Tahāfut (by Ibn Rushd), 114, 131
Taiwan, 172
Tanẓīmāt period, 79, 90, 94
taqlīd, 184
tawḥīd, 105
tax revenue, 23, 25, 26, 182
tax system, 40, 52, 75, 76, 85, 136
taxation, 24, 37, 40, 51, 62, 75, 76, 77, 79, 80, 83, 84, 89, 153
taxes, 21, 37, 38, 39, 40, 61, 70, 73, 74, 75, 76, 77, 84, 93, 122
technology, 5, 6, 7, 30, 31, 48, 91, 96, 97, 98, 99, 101, 153, 154, 167, 170, 171, 178
tīmār, 73, 148
Tīmūrids, 60, 73, 74, 146
Tlemcen, 11
Toynbee, Arnold, 48
Toynbee, Arnold J., 4, 9, 10, 14, 16, 30, 33, 34, 35, 43, 44, 48, 63, 65, 67, 166, 186, 192, 193, 194
trade, 2, 37, 41, 48, 61, 64, 65, 73, 75, 77, 79, 84, 87, 88, 89, 92, 153, 176
transport sector, 48
Treatise on Toleration (by Voltaire), 119
Tunis, 11, 12
Turks, 40, 44, 183

ʿulūm ʿaqliyyah, 97
ʿUmar, 58, 93, 137, 144, 148
ʿUmar ibn ʿAbd al-ʿAzīz, 58
Umayyads, 40, 54, 59, 60, 64, 72, 78
ummah, 36, 56, 61, 66, 120, 122, 125
United Kingdom, 51, 85, 86, 87, 89, 90, 95, 182
United State of America, 85, 86, 88, 89, 90, 101
Universal History (by Ibn Khaldūn 30
urban populations, 41
urbanization, 31, 41
ʿushrī lands, 39
ʿUthmān, 93, 137

Vaglieri, Laura, 56, 57, 66
Voltaire, 119, 131

Walīullāh, Shāh, 124, 126
waḥy, 114, 148
Washington, 167
Al-Wāthiq, 109, 135
Watson, Andrew, 41, 44
wealth, 1, 4, 8, 17, 18, 24, 25, 26, 32, 35, 38, 42, 49, 51, 56, 89, 120, 137, 150, 151, 160, 162, 167, 168, 169, 173, 175
Western Europe, 47
Western powers, 74, 83, 87, 140
Western societies, 29, 57
Western world, 28, 101, 159, 161, 176
Westernization, 178
women, 30, 35, 36, 72, 143, 144, 145, 146, 147, 148, 179, 190

Yazīd, 55

zakāh, 31, 156
Zanādiqah, 102
Al-Zarqā, Muṣṭafā, 122, 132
Zoroastrians, 42

88,

87,